BLAINE L. PARDOE

A MOST UNCIVIL WAR

BOOK TWO IN THE
BLUE DAWN SERIES

DEFIANCE PRESS
& PUBLISHING

A Most Uncivil War

(Defiance Press & Publishing, LLC)

First Edition: 2022

Printed in the United States of America

10 9 8 7 6 5 4 3 2 1

DEFIANCE PRESS
& PUBLISHING

ISBN-13: 978-1-955937-27-6 (Paperback)
ISBN-13: 978-1-955937-23-8 (eBook)

Published by Defiance Press and Publishing, LLC

Bulk orders of this book may be obtained by contacting Defiance Press and Publishing, LLC at: www.defiancepress.com.

Public Relations Dept. – Defiance Press & Publishing, LLC
281-581-9300
pr@defiancepress.com

Defiance Press & Publishing, LLC
281-581-9300
info@defiancepress.com

ACKNOWLEDGEMENTS

Inspiration comes from a variety of sources. Thankfully, I don't have to look far. I mentally picture the year 2020 saying, "The next year can't be worse than me." Then 2021 stood up saying, "Hold my beer!" Seriously. At the time of this writing, in August of 2021, it feels as if the nation is groping madly in the dark, trying to find itself. Some are angry; others wrap themselves in a cloak of intentional ignorance. In other words it is the perfect fodder for this novel.

I would be remiss if I didn't thank the mainstream media for feeding the American people crises and fear on a daily basis. I can't wait to see what they come up with next. No, strike that. I'd prefer to have them stand down and try something new—like actual journalism. Just because I wrote in a novel that the media were tools of a corrupt, despotic state, you media guys don't have to try to prove me right.

Thanks go out as well to the current administration who is demonstrating, as my father put it so eloquently, "They could fuck up a one-car funeral."

DEDICATION

To my wife Cyndi, who has always encouraged me to push the envelope. To Jamie Rife and Scott Greengold...ardent patriots if there ever were any. And to the Fawn Lake Irregulars—Jack (yes, there's a real-life Jack), Tracy, Gary, Murphy, Claire, Chad, Gavin, Bennett, and Lilly.

THE KEY CHARACTERS

Alex – short for Alexandria (no last name given). Former Congresswoman from New York, she sits on the Ruling Council and commands the National Security Force (NSF) as its Secretary. She removed her opposition and folded the Social Enforcers into the NSF. She is the Newmerica Vice Presidential candidate.

Andy Forest. Andy's father was a member of the Sons of Liberty (SOL) and Andy was instrumental in recovering the original copy of the Constitution and Declaration of Independence.

Brad (no last name given). A student at the University of Virginia.

Julius Bernstein. NSF Operative.

Rebecca (Becky) Clarke. The Director of the Truth Reconciliation Committee (TRC) and member of the Ruling Council. Was instrumental in seizing control of Congress during the Liberation.

Travis Cullen. Former Navy SEAL, now a covert operative supporting the American administration.

Jack Desmond. Former Director of the Secret Service and now the American President's Chief of Staff. Jack was instrumental in bringing the former American Vice President to power and for years was the clandestine leader of the Sons of Liberty.

Captain Gerald "Trigger" DeYoung. Officer in the Texas National Guard and the American Army.

Tess Ditka. Aide to the Director of the TRC.

Detective Dale Gallagher. Member of the NSF.

Deja Jordan. A Social Enforcer from Minneapolis.

Charli Kazinski. Current Director of the American Secret Service. For years she lived as an NSF officer named Angel Frisosky to avoid detection. She was with the last President when he died.

Caylee Leatrom. Former NSF Operative, she has flipped sides and now offers her skills to the Americans. She killed Alex's mother and brother.

Senator Earl Taft Lewis. One of the few surviving Senators after the Liberation.

Raul Lopez. Former member of the Youth Corps, his murder of a man led to riots in Detroit. As a member of the Sons of Liberty, he liberated the Social Enforcement Camp at Valley Forge.

Lieutenant Judy Mercury. Officer in the Texas National Guard and the American Army.

Jane Pistós. Employee at the TRC.

Daniel Porter. Chairman of the Ruling Council, he will be elected President of Newmerica. Daniel orchestrated the overthrow of the government during the Liberation/Fall.

Colonel Trip Reager. Renowned and scorned for his actions in San Antonio several year back, Reager is a Texan who is loyal to the American cause and one of its most recognized military commanders. Trip is an officer in the Texas National Guard and the American Army.

David Steele. Maddie's younger brother.

Grayson Steele. Former conservative member of the Virginia House of Delegates and Maddie's and David's father.

Maddie Steele. Conservative law student at the University of Virginia whose family has been living on the run since the Fall.

Tina (no last name given). A student at the University of Virginia.

PROLOGUE

"The only trust that matters is between you and the government."

Five Years Earlier
Washington DC

Rebecca (Becky) Camille Clarke had visited the Capitol on her sixth-grade school trip and had been awestruck at the splendor of the building and the stunning statues of America's great figures that were housed there. To her, then, it was the heartbeat of democracy. There was a regal air to the architecture, a sense of awe about the building. It represented power to her then, as it did this night. At the time, she remembered how history seemed to echo off every surface. That visit changed her life. *I wanted to change the world and I knew this place would play a role. I never planned to come back under these circumstances.*

This visit was dramatically different. A decade ago she had been a wide-eyed honor student from an elite suburb of Boston. This visit was not as a tourist, but as part of an army, a group dedicated to unfetter the Capitol and restore it to the people. For far too long Congress and the federal government had been oppressing the people it was supposed to serve in favor of special interest groups and big business. *Tonight that ends! This is a liberation!* She held on tight to the seat of the non-discreet, black van that weaved slowly through the crowd she could hear outside the thin metal walls.

The van she was in lurched to a halt, and the rear doors opened to a mob of black bloc garbed college-aged protesters. Her heart pounded in her ears, almost drowning out the angry roar of the crowd. Their faces were obscured, but their anger rang out into the night. She hit the ground as a sputter of gunfire, sounding like firecrackers going off, echoed out in the distance. Tonight the streets of Washington DC were alive and she was a key part of it all. *We have come to take back what is ours.*

They called her Nightingale—the voice of the ANTIFA. Getting a code name was important in ANTIFA and she reveled in having one. Only a few people knew who she really was. She covered the summer protests under the guise of being a reporter for the campus *Daily News,* with no one even realizing that she was one of the street fighters. Protecting one's identity was part and parcel of leading a revolution.

While Becky had been involved in ballet in elementary school and track in high school, she never felt that she stood out. ANTIFA changed that for her. It gave her a sense of being complete. It made her feel that her life had meaning. Where her parents tried to control her, her new family in the cell gave her true freedom, enough to change the world. She had grown up watching films like *Star Wars*, but now she was leading an actual revolution.

Part of the problem was that each ANTIFA group was separate, individual, with their own mix of goals and objectives. Getting organized had required help from within; a young Congresswoman, who went by Alex, helped get all the groups on the same page and gave them lists of targets of objectives. Coordinating them was like herding cats, but this Congresswomen knew how to do it. "When we're done there'll be a Ruling Council, a place where the groups that do coordinate with us will have a voice in reshaping the nation." It was then that Rebecca learned that you do not herd cats; you open a can of cat food and they willingly follow. That was what Alex had done.

Becky had come from a wealthy family, and it wasn't until she went off to college that she realized that her parents were part of the problem in the nation. Her father was a financial consultant, helping rich people get richer at the expense of the workers. She never fully understood that until her professors explained it. Her parents, and even her younger brother—they were all part of an inherently racist system that was built on oppression.

It had led to a fight with her father and his threat of cutting her off; again, another typical capitalist move, using money to drive influence! Outwardly she had apologized to her parents, but secretly she was frustrated and angered at how corrupt her family was. When a classmate told her about ANTIFA, she went to a meeting and became hooked.

Becky was a natural organizer and had the ability to communicate things simply. Randy, the ANTIFA leader on campus, leveraged her and soon she was in the 'inner circle,' as they liked to be called. The group was called 'Righteous Fury,' and they even had flags printed with that and the arrow symbols for ANTIFA. Becky met with other cells, some on campuses, others in cities. She helped with their messaging and straightening out their social media thrusts. ANTIFA had a long history of manipulating the media. It wasn't hard; they covertly and in some cases overtly supported individual groups. They had dozens of people filming, not what the rioters did, but the police reaction. She created a small app for uploading these images with generated tag lines that said the police were attacking, 'peaceful protesters.' Using her natural gifts and what she knew about communicating, she became a spokeswoman for the movement, all from behind a black spandex gaiter mask. It was exhilarating for her, being able to influence others to join the cause. She did not see herself as coordinating disinformation. She was merely making sure that the right narrative was communicated.

Planning and coordinating the toppling of the United States government had been difficult. Each ANTIFA cell tended to operate on their own. Some believed that coordination would actually complicate matters, but Becky had held her ground in those talks. One man emerged with a plan, one to bring down the whole corrupt system, Daniel Porter. There were power struggles between the ANTIFA cells, arguments over ideology, tactics, almost everything. One thing that united the anarchists was taking down the government and breaking the backbone of capitalism. It was a philosophy that they shared with the BLM movement. In her talks with Porter and the other leaders, she kept them focused on this concept: the United States, as it was known, had to die. Daniel was able to do what even Alex couldn't. He gave them purpose.

There was a lot of distrust between the groups and little agreement on the ultimate goals, but Porter got them to agree on one thing, taking down the United States. "Once the system is down, we can bring about a reformation and work through our differences." He kept the groups focused on a singular goal.

Righteous Fury at Yale recognized the problem and attended a live summit months before the deaths of the President and Vice President-elect. Doing it live meant that there was no surveillance, no monitoring by the government. Daniel Porter was no fool; he knew how the imperialists worked. He left them no digital trail to follow, sending messages by courier.

When the President-elect died of an alleged aneurism, it seemed highly suspicious. His death was exactly the kind of thing that the Traitor President would do—have him killed. The assassination of the Vice President-elect by a radical white separatist—that had galvanized her. It was another expression of oppression of hate—racist oppression of women. Becky cried for hours as she watched her funeral.

It was then, in that darkness, that she knew the time was finally ripe to bring down the United States once and for all.

The assassination had been a rallying cry to ANTIFA, BLM, and every other group that knew that the entire American system was hopelessly corrupt. The attack had been carefully planned and coordinated, which was a challenge that she proved equal to. As she moved into the crowd, the orange megaphone in her hands, she remembered the heated sessions Randy and she had organized for the assault.

The problem they faced was that every faction wanted to be the one that captured the Traitor President. It was Becky who held their focus. "We can't just take him down. We need a team to take out the entire chain of leadership. We need someone to tell the people that we are in charge now...that a new order is in place. Otherwise, we will be drawn into a protracted fight—and we are not equipped for that." Her words unified the thinking, and she made sure that each faction in the fight got a prize. Daniel told her she was inspiring and named her his communications officer.

Getting the activists into DC took days and they were offered shelter on Howard University, where the activists fully supported what was about to unfold. She knew that the authorities would piece together that something was about to come down, but they would not realize the scope and scale until it was far too late to respond.

They would need weapons—so the first stage of protests was aimed at distracting the authorities...some orchestrated misdirection. Molotov cocktails and fireworks brought in from Pennsylvania and West Virginia would help with that. When the police moved against that distraction, they would seize the Washington DC Armory for the National Guard. Protesters would, with weapons, become an army.

One force would storm the White House and capture the Traitor President and his staff for a speedy trial and execution. She was part of the force that came for Congress and the Senate. Their office buildings would be hit at the same time as the Capitol itself. Other teams would secure the Mint, Treasury, DHS, and other key facilities in Washington DC. They would strike in coordination, starting as 'peaceful protests' and quickly seize their objectives before the leaders could respond. Their targets were less the buildings and more in favor of going after the *people* in charge. Taking them hostage would restore authority to the people.

The summer riots, most of which they had spawned, had taught them a great deal about dealing with the police. Frozen water bottles were perfect as projectiles. Slingshots firing ball bearings could kill with a good shot. Laser pointers would be used in the front ranks to blind the police and national guardsmen.

The assault teams were prepared; bullet-proof vests—masks to prevent sucking in tear gas—all were easily available. One of the leaders from Portland, Oregon had suggested using real mortars and rockets mixed with the conventional fireworks. Even now, as Becky waded through the sea of black-bloc clad freedom fighters, she heard the explosions ringing off against the White House. Not even the vaunted Secret Service could be prepared for this kind of attack.

If all went as planned, the government of the United States would be taken out quickly and effectively. It was exciting to her, exhilarating. Now, as she moved in the crowd past the underground entrance to the visitor center, she looked up in the night and saw the shimmering white dome of the Capitol. For one heartbeat she took in the image and grinned. *Soon the people's house will return to them!* She would tell her grandchildren one day how she had been a leader in the great revolution.

Up near the top of the steps leading to the Capitol, the crowd was stalled and she could see that the doors were still in place. Pulling out the megaphone, she toggled it on and barked, "Bring up the battering rams!" For an instant all eyes fell on her and she heard one man cry out. "That's

Nightingale—do what she says!"

The rams were simple devices, logs with handholds crudely nailed on them. They were passed forward and the sound of their hammering echoed off of the buildings in the distance. Elsewhere in the city, the popping of gunfire increased.

Becky waded into the crowd, which seemed to part to allow her forward. "Kill them all!" cried several people—and it was on the verge of being a chant. *No! If we allow that, we can't control the narrative. If we kill them it will only serve to generate resistance.*

Lifting the megaphone, she barked. "No, we need them as leverage. No harm is to come to the leadership. Take them hostage! Take them hostage!" Almost instantly the crowd continued her chant of, "Take them hostage!" which gave her a sense of the power she wielded.

There was an irony to the assault on the capitol, one not lost on Becky. Members of Congress and their staff had been funneling money to ANTIFA and BLM throughout the last year. Few spoke out about the riots; they had hoped it would foil the reelection of the traitor. Now their duplicity was coming back to roost. Becky was not a fool. Senators and congressmen were playing the protesters in hope of expanding their own power. They need to be taken down just as much as the traitor and his people. *No one can manipulate us. We are an idea—a cause! We are righteous!*

There was a resounding crack from the doors above her at the top of the stairs as the battering rams completed their job. Light poured from the inside, and the crowd suddenly surged as a whole, forward and upward. She almost lost her grip on the megaphone as she twisted and angled herself forward. *I am part of history now—the creation of a new nation! All we have to do is find and secure the Speaker of the House.*

Three Years Earlier ...
College Station, Texas

Trip Reager was opening his pizza restaurant, Slice of Heaven, when the woman entered. He flashed her a smile and said, "I just started to fire up the oven, so it will be a few minutes. Please, take a seat." The heady smell of yeast filled the air as he started the prep for the lunch crowd.

She gave him a quick, insincere smile. "I'm not here for a meal, Mr.

Reager," she said. "I'm Angel Jones, and I'm with the Green Tribunal out of Austin."

The mention of Austin forced Trip to suppress rolling his eyes. It had been a hotbed of liberal thinking and support for the new administration. Since the Fall, the FedGov had tried to inflict a lot of changes. Trip was thankful that he lived in Texas and not on the East Coast, but even Texas had cities where support for the fake government ran dangerously strong. A lot of the craziness that much of the country was suffering was diminished in Texas because their Governor refused to play ball with the Ruling Council, declaring it an unlawful assembly. Social Enforcement gangs existed in the state, but only in the big cities, and they were smart enough to stay there. Any town with a university or college had some problems with SEs attempting their brand of vigilante justice. In College Station, where he lived, the students had gotten vocal and 'protesty' as he put it, but only to a point. Most understood that the citizens of Texas had little tolerance for the madness that other states seemed to be embracing.

His daughter, Jessie, went to college at the University of Texas in Austin. Trip had misgivings about sending her to a place that supported the progressive overthrow in Washington, but she had been insistent and his wife Nancy had supported the move. *She's got a good head on her shoulders...but she is surrounded by left-wing crazies.*

The thing he missed most was the ability to post what he wanted on the Internet. Big Tech had backed the coup in Washington DC and made sure that dissenting voices were quickly squashed. The Tribunals were a pain as well, but he treated them as what they were, annoyances. There were a lot of them springing up, courtesy of the temporary government in DC. The only one Trip had interacted with was the Veterans Tribunal because he was being denied coverage of a medication by the VA. They had taken the matter under advisement. It was an unnecessary layer of administration that he saw no value in. Like most people, he assumed at some point the nonsense of the Ruling Council was something that would eventually collapse or be taken down by someone else. In the meantime, you dealt with the fanatics when you had to.

"Is there some sort of problem?" he asked, moving from behind the counter and wiping his hands on his apron.

"I'm afraid you are going to have to shut down," Jones replied curtly, pulling an envelope from her business suit and extending it to him.

Trip started to chuckle but stopped as he stepped forward and took the envelope from her. "Why is that?"

"You have been identified as a polluter, second class," she decreed.

He opened the paper and his eyes swept its long-winded legal jargon. "I beg your pardon?"

"Your pizza oven burns wood. That's a violation of the new Green Act passed by Congress. I'm afraid you'll have to shut down, at least until you convert your kitchen to running on non-polluting energy." There was arrogance to her voice. Having served in the military, he had heard it before. It was the tone of a desk officer, someone who thought that rank alone carried authority.

"You *do* understand that I have a wood burning pizza oven? People come here because we have wood fired pizzas. I don't put out any more pollution that someone running a BBQ or a bonfire in their backyard." He folded the paper tightly in his now-clenched fist.

"Sir, you are a polluter and that is a cease-and-desist order from the Tribunal. You are legally required to follow it."

"First, and foremost—your Ruling Council has no legal authority to create a tribunal or anything else. They have no authority to issue orders. No one elected them. Second, the amount of pollution I generate is hardly noticeable."

"I wasn't involved with the measurement of your crime, or the decision for you to close," she said as if those words were a shield protecting her. "I'm merely here to issue the orders."

Trip took another step toward her, deliberately getting into her personal space. "What in the name of hell am I supposed to do? You can't cook a pizza with a solar panel. These are wood ovens; they cost a lot of money. Do you expect me to buy a new oven? Converting these to something you deem 'green' is going to be expensive as all shit."

Angel Jones was not the least bit intimidated by the fact that he had closed the space between them. "That isn't my problem. My job was to inform you of the violation and present you with the order."

There it is, the hippy-ass bureaucrat speaking. "Look here, Ms. Jones; I am a veteran with three tours of duty under my belt. I was wounded in the service of the United States. My wife and I built this restaurant from the ground up. I've been running it for six years. No one ever complained about me polluting. Hell, the guy across the street has a dumpster that is overflowing and draws rats, but you aren't shutting him down."

"That isn't my concern," Jones replied defiantly. "And the United States is not an entity any longer. The nation you live in is Newmerica."

That made him laugh. "I spilled blood for this country and that country is the US of A. Your friends may have killed the leadership, but you can't change reality."

"We will have to disagree on that account. I should warn you though; such talk is sedition."

How in the hell can it be sedition to speak freely? What is the country coming to? Trip wanted to push the issue, but opted not to. I need to keep focused on the issue at hand, not the fuck-ups in Washington. "If you make me shut down my oven, I'm out of business, along with my dozen employees. Where in the hell is the sense in that?"

Angel Jones shrugged. "Maybe this is an opportunity for you, Mr. Reager. You could start offering something other than pizza. You could reinvent your menu."

Trip shook his head as if to deflect the absurdity of her words. "I own a *pizza* restaurant, you moron. People come here for my pizza!"

It was almost as if she enjoyed his angst. She grinned at his words. "Well, you should give it serious thought. It really isn't appropriate for you to be offering a cultural food when it is not your culture."

"Excuse me?"

"Pizza is Italian. I doubt seriously that you family is from Italy. If you weren't going to be shut down for your pollution, it's a matter of time before you are shut down for cultural appropriation, after all."

"What in the hell do you know about my family background? And who are you to determine what I can and can't have on my menu?" His anger roared in his ears, but he managed to resist the urge to punch her face.

"I represent Newmerica," she said proudly.

"It's 'cute' that you think that means something to me. What you are talking about is outrageous and idiotic. My clients in this community love what I make. What you are talking about is shutting down, for weeks if not months, and retooling simply because it doesn't fit your idea of what I should offer. You don't have that kind of jurisdiction. You sure as hell don't have the backing to make me do it."

"Perhaps, but I wouldn't count on that, Mr. Reager. Things are changing. As for your business, well, you need to decide what to do. If I were you, I wouldn't assume that we are powerless to enforce our edicts though. As for my visit today, all I know is that a complaint was filed against you; we conducted an investigation; and the Tribunal has issued you an order to shut down."

"Who complained about me?" he demanded.

"That is protected information," snapped back Jones.

Trip took the order and tore it into shreds. "Your tribunal has no legal authority. Hell, the Ruling Council has no legal authority to form tribunals. This document," he said, throwing the shreds in her face, "is meaningless."

"We'll see about that," she sneered.

"I'm a US citizen. I have rights. I have the right to due process. I have the right to face my accuser."

"As I said before, there is no US anymore," Jones cut him off. "The United States is now Newmerica. You are clinging to a myth that is being slowly erased. I get that people like you may not understand or like that, but it is reality. America died when the people overthrew the Traitor President. You are clinging to ideals that are long outdated and racist in their origins. You may believe that the Tribunals don't have authority, but I assure you they do." He could hear the pride in her voice and it did nothing to assuage his anger.

"I won't follow your unjust orders. Go and tell your handlers there. If they want to shut me down, they will have to come and do it themselves."

She chuckled. "Oh, don't worry. If you don't shut down, you'll be hearing from Social Enforcement."

Jack grinned back. *A bunch of uppity college kids with social justice degrees.* "Little lady, you send them my way. I served in the 10th Mountain Division and this is fucking Texas. They show up here, and they will get their asses handed to them on a silver platter."

Angel Jones glared at him, then spun on her heels and walked briskly to the door. As she left, Jack looked at the torn document on the floor for a moment. *This isn't over yet. I'd better be prepared.*

CHAPTER 1

"Everything bad is systemic."

Binghamton, New York

Iris Jones noticed the car in the parking lot before she had stepped out to dinner. The man sitting in the vehicle did not seem to notice her, but the fact that he was just sitting in the late model car was enough to grab her attention. When she came back from the Sonic Drive-In, where she had walked to get dinner, the car had left. But from her balcony room at the Motel 6 an hour later, she saw it had returned—this time with a red-headed female driver who also sat in the driver's seat. Pretending to use her phone, she snapped a photo of the vehicle.

Iris Jones was a small town newspaper reporter from Cortland, New York. Her age was listed at 30, her background stunningly unremarkable. She had gotten her degree online. The few articles published under her name were small stories, the kind of local fluff about science fairs and soccer tournaments. Anyone prying open her life would find that her neighbors didn't know her at all. On paper, she paid her bills in advance, sometimes going to the offices and paying in cash. If people were asked about her, none would be able to describe her; her life was that thin. There was no reason for her to be concerned that someone was staking her out.

She carefully considered the car she had seen. *Am I being paranoid?* She knew that she was, but with good reason. Pulling up the image she had snapped of the vehicle, she finally spotted a clue. It was an issued car, a government vehicle. The license plate was coded, which told her it was from The District. *Sloppy work. I expected better.*

Iris looked at her room. *They will come tonight.* The hotel room was a trap of sorts, the only ways in or out were through the door and the window, which sat above the air conditioner/heater. Being on the second story further limited her egress if she had to move. *They could have made their move while I was on the streets, but they know the risks involved with that. Tonight will be the night.*

She had deliberately asked for a room with no one on either side, claiming that she needed to get some rest. The hotel clerk had been more than obliging; it wasn't like the Motel 6 was packed in the middle of the week. She was glad because now that request would pay off. Standing on the nightstand, she popped the ceiling tile. Cement blocks ran between the rooms, a fire break. It took over an hour for her to use her tactical knife and a metal table leg to chisel out two blocks, enough for Iris to squeeze into the empty room next door.

There was no reason for Iris Jones to own a gun, not that anyone legally could, especially her models. She had an arsenal of four weapons at her disposal. Her AR-15 had enough kick to blast through the bricks, but she wanted to be sure she took down her pursuers. The pistols, they were for up-close and personal work. She checked her gear and set up a flash-bang in the hole she had carved, tied with a string on the pin, and crawled back to turn the TV on low volume to CNN.

Now, all she had to do was wait.

It was at 2:00 a.m. sharp when they made their move. To their credit, she did not hear them approach the room, but she did catch a glimpse of one of them, the female, through the drawn curtains. There was a loud whoomp as they used a string of detcord to take out the lock and hinges. Iris was slightly impressed, if only for a second. The pair rushed into the room, and she tugged the string. The flash bang grenade she had set up at the doorway went off. She opened the door to the room she was in next door, and came in behind them.

Her first burst of three rounds hit the male she had seen in the car. He was struck above the collar on his Kevlar tactical vest. One round hit the strap of his night vision gear before continuing through his head. Blood sprayed forward in the room as the female reeled on her. No doubt her eyes were blinded by the flash bang going off.

Tossing the vision gear, the woman leapt across the bed, diving and rolling as Iris fired, hitting the wall and the horrible bedspread. She had to have been good to hop like that with the first shots. She held her pistol out and fired a spray at Iris, enough to make her move toward the door. She emptied the magazine, breaking the window and putting a merciful end to the air conditioner.

Iris sprung out before she could reload, almost immediately feeling a stinging sensation as the woman threw a knife that hit her left arm. To throw it, the woman had exposed herself, which was all that Iris needed. She sent three rounds at her center mass; one hit her arm; one hit her lower chest, and the other missed—leaving a smoking hole in the drywall.

The female dropped slowly in the narrow gap between the wall and the bed, leaving a bloody smear on the wall as she went down. Iris checked the woman's partner with a kick, then moved to the end of the bed, keeping the AR-15 on her victim.

"Nice try," she said, kicking the female's gun under the bed and out of reach.

"You're a dead woman," the redhead spat.

Iris could see blood on her lips. *That gunshot must have nicked a lung.* "Not before you I think. Certainly not tonight." She glanced at the knife cut on her arm. There was blood, but she had been lucky.

"There'll be others," the woman said, coughing as she tried to apply pressure to the gut wound. Gore oozed between her fingers as she bled out. "You killed the Secretary's mother and brother. She is never going to stop coming after you. And when we're done with you, your Pretender President will never set foot in The District. You're both dead…you simply don't know it yet."

They are planning to assassinate the President. "Really? You want to die making empty death threats? You're supposed to be better than this. I have a whole speech rehearsed for when I am in your situation."

"You won't be able to save yourself, let alone that traitor," the woman said. Her body slowly went limp; her hands drifted away from the wound; her eyes, unfocused, stared at the ugly bedspread.

Iris Jones evaporated in that instant, replaced by Caylee Leatrom. Her cover ID had been blown, so it was time to move on again. *Jack and Charli need to know what is coming at them.*

The Southern White House
Nashville, Tennessee

Jack Desmond sat at the polished table in the Estes Kefauver Federal Building conference room which served as the center of government. He twisted his aching neck. His starched shirt collar made his skin chaff. He hadn't worn a suit in a long time, and it was going to take some getting used to. There was comfort in wearing it though, a step closer toward the life he used to have as Director of the Secret Service.

Memories of that role seemed like a different life altogether. There were memories, and some he struggled not to remember. He had never asked to undertake the burden that his life had become. Like so many people, Jack had been simply doing his job. Yes, he had political beliefs, but to him, his job defined who he was. There was something honorable about protecting the President and the White House. It was a job that was steeped in history, oddly defined by the times his predecessors had failed to do their job.

Fate had intervened and inflicted itself on Jack Desmond. His family had been targeted and paid the price for him merely having the job of protecting the President. For weeks, if not months, he had wandered homeless, adopting new identities, all to evade his pursuers while attempting to find something that he could hang onto and have a reason to get up in the morning. During those months, he did things he now regretted, just to survive. It took time, but he ultimately found purpose. Some would have called it revenge, but Jack didn't use such a harsh term for his actions. No, this was justice—the very thing he had sworn his life to defend. Justice was the enemy of tyranny.

It was that concept—the restoration of true justice—that had driven him. He had sought out and found the Vice President after one of his many contacts whispered that the man was very much alive. He knew that Charli had to be alive, and he went on a quest to find her as well. Jack had orchestrated the various factions, rekindling the Sons of Liberty all across the country, with one goal—restoration. It was an obsession, one that made him leverage his more base skills and talents to achieve. *I have done many bad things to make the right thing happen.*

A lot had happened in the three weeks since the swearing in of the President in New York. The United States government had set up operations in Nashville, Tennessee while the Newmerican Administration remained entrenched in Washington DC, now named 'The District.' The Estes Kefauver Federal Building had been coined as the Southern White House, but in reality the President's temporary home was on National Park land outside of the city. Jack didn't bother to try and correct the name the media applied; it presented a sense of continuity and familiarity, even if it was inaccurate.

Jack had been named Chief of Staff and was doubling as the President's senior advisor. He had not asked for the job; in fact he argued it was best served by a senior politician. The President had disagreed. It was hard to argue with the man, since Jack had been instrumental in getting him the position in the first place. After only a few weeks, it seemed like a lifetime ago.

Some state governors refused to acknowledge the return of an American President, where others begrudgingly acknowledged the former Vice President's broadcast inauguration. The President swiftly federalized all National Guard forces, but in those states that refused his existence, it remained to be seen how or if that order would be complied with. Some were in open defiance. In Washington State, the Governor had crudely said that the new President could 'fuck off.' In California, the Governor called for his own activation of the National Guard. In New York, the Guard was busy providing protection for the riots that broke out after the President had been sworn in.

The US military did acknowledge the President but rode the fence as to whether they could be employed against those states that stood firmly with the false Newmerican government. The military refused to commit to either side of the coming conflict. They had trotted out a liaison officer from the JCS, but that was the depth of their loyalty. *They've dug themselves into a hole. They stood by and did nothing to save the last President, and have tacitly backed the Ruling Council. No doubt more than a few generals are worried that their role in the coup will be revealed. So they play the middle of the road.*

There were rumors of troops and entire units essentially defecting to Newmerica—a disturbing allegation that the Defense Department refused to acknowledge. Likewise, some units had mobilized and had come to Tennessee on their own accord. The Joint Chiefs possessed the ability to defend the nation, the nuclear launch capability, independent of the Ruling Council or the President at this stage. To Jack, it was clear that the current split of the nation was one that would not be resolved politically. *They took us out by force, and we are going to have to use force to take it back.*

The President immediately called for fair and free elections. It had been five years since The Fall, when the government had been toppled by a coup d'état. The last election had been highly contested and while the results had been certified, many members of Congress and the Senate were serving far beyond their terms of office. Some had been sent to Social Quarantine camps, some to prison, while many simply disappeared—presumed killed during the seizure of the Capitol. One thing was certain; the ruling party could ill-afford opposition.

As the white-haired leader of the fractured nation entered the room, Jack instinctively stood. The President's advisors entered as well, taking their seats in the interior conference room in the heart of the federal building. At the doorway stood Charli Kazinski, the acting head of the Secret Service. She gave a nod to Jack, clearly suppressing a wry smile as she did so. Jack nodded back. *We've both been through hell and back to get to this point. Charli's scars run deep.*

The President carried a yellow, legal notepad with a long list of blue-ink notes; some were highlighted in pink and green. "Alright then," he said, adjusting himself in his seat. "Let's start with the current state of our Union."

Jack took out his iPad and pulled up his report. "This morning the Ruling Council announced that they too support fair elections. Big shock, I know. Of course they are in favor of them as long as people vote for their candidates. According to their press briefing, this is, in no way, a response for our call for the same thing. Oddly enough, they didn't even mention us."

The President chuckled once, silently. "They didn't have a choice. We've been flooding the Internet with this and some local reporters have gone out with the story. Jack, what does it mean for us?"

"The last election was rife with cheating, all of which they conveniently covered up after the coup. They labeled anyone that contested the results or the process as a traitor. When you are in charge, you can redefine the rules of the game. Sir, I believe they mean to have elections alright, and they aim to win them across the board…no matter what it takes. For them, it will legitimatize their government and allow them to move forward with this Constitutional Convention that they have called for."

"There will be no new Constitutional Convention," the President replied flatly. "I will not give them the chance to throw out our way of life by rewriting the Constitution to cover up or justify their crimes."

"Agreed," Jack said. "All they are trying to do is legitimatize what they have done. So our priority is to make sure that this election is fair and just. It is complicated with their declaration of Voting Sanctuary Zones and Cities."

"A thinly veiled way of saying, 'we intend to cheat in these communities,'" the President said with a hint of humor. The Ruling Council had claimed that the President didn't have the authority to govern voting. Instead, they established areas where they claimed that valid voting would take place. Votes cast elsewhere would be discarded. Most of those locations were in big cities that had the greatest concentration of supporters.

"How do we counter attempts at fraud?" the Vice President said from her seat. Jack admired her when she had been the Governor of South Dakota. She had a reputation for being tough and blunt; two qualities that Jack admired. Her state was one of the few where the Social Enforcers had been put in check quickly, usually by the police, if not, the locals. She had refused to federalize her law enforcement under the auspices of the NSF, and the Ruling Council seemed satisfied with labeling her a traitor to the nation and resorted to a guerilla war against her administration. Twice 'radicals' disavowed by the Council had tried to assassinate her, and twice they had failed. *She's tough as nails…what we need a heartbeat away from the President.*

Jack locked gazes with her. "We'll do a little fighting fire with fire. Just prior to the election, we will issue an Executive Order federalizing the elections, taking them out of the states' hands. We will then declare our own 'Free Voting Centers' manned by our people. We use the National Guard and, if practical, the military, to enforce that proper procedures are followed. The Sons of Liberty will muster additional forces, both in the cities and rural areas. We will use methods that ensure no one votes twice. Votes cast in the Ruling Council's sanctuaries will not be counted, and we will make sure that message gets out. That means we limit the number of voting places—we validate all voters with identification, and we make sure that any 'shenanigans' are dealt with swiftly.

"Our focus will be on the cities. In most states, the majority of the progressive power is in the cities. Look at New York. Most of the state is still likely conservative, except for Albany and New York City. We will go in, establish a dominating presence and ensure a fair vote."

"Just going into those cities with military force will keep a lot of people at home," the Vice President stated.

Jack understood that thinking and approved of it. "That is true. People will be less likely to go where a riot might break out or shooting might take place. At the risk of sounding callous, it works to our advantage if less opposition party voters show up."

The VP turned to the President. "They will say we are suppressing the vote."

The President winced, but only slightly. "They will say a lot of things, Kristi. Of course they will say that. The truth is always the first victim with these people. It's a veiled way of saying we are racists. It is their pattern. Anything they don't support is racist and a threat. They will call us every name under the sun. We can't be swayed. Our cause is just. We will establish voting centers. If their supporters don't show, well, then they get less votes. We will not deny legitimate and identified voters the right to cast their ballots. We are better than them."

"They will use force and intimidation." The voice came across the table from the National Security Advisor. He adjusted his eye patch as he spoke.

Jack nodded once. "They will. Be assured of that. I would if I were them. If they lose this election, their entire fraud of a government is lost. They have spent years painting all of us as criminals for what we believe in, but now they are facing the reality that they might be held accountable for their crimes. Damned right they will attempt to use force, intimidation, terror tactics, whatever it takes to hold onto power. We, in turn, must be prepared to fight back." His words weren't hollow or in vain. They painted the stark reality of the enemy that they faced.

"We will face force with overwhelming force," the President replied. "The American people are done with being intimidated by black-hooded goons using street tactics. People will come out and vote."

"What if that leads to another San Antonio?" the VP asked. Jack admired that she had the sand to ask such a question. What had happened in San Antonio four years ago had been vicious, but had spared Texas much of the agony that the rest of the nation had been facing. The message to the Ruling Council had been clear…Texans were not going to knuckle under like most of the nation had. That came with a price, one paid in blood.

The President drew a long breath before responding. "No one wants another San Antonio. By the same token, these Social Enforcers need to come to an end. I intend to grant full authority to the local commanders to use whatever force they deem necessary to ensure that voting takes place and is fair. If these enforcers try anything, and they will, they are not going to be facing pepperballs and rubber bullets. We learned that approach only encourages more bad behavior." Jack understood completely; he and the President had spoken about it in depth. *If they push, we will push back ten times the force.*

"Tell me about my opponents," the President changed subjects.

"You already know that Daniel Porter is the Chair of the Ruling Council. He ran a large cell of ANTIFA in Portland before the Fall. He organized the attack on Washington DC. For the first time ever, he coordinated all of the factions that wanted to bring down the government. So far he is holding the reins of power, sharing it with his council members. But his running mate, who we all know, is the Secretary of the NSF—an ice cold bitch if there ever was one. Porter pulled off a miracle during the Fall, coordinating all of the people that hated the government. *She's* the one to be worried about. I would if I was Porter; she killed almost 200 people overnight to seize control of the Social Enforcers. With the federalization of the police and absorbing the SEs, she commands an army, one used to not playing by the rules," Jack spoke without even glancing at his notes.

"I thought what was left of Congress was looking into her and her thugs?" the VP asked.

"There's not much left of Congress, and those that are there support the Ruling Council. Our intel points to her being the real power behind the proverbial throne. One of our party's former leaders, Blackburn, sits there heading the Treasury, but she's more a hostage than anything… propped up as a token. The real power resides with the NSF.

"There are a few exceptions, but these people used fear to seize control, so fear is all they know. Congress might poke a little bit into her activities, but our estimate is that nothing tangible will come of it."

"What if we lose the election?" the national security advisor asked. "We are talking about a people that undermined the last election…not as a grand strategy, but at the local level. Collectively, these efforts undercut any hope that elections were fair and just. People may not vote simply because they don't trust the system." Simply saying the words stirred the people around the large, oval table. It had been a spark, an impetus for rebellion. The media and Big Tech had conspired to paint anyone that even questioned the results of the election as a dangerous seditionist. Most of those around the table carried the mark of traitor as a result.

The President was undeterred. "We *won't* lose. Fear has been the Council's primary weapon from the start of this nightmare. It worked too. People were willing to give up freedom to reduce fear; it was a means of control for them. Over time, they have gotten Americans to turn on each other, all for Reparation Points. Short term, it works. Over the long term, however, people start to hate living afraid. People want freedom; it's in their very nature to crave it. For the last five years or so they have used fear as a club to beat people into submission. A just and fair election could change all of that. The Ruling Council may believe they are in control of this situation, but in the end, the people should and will control their government again." The words flowed from his mouth as if he were at a political fundraiser. Jack could not help but feel proud to be a part of it all.

He weighed in quickly to support the President. "Our ground game has already started, thanks to the SOL and other groups. We will get out our supporters and protect them."

"Where do we stand with Congress?" the President asked, changing subjects quickly.

The new Vice President stiffened slightly with that question, given it had befallen her to coordinate. "I've reviewed it with the Attorney

General. It's not the most stable legal ground we could be on, but it will work. Those states that don't respond to your call need to be labeled as 'states in rebellion.' You will need to declare this as a crisis and convene Congress with those states that recognize you and that government as legitimate."

Jack knew that they were on thin ice legally, but that the Ruling Council had no true authority whatsoever. "Legalities aside, Mr. President, we can do little to avoid conflict,"

"I had hoped civil war could be averted," he said slowly, almost wearily.

"Mister President," the National Security Advisor, Dan, said solemnly. "That's impossible, I fear. They have been attacking half of our population in one manner or another for five years."

"Hope is not a strategy, unfortunately," Jack added.

The President nodded. "The problem confronting us was one of our own making. When I was a Governor, I read the 9/11 Commission Report," he said thoughtfully. "One thing struck me. We were at war long before 9/11; we just didn't know it until they flew the planes into the Trade Center towers and the Pentagon. Our enemy was at war with us, but we ignored everything until people were killed. That is what has happened again. We refused to see the obvious: that the left was at war with us, but we were not at war with them. That's how they took control so completely and swiftly. We were convinced that we could arrive at some sort of middle ground, that we could compromise our way out of this, but in reality; they wanted nothing short of our eradication. They had no intent on compromise. We assumed that once things calmed down, we could restore the nation to a semblance of itself; they wanted our history rewritten so there was no going back.

"I look back now and see that the liberals were waging war with us long before the Fall; we just wrote it off as partisan politics. We looked the other way. In reality, they were waging war and we were oblivious."

Jack heard his words and understood. The signs had all been there, during the virus with the riots and how they turned a blind eye to ANTIFA and other groups that were destroying the cities and mauling the police forces. *He's right; we kept trying to work with them, but they had no intention of ever working with us. We convinced ourselves that they could be reasoned with when they never intended to use reasoning.*

"What are we looking at Jack if this becomes a full-fledged conflict?" the Vice President asked as she shuffled in her seat.

Jack drew a long breath and sat up rigid in the chair. "This will be a civil war unlike others. Yes, there is a geographic nature to it, but the liberal bastions tend to be in the big cities. Look at New York. The vast majority of the state geographically was conservative, but the massive population of the city made the representation appear to be far left. Georgia is on the fence in terms of supporting us, mostly because Atlanta and Alpharetta are hotbeds of progressives with strong SE presences. Pennsylvania is with us as is most of Pittsburgh, but Philly is split along political lines, almost block by block."

Jack paused for a second, and then continued. "Unlike a traditional civil war, where armies will clash—a lot of this will be fought in small skirmishes. It will also be fought digitally. For the last five years, the Ruling Committee has done a remarkable job of crushing conservative voices and rounding up anyone that opposed them. Anyone that dared question their activities was either killed or shipped off for Social Quarantine. Big Tech companies made sure that there were no counter-voices to the Democratic Party line. They erased our symbols, our flag, and even blocked the Constitution from the Internet. There was no reality check with the media—they only tell one side of the story, signed, sealed, and stamped official by the Truth Reconciliation Committee. With Social Enforcement mobs that could beat people physically or emotionally, people that held their conservative values were silenced with fear and intimidation. Throw in the National Security Force members that stay loyal to Newmerica, and their Secretary has a domestic terror army at her command.

"They took away our means to protect ourselves by seizing our weapons. They rewrote our history. Over the years they have seized control of our colleges and have turned them into indoctrination centers for their ideology. I hate saying it, but they were brilliant. They made one major mistake."

"Which was?"

"Our supporters are still out there. The other side wanted a genocide of conservatives, but that was too difficult to pull off. Instead they went for suppression. Ultimately their mistake was that the tighter they tried to choke us, the more determined our people have become. Many of our people have been patiently waiting for the right opportunity to rise up and take the nation back. You saw that the night you were sworn in. While there were state-sponsored riots the following day, that night, a lot of our people took to the streets in support of a return of America."

The President nodded in response. "Alright Jack, so how do we fight this war?"

"History has shown us that to defeat evil, you must be willing to do some fairly dark things. In WWII, as much as we like to paint ourselves as honorable, we firebombed Dresden and Tokyo; we unleashed nuclear weapons on the Japanese. I'm not suggesting anything that brutal, yet, but I wouldn't be doing my job if I didn't tell you that we are going to have to fight full-on-ugly before this is over. If we try and play fair, they will defeat us." *And if they defeat us, we are all dead.*

The Vice President seemed to draw power from his words. She leaned over the large wooden conference room table towards the President. "He's right. It eats me up to think about what we have to do to win. We will have to get downright nasty in some instances, even against our better judgment. We will have to make them experience some of the pain and suffering we have endured. If they don't feel the anguish or suffer some consequences for their actions, they will simply continue on. Our means of fighting will be vicious and brutal, but actions are tempered with the knowledge that at the end of it all, we have to have a united nation again."

The President said nothing for three seconds, and then he spoke. "I don't disagree with your assessment Jack. But we all have to understand one thing. When this is over, we have to have a country left to run. I don't want to destroy America to save America. That being said, our enemy has shown themselves to be ruthless. They have illegally imprisoned hundreds of thousands of people simply because they don't like what they said, or what they might say. They have killed, intimidated, and turned neighbor against neighbor. We all need to understand that our enemy will not have an issue with going low. They will burn it all to the ground if they have to. Losing, for them, means what they face is justice."

University of Virginia
Charlottesville, Virginia

Maddie Steele sat in her dorm room in Metcalf Hall; her eyes were glazed over reading a textbook on her Kindle. She was studying *The History of Law in the Nation*, and knew that the textbook that she was reading was a joke, which was more knowledge than was possessed by most students who attended the illustrious University of Virginia. It was another Post-Liberation book, one that made out the Founding Fathers to be a corrupt group of capitalists who formed a nation to exploit its people and natural resources. Almost every other sentence in the book was twisted to fit the narrative that the FedGov pushed, one where the old United States was little more than a racist construct. She had heard the narrative so many times, it made her eyes roll.

She had known what she was getting into when she came to UVA. Her father, a former member of the Virginia House of Delegates, had warned her and had tried to get her to one of a few colleges that still existed in Newmerica that did not knuckle under to the rewritten history. He had gone to great lengths to protect his family, even changing their last name several times with a friendly small-town judge so that they would avoid the SEs and the Social Quarantine camps. For three years, they had moved four times to further blur their trail from anyone looking for them. Grayson Jones, now Grayson Steele, wanted to protect his only daughter, and having her go to school in a hotbed of progressivism was not what he wanted for her. Maddie, however, was insistent. UVA's law school was one of the best in the country and she wanted to be a lawyer like her father had been.

She had been a sophomore on campus during the horrific night of the Liberation. The mob had cut off the legs of the statue of the university's founder, Thomas Jefferson, as part of their celebration. They went after the members of one of the secret societies, the Sons and Daughters of Liberty, beating eight members to death in front of the law library…the irony was not lost on her. Maddie had stayed in her room that night, not out of fear, but more because of not wanting to be a part of the chaos on campus. From her window she saw the campus security force and the Charlottesville Police doing nothing to help the victims as they were beaten to death. They seemed concerned that the violence was contained on campus and didn't turn against the local businesses.

The 'reforms' that followed at the university had been swift, to the point where Maddie wondered how much they had been planned in advance. The secret societies, long a staple at UVA, all but disappeared—having been labeled in some manner or another as racist or prejudiced. A student Social Enforcement force, The Grays, appeared within a few days of the Liberation. They targeted the campus Republican groups, forcing most of the members to leave out of fear for their lives. New secret societies emerged, like The Uprisen, which were more militant in their actions—bombing the local Republican Party HQ as one of their 'events.' One group, the Scarecrows, didn't make threats. They left handfuls of straw at the doorsteps of students that were suspected of being conservative. It was a warning. 'We know who you are and where you live.' Most packed their bags and left, even if the charges weren't true. *The truth no longer matters. What matters is what they feel.*

Maddie was conservative, but she knew that the secret was to not share her beliefs with anyone. She was there for the degree, nothing more. Her roommate, Pris, was a huge supporter of the LGBTQFM community, but Maddie always managed to find a good excuse not to attend the events she was invited to. She was proud of the fact that she was true to her ideals, but not a hypocrite. Maddie refused to pretend she was something she wasn't; she merely hid who she really was.

When the former Vice President was sworn in on live TV, she felt like cheering. Five years of darkness and now there was a glimmer of hope! The campus, however, began a stew of anger, frustration, crying, and protests. The Grays called for the new President to be hung; they even made a scarecrow in a tattered suit—with a noose around its neck—the night after he took the oath of office. She had seen it from her dorm window as it was paraded around campus with cries of 'Kill the traitor!' ringing in the night air. That night, she had hidden her smile. *They are afraid...afraid of what he represents. He can bring back normalcy and if he does, their kind will face some sort of justice.*

Her phone beeped indicating it was time for a meeting with her counselor and she gathered up her Kindle and her notepad and set off across campus. The electronic signboard on the campus flashed the slogan du jour, "Your degree…your right!" She made her way to Doctor

Morose's office, knocked lightly and was invited in.

Morose was a skinny man, bald, with thick, black rimmed glasses. He gestured to the chair in front of his tiny desk; there was barely enough room to avoid hitting her knees on the laminated wood in front of it. "Maddison, thank you for coming to see me."

"Is there something we need to address?" she asked.

"Well ..." he said opening a red file folder on his desk. "There's no problem with your grades. You should be set to graduate this spring, if all goes as planned."

That's a relief. "So why do you need to see me."

Morose shifted in his seat. "Well, it has been brought to my attention that in your entire time here, you don't take part in any extracurricular activities. You are not a member of any campus organizations or groups."

"I prefer to focus on my studies," she said, issuing forth a half-truth.

"So you say. Still, it makes you stand out."

"I'm confused, sir. Am I required to take part in such activities?"

"There's no formal requirement. I will tell you that some law firms look at what you did while outside the classroom. The choice of the right activity could help you when it is time to get a job."

"But it isn't required."

"No."

"So then sir, how do I stand out? Those were your words. If I am not taking part in outside activities, how could it draw attention?"

Her words made his bald head turn pink. "Because everyone else *is* a part of something. Almost the entire student body is involved with some sort of political action group or another and you are not. You take part in nothing outside of your studies. It looks…suspicious."

"What I do in my out-of-class time is my business," she stated flatly. "It is a choice whether I take part in some group. I simply choose not to."

"Madison, appearances are everything. If you are not supporting something, it makes you look as if you are opposed to the things that others *are* supporting. You need to join some sort of club or activity. I am simply trying to help you make good choices for your career and your time remaining here at UVA."

There was no sincerity in his voice. She heard what he was really saying. There was a risk that she might be a conservative. Worse yet, it might be noticed, and that would draw violence. "I have zero interest in politics. I am here to study law. That's it. I am not going to spend my downtime protesting or whatever it is these groups do—I simply don't have the time. Law school is hard enough without distractions."

"Very well. I'm your counselor and it is my job to give you advice. My advice to you is to take part in something outside of class. I've seen this before. If you don't, well, things can get ugly."

"There is something you can do to help me," Maddie said. "Who brought this to your attention?"

That flustered him. He closed the paper file, as if she could read it. "That is privileged information."

"No sir, it isn't. I have been accused of something. I still have the right in this country to confront my accuser. Who was it that felt it was so goddamned important to reach out to you?"

Morose shook his head as if that would deflect her words. "I'm under no obligation to share that with you."

"You counsel law students, Doctor," she reminded him. "I have the right to know."

"You have what rights we decide you have. And in this case, you don't have the right to know. What you need to know is that people are watching you, Maddison. You're under scrutiny, and not the good kind."

As if there were a good kind of scrutiny to be under.

"You did your job then. You've told me, and I have responded. I appreciate your concern, but it isn't necessary. I'm not some closet-conservative or anything else other than focused on my schoolwork. Now, if you don't mind, I need to study for a test in international law." She rose to her feet and Morose did as well. She did not thank him, though; as she stepped out of the building, she realized that she should have. *He was warning me, and that's a favor.* But thanking him might have only confirmed the suspicions that people had voiced about her. *I need to be careful from this point forward. There are eyes on me.*

The District

The Secretary of the National Security Force entered Senator Earl Lewis's office as his aide held open the door. Alex, short for Alexandria, hated being in the Russell Senate Office Building, but the meeting was necessary. The building was bland except for the atrocious modern art on display in the lobby. *What a waste of marble.*

She had been in a dark place since the murder of her mother and brother and would have preferred to avoid the meeting, but felt it was important. She had always been a firebrand, a lightning rod of controversy. That was deliberate. In her early years in Congress, it had been useful to say outrageous things. It ferreted out her enemies who were compelled to respond.

She had carefully crafted her image. She had started as a bartender and ended up in Congress. Then she had helped plan the Liberation. That changed many people's view of her. No longer was she a babbling fool; there was a level of craftiness in her character after the Capitol had been taken down. While some people still thought of her based on her early years, she had slowly forced them to respect her…if not for her accomplishments, then out of fear.

Throughout her ascension to a place on the Ruling Council, her mother and brother had been supportive. To her, they were the one genuine part of her life. Everything else was staged, created for public consumption. With her family, she could be who she truly was. That had been ripped from her, leaving her with the fabrication of her life as the only reality to cling to. They had been killed by a sick, rogue operative. It angered her to whole new levels, causing her to smash more than one piece of china or glass in her home in The District. *They deserved better…I deserved better.*

It had never dawned on her that she was placing them at risk. With all of the resources of the NSF at her disposal, she had never thought to put protection on them. *Until a few weeks ago, no one would have dared go after them.*

Now she was constantly haunted by her loss. On Sunday mornings, when she usually called her mother, there was a void—a dead time in her ever-packed calendar. As much as she knew she had to move on, she couldn't. Gabe's wife had pleaded with her to bring the killer to justice, but thus far Caylee Leatrom had proved elusive. Her people had gotten close two days ago, but now that was another dead end. Finding Leatrom was a new purpose in her life, filling the gap that had been held by her family.

The Secretary embraced her new motivation with zeal. Revenge. Not just against the rogue operative that had turned against her and the nation, but against the Pretender. *A people that would sanction the killing of innocents like my family can never hold the reins of power.* If she had to, she would have them all murdered to prevent the downfall of Newmerica.

For now, she had to deal with some of the fallout that Leatrom had caused, more justification for vengeance. Senator Lewis was calling for hearings, investigations into the NSF and her recent activities. *It is bad enough we have to deal with this Pretender and a forced election, but now our own people are pursing these pointless activities.* As with everything, she tackled the threat head-on, going to visit him directly. She sauntered into the Senator's office and took a seat opposite of him as he rose to greet her. "Madam Secretary, it is a bit irregular…you coming to visit when I have hearings on the docket into investigating your department and your activities." He took a seat and looked remarkably calm. *You are so smug, thinking you can come after me.*

"These hearings you've called for, they have no standing," she said flatly. "In fact, your elected term elapsed. You have no authority over my actions."

"I see," he said, shuffling in his seat. "If we are going to play that game, you have no formal role since the NSF nor the SEs are true legal entities. We both know that the Ruling Council and the actions taken since the Liberation have no basis in the law, so let's not dance around technicalities. But, until elections do happen, I do hold a seat—the Governor of my state has said so. The people of Newmerica are going to want answers. So we can play this game all day about who has what authority, or we can move forward."

"Senator, I am here as a professional courtesy. I had hoped to spare the nation something that would be embarrassing and unproductive."

"Unproductive? You have a great dealt to answer for. The bombing in Northern Virginia, the poisoning attacks of several of your key investigative facilities including Quantico—the destruction of Bumblehive…not to mention the swearing in of a man we all thought was dead. Then there is this matter of your covert operatives committing assassinations, apparently under your direct orders. From my seat, it looks as if the investigative arm of the NSF has been given a kick to the crotch. As the leader of the NSF, you have a great deal to answer for."

His rant bothered her, not because he had done it, but because of what he knew. The Bumblehive incident had never been made public. *He is getting information from someone within my organization, or from the people responsible for these attacks.* "It is…amusing…that you believe I need to be held somehow accountable for the acts of terrorists. It leaves me wondering how you amassed your intelligence information. Is it possible that you are somehow connected to the parties responsible for these incidents?"

He shook his head and grinned. "If I were, do you think we'd be having this discussion at all? Fish all you want Madam Secretary; they simply aren't biting today."

Given the sensitive nature of these incidents, I would prefer we discuss them behind closed doors—especially since they are part of ongoing investigations."

"That seems reasonable—but that portion only. Some of this needs to be public. The information is out there already, and the answers for those alleged crimes need to be out there."

"You're referring to the documents that were released on the Internet?" Caylee Leatrom's release of classified material was beyond embarrassing. It implicated the Secretary personally in illegal activities. *That bitch will pay for the damage she has done.*

"Damned right I am," he fired back. "I've read them, as have a lot of people. The accusations they make are astonishing."

"If they were true."

"So you claim they are not?"

"Those documents that have been posted to the Internet were completely fraudulent. They are works of pure fiction," she said with confidence. She knew they weren't, but did not say more than that. Caylee Leatrom had posted them after Alex had sent a team to kill her—after Caylee had killed her mother and her brother. Even thinking of the former operative for a millisecond raised the Secretary's blood pressure.

"Well, they were up for almost two weeks, and a lot of people saw them," Senator Lewis said, leaning forward over his desk and resting his elbows with arms open between the two of them. "Copies of them were downloaded and pop up every day or so. Until our friends in Silicon Valley take them down and keep them down people are reading them and wondering what kind of operation you are running. Too many people have seen them and want answers."

"I don't see why we would waste time looking into some things that are clearly fake," she replied.

"If they are fake; we need to make that known," he replied. "But if anything in there is true, you were responsible for ordering the murder of people without a hint of due process. *That* is something that cannot be ignored, no matter who is in charge of the NSF—don't you agree?"

She glared at him. *He believes he is immune. He thinks I can't touch him.* Part of that was true. Lewis had been a Democrat at the time of the Liberation. He was a church going man who actually followed his faith, a rarity in The District. Unlike most people in positions of power, she had dirt on them. Not so with the Senator. He didn't watch pornography, have a lover on the side, or shady financial dealings—at least none that the NSF had uncovered yet. Those things alone made him the exception to the rule when it came to senators.

"All you are going to do is spark conspiracy theories and speculation. There is no proof that I or anyone in the NSF was involved in the activities that those documents claim."

"We have subpoenaed a number of witnesses," Lewis countered. "I am confident we will get to the truth."

"Truth?" she said and then chuckled. "I'm not some naïve intern, Senator. The truth is what we say it is. It's been that way for half-a-decade now and has worked out pretty well…for both of us. All your hearings are going to do is be a distraction, one we can ill afford at a time like this."

"The NSF needs oversight, Madam Secretary," he replied. "If you won't allow it willingly, then we will have to do it the hard way."

She rose, tossing back her long black hair with her left hand. "It is interesting that you believe that senator. Before I go, I need you to consider this. If those documents are true, even in some small part, that means I have a group called *operatives*. It means that I order them to eliminate people that are a threat to the stability of the government. It means I have ordered murders, in some cases, of high ranking officials."

Lewis said nothing as she paused and started to rise from her seat. "If they are true, that means you are threatening someone that has no qualms about ordering the deaths of others. Tell me Senator, is that a smart move on your part?"

Before he could respond, she walked out of his office.

CHAPTER 2

"There is nothing that cannot be fixed with government intervention."

The Southern White House
Nashville, Tennessee

Caylee Leatrom entered Jack Desmond's office and her instincts kicked in. There was a window, no doubt bulletproof—making egress through it difficult if not impossible. Jack had a lot of items on his desk that could be used as weapons, if needed. Desmond was older than she, no doubt slower, but still he was trained in combat. One leap over the desk, and she could take him down quickly—then exit through the office door…if she had to. *Old habits die hard—someday I will be able to enter a room and not think about how to kill everyone in it.*

Desmond flashed her a grin and gestured to the guest seat. He wasn't pretentious; the seat wasn't deliberately uncomfortable or lower than his own chair. Jack liked looking at people eye-to-eye, which was one of the things that she respected about him; that and he got things done. *Most people can barely handle one thing at a time—Jack is a rare one. He juggles a lot of balls at once.*

"Good to see you, Caylee," he said.

"You as well, Mr. Desmond. I trust that this is not a social visit."

"There's no reason it can't be that as well as business," he said, leaning back in his chair. "I saw your last report. I take it you have healed after that attack."

She glanced down at her arm, still bandaged, where the knife had hit her. "No permanent damage. I can't say the same for the operative that attacked me." She allowed herself to crack a smile. "I met with Charli and passed on the information regarding a potential assassination attempt."

"Good. We expected some sort of violent reaction on their part. An assassination doesn't entirely shock me. They have a lot to lose."

"They are not the only ones," she said, rubbing her bandaged arm slightly.

"One thing is sure; the Secretary you pissed off isn't going to let up on you. She's going to keep throwing people at you. You made it personal with her."

As was intended. "I anticipated that," she replied, relaxing slightly in her seat. "The material I released was damning. Even if they take it down, a lot of people are talking about it."

"It's not helped that you killed her mom and brother," Jack added in a softer tone of voice, almost fatherly.

"No, it probably isn't. I needed to send her a message…if you send people to kill me, I will come back at you."

"A lesson she hasn't learned apparently."

Caylee nodded. "Sooner or later they will run out of operatives to send after me."

Jack chuckled. "We can only hope. I am glad you're doing alright though. It can't be easy, always looking over your shoulder."

"An occupational hazard. But you didn't ask me to pop in because of this, did you Mr. Desmond?"

"No, I didn't," Jack replied. Caylee liked that about Desmond; he was courteous, personable, but didn't play games. *So few people in the circle of politics are like him—then again, he isn't a politician—he's Secret Service. That must be it...the source of his integrity.* "I have two missions for you, if you're willing."

"We share the same enemies, Mr. Desmond. I wouldn't be here otherwise."

"I would prefer being allies."

She considered the word carefully. *Are we allies?* She had helped Charli and Andy because they stood against the Newmerica government. So far, Jack had only asked her to do things that were mutually beneficial. At the same time, having no friends in high places could be dangerous for someone in her occupation. "I believe that word is accurate. For now, our relationship is mutually beneficial."

"Good. First, I'd like you to the safety of a young man named Raul Lopez."

Her mind ran through her mental Rolodex, but the name was not familiar. "And he is?"

"That incident in Detroit a while back, with the Youth Corps; that was Raul Lopez. As it turns out, he was one of the leaders that helped liberate the Social Quarantine Camp at Valley Forge."

That she had heard of. The images of the freed prisoners had made it on the Internet for a few days, enough for a lot of questions to be asked about the camps. "What is the risk to him?"

"The Philadelphia SEs got his picture from the background of one of the videos that was released showing the prisoners. It was a simple slipup on their part. It's really a matter of time before they piece together that Mr. Lopez is the same person that the Detroit authorities are looking for. I'd like you to get him out of there before they find him. Relocate him someplace we have picked out that is safe here in Nashville."

"That seems easy enough," Caylee replied. Deep down she knew it probably wasn't. *If it were a simple transport job, he would send someone else. This must require an operative's touch. This Mr. Lopez is a hot potato with the NSF and SEs all looking for him.* "If you give me his info, I will take care of him…keep him out of the hands of the government."

"Excellent. I will send you the data. I appreciate it. This young man has been through a great deal, and I fear he is about to undergo a great deal more."

Caylee understood. She knew what the Newmerica government could bring to bear on a person identified as a target or a threat. She had been an implement of that kind of retribution. *That's probably why he is asking me to undertake this.* "What is the second mission?"

Jack shifted in his seat, telling her the gravity of the request he was about to make. "Caylee, the President is pushing for free and open elections. At the same time, we also need to blunt this push by the Ruling Council for a new Constitutional Convention. It is nearly impossible for us to get our messages out to the people. Silicon Valley takes our stuff down, routing it all to the TRC for instant editing. That's the problem—the TRC—they stifle everything we try. They paint us as insurrectionists, the product of conspiracy theories and racism. They discredit every message we attempt to get out."

"I would say that people are smart enough to know the difference between propaganda and reality, but I won't insult your intelligence, Mr. Desmond."

"They have been fed so many lies that they can't tell the difference," Jack conceded.

"That was always the intent. The TRC was put in place to remove the voice of any opposition. The Truth Reconciliation Committee is misnamed like everything coming out of the Ruling Council," she said. "It was created to effect government censorship and is highly effective, though it has little to do with the truth."

"Agreed. A few news outlets out there do support us, but the TRC makes life hell for them. They revoke their operating licenses and put up disclaimers on their stories saying that they are not approved content and may be false and misleading. When that doesn't work, the Social Enforcers jump in and destroy transmitters and broadcast stations, or they target the newscasters. The TRC is a cornerstone of the Ruling Council holding power. It allows them to twist every fact and statistic to their agenda. There can't be free voices speaking out—they squash them."

"As an operative, they were useful. They covered my tracks. Now that I'm living on the other side of the proverbial fence, I hear what you are saying and agree. Where do I fit in with them?"

"I want you to take them down," Jack said firmly.

For a long moment, Caylee said nothing. Her mind raced with the words he had spoken. *How would I take them down? Is this a matter of killing the Director—or does he have something bigger in mind?* The TRC was one of the largest agencies in the FedGov and also one of the more secretive departments. *This is a big job. For him to ask me to do it tells me how important it is.* "What would be my mission parameters?"

Jack rubbed his chin for a moment in thought. "None. I'm not going to tie your hands with this one. I learned a long time ago that people who do your kind of work are only frustrated with a lot of rules and guidelines. I need the TRC to come to an end, period."

"Mr. Desmond, you are asking a great deal. First, it is a large organization and pretty much a black box—no one really knows their inner workings. Second, they have offices in The District, Chicago, New York, and LA. That means they may have some redundancy. Third, their HQ is in The District, where I am, dare I say, less than welcome."

Jack nodded. "I know. I am asking a lot from you. I also know from experience that sometimes the best place to hide is right in plain sight. Ask Charli—she can tell you. You being in The District will throw them off. It is the last place that they would look for you."

"When you say, 'Take them down,' what do you mean exactly? What is your ultimate goal with this?"

Jack paused, no doubt picking his next words carefully. "The TRC claims to be impartial, but we all know they are the voice of Newmerica. We need them to be unable to function just prior to the election. We have a number of news people out there that want to report the truth, want to put our stories out there, but they can't. If the TRC can't do its job, they can at least try. On top of that, we know one thing about these liars; they will spread their falsehoods heaviest immediately before the election. If they are crippled, unable to work, the truth will get out there. People deserve to know about those that have been holding them down all of this time. So, I want them unable to do their job—period."

Jack answered by not answering. *In other words he's leaving the 'how' of this up to me.* "The SEs will still go after your reporter friends, even if I am successful."

"As you know, your former boss did a late night purge of the SE leadership," Jack reminded her. "The Secretary likes to think she has brought them into her house, but no one trusts her now. The SEs were just ANTIFA thugs and punk Social Justice Warriors until the Ruling Council legitimatized them. Now the Secretary has pulled off a little coup of her own to control them. They are chaffing at that. We are going to keep pressing the buttons on that tension between the NSF and the SEs. Hopefully, we can keep them at each other's throats long enough to get our word out."

Caylee appreciated the insight, but it did not make the task in front of her any easier. "Mr. Desmond, this has the potential to get messy on my part. My tactics may result in significant loss of life."

"Consider it authorized," Jack said in a low tone. "I don't know what choice we have at this point, Caylee. I don't like it, but we are at war now. The TRC is like a battalion of enemy troops we are facing across the battlefield. These people have no qualms about ruining lives or taking them. The President recognizes we are in a civil war now. He'll never say it publicly, but he knows. Wars have casualties."

She understood completely and was relieved to hear that the President understood the nature of the conflict as well. I fought on the other side of this, thinking I was doing what was right. It wasn't until they turned on me that I realized the truth about the people I was working for. Her mind moved past the morale dilemma and into an operational mode. "If I am going to do this, I need to do it from the inside. I will need a new ID or two, one that will pass muster when I go to find this Raul Lopez. I like having a few at my disposal."

"That can be arranged," Jack said. "The more they overthink their security, the more doors they crack open for us."

"Good," she said. "Anything else?"

"No. Other than, 'Be careful.'"

Caylee rose. "It's nice to know that you care, Mr. Desmond."

Minneapolis, Minnesota

Deja Jordan got out of bed slowly and glanced at her alarm clock with a menacing eye as she shut it off. She had hammered the snooze button several times before finally getting up. Now she would not get to work until at least 10:30 a.m. A month or so ago, that would have been cause for concern. Her manager had recently died in a car accident, at least that was the story that was conveyed to her Social Enforcement unit, The Como Ave Avengers. Since then her division had been virtually leaderless. They were given a contact number in the NSF if they had questions, but mostly what they had gotten was silence. *Why would we call the NSF to ask questions about the SEs?*

Years ago, during the pandemic, Minneapolis had been the epicenter of racial unrest. She had been on the forefront of it, joining in quickly with ANTIFA when the protests turned to riots. *The city deserved what it got*—she felt that then and still did. Back then, it was anger that had driven her. The Liberation…the death of the traitor president—that had been exhilarating. The Ruling Council had formalized the ANTIFA and BLM, allowing local Social Enforcement teams. *We whipped the neighborhoods into shape then too!* Deja had helped round up dissidents…closet racists and anyone opposed to the Liberation. It had been easy at first; people turned in their neighbors with wild abandon. There was no investigation like the police did. Justice got handed out street style, the way Deja liked it. If there was some question about someone's guilt or innocence, well, they got sent off to the Social Quarantine Camps. *It was for their own good. They weren't safe staying in their homes after being doxed. We did them a favor getting them out of the city.*

She thought fondly back to those early months of the Liberation. Homes that had been owned by bougie whites who had long flaunted their wealth had been vacated by the SEs and turned over to the people. Deja's mother had gotten one of the houses the Como Ave Avengers had seized as part of social reparation. She remembered how her mother had cried when she had taken her there for the first time. *For far too long they lived in luxury while we struggled in run-down federal housing. Well, we changed that!*

Things had changed though; the flood of people turning in their neighbors turned to a trickle. The Reparations Act had gotten people to turn in social offenders for points worth money. The result was a surge of people that continued turning against their former friends. That had helped keep the SEs going. She often suspected that some of the people being turned in were being falsely accused of crimes, but that wasn't her problem. *If they weren't guilty of the things they were turned in for, they had probably done something worth bringing the pain.* Still, she had a nagging feeling at times that social enforcement, now that it was legitimate, was losing its direction. Now, with the death of Margaret, she wondered who was going to lead her team.

Deja had earned her reputation as a Digger—slang for someone that was good at locating undesirables. She was excellent at finding people that didn't want to be found, people whose ideology was corruptive and dangerous. There was a bit of technique in what she did, but her true secret was in being persistent and stubborn.

Deja stood in the shower, staring aimlessly in thought, nursing her memories. Try as she might, she could not shake the thought that something was off in Margaret's death. Everyone in the unit knew that Margaret had not died driving a car. *She didn't have a driver's license.* To travel, she relied on Uber or other members of the unit to chauffer her around. Deja doubted that she even owned a vehicle. The NSF was lying; she was sure of it.

She and Margaret weren't particularly close—Margaret wasn't friends with any of the SE team. What she lacked in comradery she made up for with respect. Deja had been recruited by her at the time of the first protests. Margaret had earned her position—she had been there from the start. She had been old school ANTIFA—*not like the pussies that were joining now.* She wasn't afraid to knock heads with the cops. If anything, she liked it.

She got out of the shower, put on deodorant and pulled out a T-shirt from the pile on the floor, one that she was pretty sure she had only worn once. She worked her hair—forgoing most of the usual makeup. Almost overnight the SE leadership seemed to have disappeared. *Why was the NSF lying? Did Margaret get into some shit and someone took her down?*

She biked in. Not so much because the weather was good, but because she had used up her gas ration for the month. *Next time we get called in on someone, I need to lift their ration card.* When she arrived at the former police precinct that the SE had taken over, she locked her bike and went inside.

Before she reached the break room, Lexus moved up to her and pulled her aside. "Girl you are late."

"Don't be giving me shit," Deja replied wearily.

"We've got company this morning," Lexus said in a heavy whisper. "Some big shot with the NSF."

"What do I care about the NSF?"

"Girl, you had better. He says we report to the NSF now."

"What the fuck?"

Lexus nodded. "We roll up under them now. It's all official. I heard more. My sister in Chicago—they lost their Division leader the same night that Margaret supposedly went for a drive."

"That doesn't sound like coincidence," Deja said in a low tone so her voice didn't carry.

"It ain't. They weren't the only ones. If my peeps got it right, most of the leadership had some sort of accident or just up and died in one night."

"Why wasn't it on the news?"

Lexus tilted her head and looked at Deja as if she were a fool. "Seriously? You think they are going to broadcast that kind of thing?"

Suddenly the door to Margaret's old office opened and a white male stuck his head out. "And you are?" he asked, looking at her.

"Deja Jordan," she replied. She looked him over and he did not look at all like a social enforcer. He wore khaki pants, an ironed, blue button-down shirt. His hair had been cut short, not a crew cut like some of the enforcers—his was more pristinely trimmed. She knew in an instant he did not come up through the streets. He smelled like a cop…a white cop. Instantly, she didn't trust him.

When he made eye contact, he flashed a thin smile. "I missed you in the group meeting this morning. I'm Foster Recht." He extended his hand and she reached out slowly to shake it. "Why don't we step into my office?"

This isn't his office—it is…was…Margaret's. Entering, she took a seat as he slid behind the desk. Margaret's things were gone, boxed up next to the desk. She could smell Recht's cologne, mingling in the air with the cheap perfume that Margaret used to wear. "I'm sure that is a little confusing. I'm with the NSF and I've been ordered here to step in and manage this Division."

Deja crossed her arms and locked her jaw forward. "So we all report up to you then."

Foster nodded as he sat in Margaret's chair. "That's the long and short of it."

"What happened to Margaret?" Deja blurted out.

His face didn't betray surprise at the question. "I was told a car accident. If it helps, I'm sorry for your loss."

It doesn't help. "Since when do SEs roll up under the National Security Force?"

"As of a few weeks ago; it has taken time to get the word out," he said. "Is that going to be a problem?"

For a few moments, Deja said nothing. She fumed at the man sitting across from her. Finally, she crafted her words, choosing them carefully. "OK. You're in charge. Is there anything you need from me?" Getting out of that office was all that mattered to her.

"Actually, I do need something from you," he said. "From what we have been able to learn, you are the best Seeker in the SEs."

"Digger," she corrected him. "Seeker is from that Harry Potter bullshit."

"Right, Digger. My bad. From what I have heard, you can find just about anyone. You're a regular bloodhound."

She hated the comparison to a dog, but let it go. "I get the job done."

"Excellent. I have an assignment for you."

Deja glared at him, narrowing her gaze. "Assignment? Social Enforcement doesn't have assignments. We do responsibilities."

Recht did a slight shrug. "Sorry. I'm new in this role. It wasn't something that I lobbied for. The leadership asked me to jump in here."

She sighed and relaxed a little in the chair, uncrossing her arms. "What do you need, sir?"

"First, it's not 'sir.' You can call me Foster. Second, from what I have been able to gather, you are pretty good at working alone. At least that's what I was able to piece together from the assessments that Margaret had in her files."

"Yeah—I do pretty good by myself. Why?"

"We have a situation in Philadelphia. I'm hoping you are the right person to handle it."

"I work out of here—Minneapolis."

"Senior leadership wants us to start getting people exposure outside of their normal duties. Given your, shall I say, unique talents, you are perfect for the job. I'm not asking you to move or anything, just to handle a situation."

She didn't like the thought, but couldn't put her finger on the reason why other than that the request had come from Recht. "What do you need me to do, Foster?" She emphasized his name enough so that he would notice.

"You heard about Valley Forge?"

"The Social Quarantine Camp thing? Yeah."

"Our investigating capabilities have been hindered lately—a lot of stuff happening above my pay grade. Anyway, in the background of one of the videos we spotted one of the raiders. It took a while to get the image sharpened. When we did, we ID'd him as Raul Lopez. We did some digging into his background and he was in Detroit working with the Youth Corps—the same troop that was involved with the riots there. I want you to go, find this guy, and bring him in."

A Digger job. "Sounds like an NSF task."

"The word from on-high is that they want an SE to handle it. If the NSF brings him in, he has rights and will lawyer up. As you know, Social Enforcers don't play by those rules."

"Why not have someone local handle it?"

"I asked that too," he said, far too casually for her comfort. "Word is that the Secretary herself has ordered a shakeup in Philly of the SEs there, now that they report to her. That whole raid and the videos that went up—it was a big, damned embarrassment for the Ruling Council. They want a fresh set of eyes in there. On top of that, you have the skills to get the job done."

She didn't want to think about what the Philly SEs were going through. If half of the rumors she had heard about the Secretary were true, they were getting a first-class ass reaming. A part of her thought they had it coming. *That whole Valley Forge incident was a clusterfuck. You don't embarrass the people in charge, and they messed up big time.* "You have some info on this Lopez?"

"We do," he said sliding a red folder in front of her. "We have someone tracking down his family for questioning too...you know the routine."

She eyed the crimson folder for a moment before picking it up. When she opened it, the top image was a photograph of Lopez. *Stupid punk-ass Latino.* "Alright. I'll go and see if I can find this kid for you."

Foster Recht flashed a smile. "Thanks Deja. I'm sure this will be a cake walk." There was something in the way he said it that made her wonder how big a mistake she had made.

Houston, Texas

The former Texas Congresswoman was making a gurgling sound as he stood over her. Julius Bernstein could have made the shots from a distance; he had been trained in the army as a sniper. The problem is that long range shots mean you hit the target, but sometimes they live. There were so many variables—heat, wind speed, even the deflection of the window. He would have had to fire through. No, such jobs required the precision and confirmation that only close range shots could provide.

She looked up at him, eyes wide, as the life oozed from her body. "Why?" she asked in a raspy voice.

"A fair question," he said, surveying her apartment slowly to make sure he had not overlooked additional threats. "You don't really deserve an answer to that, but you were an easy kill, so I will give it to you. You are a member of a traitorous political party, one that is opposed to everything that Newmerica stands for." Julius took a seat on the sofa next to where she lay bleeding to death. "Somehow you didn't end up like the rest of your accursed political party during the Liberation. I admire how you dodged that. You must have known that people would come to kill you, given your support of the Traitor-President. Now, you have come back into the political limelight, publicly announcing your support for the Pretender-President."

He paused, bending down close to her, talking a little softer. "It is as if you are not thankful for what we have done for you." She tried to move; her hand slipped on the pool of her own blood that was still growing.

"If it helps, your death will be of assistance to Newmerica. Oh, it's not that you were that important, but it will send a message to other traitors out there. They will know they are not safe from people like me. They won't sleep at night."

Her last breath was not a gurgle but a death rattle. Julius had heard it before. It was part of being an operative; you got used to killing others. He had left the army after four tours of duty, hating the dangerous thinking of some of the soldiers. Some had tattoos of Confederate flags; others were offensive every time they opened their mouths. Extremists were everywhere. Julius's own lifestyle choices only garnered hate from some of his colleagues. Those that supported traditional families were enemies in his eyes; they didn't approve of the lifestyle he chose. It wasn't enough for him that he could live the life that he wanted; everyone needed to openly accept it.

That was the appeal of the Newmerica government. When the Liberation had taken place, he was glad that the Pentagon had not sent help to the White House to save the Traitor President. Watching the old building burn in those early morning hours was a symbol of hope to him, as were the events that unfolded at the Capitol. For years he had tried to fit into society, only to occasionally face scorn. That ended with the Liberation and the months that followed. The people that backed the hate were sent off for Social Quarantine and the real offenders, like the former Congresswoman at his feet, well, they were eliminated. *The world is a better place without people like her. No more dissent.*

The NSF had recruited him as soon as he mustered out. Julius returned to war, this time fighting for Newmerica against threats from within. Being an NSF operative meant that he was doing the most patriotic of duties. *The only real enemies we have are those within the nation that refuse to yield.*

Julius remembered the day that his parents had been sent off to quarantine. They had never been accepting of the life he was living. Turning them in had not been hard at all. *Intolerance is an enemy of the state*—that's what one of the daily slogans had been at the time. It resonated with him deeply when it came to his family. They had not been members of the traitor's party, but in that first year of the great Liberation, things like that didn't matter. They professed being liberal until they learned of his life orientation. Suddenly their so-called ideals had been cast aside. That was the problem with many on the left; their values were always changing, morphing to their own situations. Even thinking of them still made him wince. *They never understood me or how their thinking landed them in quarantine.*

He pulled the magazine that he had used, swapping it for a fresh one when his phone buzzed in his jacket pocket. Pulling it out he saw that the number was the National Secretary. Holding it up, he pressed the connect button.

"To what do I owe the honor?"

"I take it your current assignment is near completion?" came the crisp voice of the Secretary.

"Op 621 is complete."

"Good. I have another assignment for you...perhaps the most

important one I have ever asked you to undertake."

He could not suppress his pride that he was being personally chosen. "May I ask what is my target?"

"The Pretender-President," she said.

Julius leaned back on the sofa, almost as if he were pushed back. *Such an honor!* "Thank you, Madame Secretary."

"Mission parameters are in an encrypted folder on the NSFCloud. Study them carefully. You are not to make your move until I personally authorize it. Understood?"

Julius grinned broadly. "Understood. I will not fail you."

"I know," she said. "That was why I chose you."

CHAPTER 3

"Someone else is always to blame."

Texas Military Department (TMD) HQ, Camp Mabry, Austin, Texas

Colonel Trip Reager had come to realize that wearing his fatigues was probably one of the more comfortable feelings he enjoyed. Putting them on every day was a simple act, but it made him feel complete. He had never planned to put them on again, but the events of four years ago changed things. *I lost everything for no real reason other than I didn't play along.* For a while he had kicked himself for standing up to the government. That didn't solve anything. *It was not my fault…it was theirs. The rat-bastards couldn't leave me alone. They had to make it personal.*

Rejoining the Texas National Guard had been easy for him at the time. Three tours in Iraq had more than prepared him for duty again. He had walked away from the military life, opened a restaurant, and tried to fit in with his own little corner of the world in College Station, Texas. That all had fallen apart, leaving him alone in a nation in turmoil. At least with the National Guard he had purpose; he was back in the saddle again.

He had buried himself in his first assignment, the creation of an armored rapid deployment battalion, using the 278th Armored Cavalry Regiment as its core. The unit had been outfitted with tanks and armored vehicles brought back from Iraq, and Trip's experience as a front-line armored commander made him perfect for the job. With no home, no marriage, and no business, he had buried himself in the work of forging the unit.

Brigadier General Ronald "Nutbuster" Baker motioned for him to enter his office. Before he could get to attention, the General handed him a cup of coffee. "Good to see you Trip. I hope you had no problems getting here."

"None, sir," he said, taking a scalding hot sip. The heat from the cup penetrated his hands as the General paced to a spot at the far end of the office.

"The last time we saw each other was in the city, the night after the Alamo," Baker said.

San Antonio..."Yes, sir, it was."

"That was a hell of a scrap."

"A bit one sided as I recall," Trip said taking a sip and remembered the events of that night. It had been brutal at first, especially the fires. The riots had gotten out of control and the troops were outnumbered. If not for Trip's quick thinking, a lot of men and women in their commands would have ended up dead.

Baker chuckled. "It was when the gloves came off." He moved to his own plain chair behind the desk and took a seat. Trip did the same, sitting across from him. "I didn't call you here to reminisce Colonel. I have a request from the Commander in Chief himself. I think you're the right man for the job, and so does he."

For Trip, there was only one man that held that title—the true President, the one that took the oath in New York a few weeks ago. "What is the op, sir?"

"There's going to be an election. The President wants it to be fair. Needless to say the Newmerica-powers-that-be think otherwise."

"I bet," he said, taking another hot sip.

"Our Governor has committed our forces to assist the President, and by God that is what we are going to do. I want you to mount up your battalion and move into Chicago. Once there, you will restore order and ensure that the voting is legitimate."

"Chicago? Isn't that one of their Voting Sanctuary Cities?" He wanted to chuckle at the title, but held it back.

Baker nodded. "It sure is. The President is sending you to provide a message to them. They can't declare that a city isn't going to follow the law of the land."

Jack shook his head. "Hell, they are asking for another San Antonio all over again. Daniel in the fricking lion's den."

"You got it. I saw what you did in San Antonio. You think and act quickly. You made a tough call then, and it was the right one. I'm sending you into a Newmerica hotbed because I know you can handle it."

Memories of San Antonio made him physically wince. He wasn't proud of what he had done that night. *I already have a lot of blood on my hands, and now he's asking me to possibly paint more on.* None of his combat in Iraq measured up to the emotional impact of what he had experienced in his own home state that night.

"Is a battalion going to be enough?"

"It has to be, at least from Texas," he replied. "This isn't our only op. Chances are you'll get some reinforcement."

Trip set his coffee on the General's desk. "Sir, are you sending me because they know who I am?" The news media, fed by the TRC, had labelled him a 'war criminal' after San Antonio. Death threats came from around the globe. While exonerated for his actions by the TMD, Trip was a public figure whether he liked it or not.

He could cope with being labeled "The Butcher" because he knew it wasn't true. He hated being recognized on the street by his fellow Texans who saw him as a hero. They slapped him on the back and tried to buy him drinks. It reached the point where he avoided going out in public and often went out only at night so it was harder for people to identify him. To Trip Reager, the limelight burned far too hot for his liking. *I'm not a hero. What I did, I had to do. God knows I paid the price for San Antonio, every damn day.*

To his credit, the General didn't flinch. "Yes," he said. "I'm not going to lie to you Trip. Hell, the President himself dropped your name. He and I both know that if you go, it might scare the Newmerica thugs into submission."

"Or it will make it worse," he said flatly. "They have a bounty on my head. Some of my people might have to pay the price for that."

General Baker nodded. "It would be the same no matter where I send you. Do you think St. Louis would treat you any differently—or Chicago? You hurt them and they haven't forgotten that. Americans know what really happened; they know you are not 'The Butcher of San

Antonio.' Newmericans, well, they know that if you are there, we mean business...we aren't pussyfooting around."

I'm no longer just a unit commander; I'm a damned public relations figure. That realization made him uncomfortable. He wanted to be mad about it, but Trip also knew that his reputation might scare away some troublemakers. If his wife were still with him, she would insist that he not go, which tore at him as well. *She was always worried about me, but we both should have been more worried about Jessie.* "Chicago's a hotbed of SE activity," he said. "What kind of support can I count on?"

"We will likely have rapid response National Guard troops at the ready if things get dicey," Baker replied. "Realistically, you may be on your own."

Trip understood completely what he was hearing. *We will be operating by ourselves in a hostile urban environment. They are putting me there with my men and women to send a message to the people in DC—we mean business...we are not afraid.* "I went to Chicago once. It was a war zone in some of the neighborhoods back then and that was before the Fall."

"You can assume it hasn't gotten any better, Colonel."

"What are my rules of engagement?"

"Your own common sense," he said. "There was talk about giving you some ROE, but I argued against it. If we had that in San Antonio, we would have been killed. Obviously we don't want a bloodbath there, but I'm sure as hell not going to tell you to let an angry mob attack you."

"Common sense," Trip said, repeating the General. "My dad used to say that was the rarest of commodities."

"Smart man."

"When do I go?"

"Soon," the General replied. "Transport is tricky with parts of the country pledging themselves to support the Newmerica government. We're working through the logistics. In the meantime, I need you to go over the plans for how voting will be done and come up with how you want to deploy your forces."

Trip rose to his feet. "I'd thank you, sir, but I'm not sure that's warranted."

The General rose to his feet and extended his hand to shake it. "The last civil war started when the south fired on Fort Sumpter. This one started when they stormed the White House and Congress. We didn't want or ask for this fight. If they want to press the issue Trip, you press it right back at them."

"San Antonio," he said in a low tone, shaking his COs hand.

"Goddamned right, San Antonio."

Philadelphia, Pennsylvania

Raul Lopez felt horrible, even though Jayden had assured him it was not his fault. After their stunning liberation of the Social Quarantine Camp at Valley Forge, the Order of the Bell—the Sons of Liberty resistance cell he was in—videoed some of the survivors, capturing their stories. One shot caught Raul in the background. It slipped past their editors and made it on the Internet. When they realized the mistake, they pulled it down, but Jayden said it was too late. "By now the NSF will be trying to identify you as the means of getting to us." He felt as if he had betrayed his friends and colleagues, despite assurances to the contrary.

They had evacuated everyone from the warehouse where they trained the day before and had been piling up trash to aid in the arson that was about to come. Sasha stood at his side as the building was set ablaze. Jayden had said that it was the only way to make sure no evidence was left behind. It was a filthy place; it reeked of oil and was wet and cold... but to Raul it had been his home since what had happened in Detroit. Seeing the flames roar through the old building bothered him.

Raul looked around the big empty warehouse that had been his home, realizing he would never see it again. *I feel like I have been on the run for months.* He turned to his good friend, Sasha, who seemed to understand. "We need to get on the move," Sasha said, tugging at his hand as they reached the old truck that had been assigned to them for the evacuation. Jayden, the leader of the Order of the Bell, joined them next to the pickup, sliding into the driver's seat. He brought a mix of sweat and a hint of gasoline with him in the night air. "We need to get some distance. They aren't going to show up fast, not in this neighborhood, but we don't want to be here."

The three of them slid onto the bench seat of the old Ford F-series truck as it coughed to life and pulled away. The reflection of the orange and yellow flames lapping skyward lit up the cab of the vehicle. Raul caught a glimpse of Jayden's scarred head; a bullet had glanced off of his skull at Valley Forge, leaving a scar where his hair refused to grow. They had gotten almost five blocks away before the distant wails of sirens could be heard. Raul knew they were too late to save anything of the building at this point. As an abandoned structure, the fire department likely would make sure that the conflagration didn't spread.

Jayden turned the truck in the opposite direction of where the Order of the Bell had settled, in an old steel fabrication plant at the other end of the city. "Where are we going?" Raul asked.

"I'm going to take you to a safe house," he said with a firm voice. "You're a hot commodity now. He said it is best that only a few of us know where you are."

The revelation stunned Raul. Glancing over at Sasha, he saw her head dip slightly. *She knew too!* Suddenly it made sense, why Jayden had the two of them come with him when he could have set the fire alone. "You knew?" he asked her.

Sasha nodded. "Since the video got out, your face and name are known. It puts us all at risk," she replied sadly.

It was the right decision, but he hated it. "So I'm going to be locked away?"

"Just for a while," Jayden said. "And it's not locked away. We can't afford to have you on the street."

After the rioting in Detroit, the Newmerica government had plastered his face on digital billboards everywhere. He was thankful that it was so blurry there was no way they could have enhanced it enough to identify him. Things had changed now. They had a good image, and a name associated with it. Jayden had shown him the media coverage, and it made him blush and cringe at the same time. *Now I'm putting my new family in danger.* It wasn't like the danger at Valley Forge. That was up-front, in your face. The enemy was visible. *The Newmerica government isn't just the people working for it; it is everyone that profits by the government being in place.* People turned in neighbors for any infraction, real or imaginary, to get reparation points that could be converted to cash. It made everyone a potential informant.

The truck passed an onramp onto I-476 and he turned back to Jasper. "Not taking the highway?"

"Can't," he said. "They have cameras everywhere on the federal roads, snapping pictures of car occupants. You are on the NSF's Most Wanted List."

Raul pulled out his phone and Googled the NSF's list. His face was there, along with his name, his home town in Texas, everything. In the darkness of the truck cab, the phone lit his face as he scrolled through the details. They had finally connected him to the riots in Detroit. The words, 'domestic terrorist,' hurt. "I am not a terrorist!" he blurted out, shutting the phone screen off in disgust.

"Of course you're not," Sasha replied. "None of us are."

"I might be," Jayden said with a chuckle.

"Now isn't a good time, Jayden," Sasha snapped back. "He feels bad enough as it is."

"Do not worry, Raul. I sent word to an SOL group in Texas to protect your family," Jayden said, trying to calm him.

My madre...he hadn't thought of her. *And his sisters!* They would see the news—no, worse! The NSF would show up and interrogate them. They would think that he was a murderer, or worse. A wave of sorrow swept him. "Will they be OK?"

"The SEs don't have much sway in Texas," Sasha said. "The NSF is there, at least for the time being, but I'm sure our people will protect them," Sasha offered. The words were the right words, but they did not abate his worry. *What will they do to them?* He had seen what the Social Quarantine camps were like, how they tortured and starved people to break their will. *What if they send them to a place like that?* His mother was strong, but not that strong. His younger sisters were kids—but from what Raul knew, children were not spared the wrath of the government. His enemies knew no limits—no rules applied to them, no restrictions. *Because of me, they will suffer.* Suddenly he felt as if the weight of the world had returned to his shoulders. It was worse than when his actions had triggered riots in Detroit. This time it was deeply personal.

"I have to get to my family," Raul said.

"No, no, my friend. That is exactly what they would want. You need to stay away from Texas for now."

"But from what the news said, Texas is now loyal to the true President. It would be safe there."

"There are very few truly safe places," Jayden said. "Even in Texas, there are SEs and the NSF, though I heard that the Texas Rangers are still independent. Even so, Newmerica is everywhere. It is like a hunt; they will try and drive you from cover so they can capture you."

"We didn't do anything wrong," Raul protested. "We freed those people. They were being treated horribly, and we got them out of there."

Jayden turned the old Ford onto a dark street of older buildings, warehouses and long-closed factories that were little more than brick canvas for graffiti. It wasn't even an old part of Philadelphia, from what Raul knew. It was a neighborhood that had been gutted by the riots during the first year of the Liberation. One store they passed, an auto parts supplier, had been gutted by fires and left to rot. "The people that put them in those camps don't like having their noses rubbed in their own *mierda*. What we did was the right thing to do, but not to the government that set those camps up in the first place. With the Big Tech companies scrambling after the attacks on them, our images and videos got out. The country saw what the camps really were. A lot of people refused to believe it, but they can't shake those pictures we posted. That hurt the leaders of Newmerica and they want revenge." His voice rang with conviction and Raul knew what he said was true.

"How long will I be staying at this safe house?" he asked, as Jayden made another turn onto a street that led to long rows of houses that all looked the same.

"Not long," Jayden said, giving him a moment of hope. "I have reached out to our leadership. They are sending someone to escort you to a safer state than this one."

Those words hurt as well. It wasn't just that he and Sasha were close; the entire cell was like family to him. He had felt that way in the Youth Corps and had been forced to flee Detroit. Now he was being ripped away one more time from people he knew and trusted. *This isn't fair!* "I don't want to go, Jayden," he protested. "You are my family."

Jayden nodded as he drove. "And we see you the same way, Raul. The only way to keep us safe, is for you to move on. It isn't forever, just until things calm down. If they were to capture you, they would know who we are and be able to round us up as well."

"I would never talk."

The leader of the Order of the Bell shook his head. "They would eventually break you, Raul. Even the strongest person would talk eventually. We all like to think we could hold out, but in the end, almost everyone snaps. Even I would.

"I don't like having to do this, but it is the only way to preserve us." As he rounded a corner, he stopped the old truck, and its brakes squealed slightly as he did. Jayden nodded at the house they had parked in front of, a small, red, ranch-style home with a tall, wooden fence surrounding the backyard. The lights were off and the drapes were drawn. The place looked abandoned. "That's the place. Knock twice and they will take you in."

His body felt limp as he put his hand on the door. Sasha stopped him, touched his face and pulled it to hers. She kissed him, deeply, her tongue twisting around his. He pulled her close and held on for what seemed like a minute. Slowly she pulled back. "We will see each other again, Raul," she whispered.

Opening the truck door, he numbly stepped out into the darkness and walked away.

The District

Rebecca Clarke, Director of the Truth Reconciliation Committee, sat behind her sleek, black topped modern desk and found herself grimacing at the events of the last few weeks. The anniversary of the Liberation broadcast had been hijacked by terrorists, and they had sworn in a President—the former Vice President, who was supposed to be dead. Five Social Quarantine Camps had been raided by the Sons of Liberty, a group thought to have been extinguished, and their inmates were put on the Internet and they told tales of mistreatment and abuse. Then a disgruntled NSF staffer named Caylee Leatrom had released hundreds of classified communications showing that the Secretary had a covert private force, operatives, which were used for assassinations, torture, and worse. While rumors of operatives had been out there for years, this confirmation and the implication that the government had been murdering people was damning. *Any one of these things I could deal with, but together, they are daunting.*

She brushed back her short, black hair and stared at the screen of her laptop that showed the overview of the plans for dealing with each issue. The government's allies in Big Tech normally would have blocked the material, but they had been attacked and had been slow to respond. *Those insipid geeks are all afraid after the bombings.* Everything had been going so well. *Our call for a new Constitutional Convention has been ruined by these events.* On top of that, the Secretary of the NSF blamed Clarke for the hijacking of the Liberation celebration. She knew the Secretary well; they both served on the Ruling Council. *The last thing I needed was for her to lay the blame at my feet. This was a security matter—that's her responsibility.*

The biggest threat was not the doubt that the information generated, but it was the sudden reappearance of the man who claimed to be President. If he did manage to somehow consolidate power, she and the other members of the Ruling Council would be painted as insurrectionists and traitors. The justice they had been delivering on others would be turned against them. *I will not be paraded like a criminal. That will never happen!*

Rebecca handled the reappearance of the Vice President according to the playbook that she had written. *Delegitimize, label, discredit, generate fear, and intimidate.* It was a combination that worked most effectively. She knew that arguing the facts was never a good stance for the Newmerica government. If he was the legitimate Vice President, challenging that would prove to be unstable ground. *Even in the early years of the Liberation, we never allowed ourselves to get bogged down in facts.*

The first step was easy; call the man a liar. "Is this really the former Vice President? How was that possible when his body had been recovered?" Labeling him became important. Words like, 'fascist,' 'coward,' 'homophobe,' 'Alt-Right,' 'betrayer,' and 'racist,' were woven into every newscast Rebecca had influence over—which was most of them. *People are weak minded. If they hear or see something enough, they will believe it, even if it isn't true.*

The next step was to discredit him in the eyes of the public. That was easy; he was second in command behind the Traitor President whom she had been smearing since his election. Ruining This upstart's reputation was ruined so that no one could possibly trust anything he said. Stories were crafted that linked him to extremist groups that no longer existed, and a handful of new ones that her people had written backstories for. She wanted to paint him as a pedophile, a terrorist, a baby-killer, anything that might erode the image of him as leading the nation. It had worked before; they were the same tactics that had been used just prior to the Liberation and the death of the Traitor President. Labels gutted reputations and gave the masses reasons to not trust or believe someone. Sometimes that was all that it took, planting a doubt. *No one wants to support someone that others are calling a pedophile or a domestic terrorist.*

Smearing him was a tactic that Rebecca had at her disposal and one she loved. The problem was that the former VP had not been involved or implicated in scandals or criminal incidents in his past. That was no problem for her; it simply meant working with what they did have. He was a Christian and that would do. Devout Christians tended to favor conservative ideals, which was why the Newmerica government had targeted their churches. Christian had become synonymous with homophobe, standing against a woman's right to choose, or any alternate lifestyle. His faith was twisted to make him look like a crazed radical. She made sure that when he was referenced in new broadcasts, his Christian backing was part of his description, hoping to stir the pot of loathing even more. *It isn't enough for people to be uncomfortable with him. I need them to hate him...every single aspect of his life.* She had done it before, many times, with great success. She ensured that in every image of him he was frowning or he was pictured with the Traitor President.

Threats and intimidation were the next Chapter of the playbook. The Ruling Council gave her the ammunition to fire those shots. They were mobilizing some loyal National Guard units and declared that if this so-called President did not turn himself in, it would lead to civil war. Images of troops, tanks, and barricades in places like Times Square were intended to bully this pretender to the throne. *I want people to associate his return with violence.* Having the Social Enforcers in major cities marching in the street, holding banners and calling for him to step down, made people fear that riots might follow. *We will lay that fear at his doorstep. It is his fault, not ours.*

There were problems, however, ones she could not escape. People fondly remembered him as a VP despite his association with the traitor. In the videos he released to the Internet, he sounded firm, convicted, and righteous. He spoke of love of country. Patriotism had been painted for five years as 'fascist thinking,' but many in the nation seemed to crave it. His return had stirred feelings that the Traitor President was some sort of martyr, someone who had given his life for a failed cause. Six months ago everyone hated the man; now, with the return of his former Vice President, people began to question the story that he had died in prison. The polls that Rebecca had commissioned showed that his messages were resonating with people, and that was a problem. *We had the entire world at our feet; now everything is unraveling. This pretender has formed a government and is screaming for new, fair elections. We don't have things in place like we did before when we skewed the voting to our favor.* For the first time since the Liberation, Rebecca felt as if she and the Ruling Council were on the defensive and she hated that.

Larger concerns were in play. What had happened in the United States had ripple effects around the world. When the Liberation happened, similar moves had toppled the governments of Spain, Italy, France and the UK. The British Royal Family were living in exile as ANTIFA-backed forces stormed their castles and plundered the nation's museums. Three times the German President had been targeted with assassination attempts. His response had been a brutal smack-down of the freedom fighters. Now that the Pretender-President had emerged and had claimed the role of his predecessor, international concerns might trigger counterrevolutions in Europe as well. *This has the potential of getting out of hand globally.*

This was not Rebecca's first rodeo—though the stakes felt oddly different to her. *We have always fought the information war against our enemies. Now, they are striking at us. People had doubts about the government and our leaders, and they are giving them substance.*

The knock at her door indicated that her 10:00 a.m. meeting had arrived. "Enter," she said, closing her screen on the laptop. One of her top people, Tess Ditka, was handling it, but Tess had been smart enough to know she had to coordinate with her.

Tess led the other two people in and gestured to the guest chairs. Rebecca did not stand for her visitors, but she offered her trademark smile. "And who do we have here?" she asked, darting her eyes at Tess.

"These are the Detectives Reese and Gallagher," Tess said. The male, Dale Gallagher, extended his hand to her, but she waved it off. "I don't shake hands, Detective," she replied. "Old habit from the pandemic."

Tess continued. "They are the Detectives working the Raul Lopez case."

"Ah, yes, you're the ones going on *Sixty Minutes* this week," Rebecca said.

"Yes. We want to make sure that we get our perp's face out there," Gallagher said, shifting in his seat. She eyed his short-cropped, salt-and-pepper hair, his perfectly split chin, and saw an old school cop. Even his choice of clothes, a non-discrete tweed sport coat and a button-down blue shirt made him easy to see as a law enforcement officer. "This script that you sent us, well, I was under the impression that this was an interview by the media."

"We can't have you out there free-wheeling your answers, Detective," she replied.

"Ma'am—" Detective Reese started, but Rebecca cut her off. "Don't use that pronoun, please. You may refer to me as Director."

"Director," the younger Reese corrected herself, her light skin blushing slightly. "Some of these answers your people have written for us, well, they are not right."

"Such as?"

Gallagher cut in, "Like the part where you have us saying that Lopez was inspired to action by the so-called President and other radical groups. We have found zero leads to link him directly to organizations other than the Youth Corps and the Order of the Bell."

"No doubt the attack at Valley Forge was timed with the Pretender-President being sworn in. So the link is there." She corrected his manner of referring to the former Vice President. *And even if you don't think it exists, it does, because I say so. It fits our narrative.*

"I don't care what you call him," Detective Gallagher replied. "We haven't found the link."

Tess spoke up. "You can see what I have been struggling with Director," she said, which earned a scornful, side glance from Gallagher.

Detective Reese spoke up, perhaps hoping to diffuse the tension that had emerged. "And this piece where you have us saying that Lopez is suspected in the murder of his entire Youth Corps team. While it is true that we have not been able to locate any of them, nothing that we have seen or heard points to him as having killed them. If anything, our investigation has shown that he was *defending* them when that Dearborn SE Team attacked them."

Gathering her thoughts, Rebecca said nothing for a moment. "Detectives, I appreciate your perspective. Let me share mine. You seem to think that this is about sharing information with the public to apprehend an enemy of the state. That is admirable but short sighted. When you are on TV, you will be representing the Newmerica government. Our narrative is important for people to hear, to reinforce other stories that are out there. People want comfort in consistency. For them, they need to hear that this Lopez is a threat, a heartless killer. They need the fear. When the people have fear, a fear they can attribute to an enemy, it makes them feel they are part of a greater solution. So the script is important. Your following it is critical to ensuring the consistency people crave."

Now it was Detective Gallagher's turn to blush. "I'm a detective. My job is solving crimes. I'm not here to be a mouthpiece for narrative." He rose to his feet and the younger Reese did the same. They left the office, which suited Rebecca fine. She turned to Tess Ditka. "Reese understands and fits the image we want for women in power. Get her hair cut shorter before the interview, more man-ish so that it plays well with our transgenders and binaries. See if you can get a little streak of pink in it. She's blonde, so that will show that we are progressive in the NSF."

"I was thinking the same thing. I have some folks working on her clothes too. I thought something dark blue, not flashy, but crisp—you know, professional."

"Agreed. As for Gallagher, let's replace him with an actor. I want someone younger. Get someone with a bun or a ponytail. A scraggly beard is good too. We want him to appeal to both men and women."

"Very good, Director," Tess said.

"And make sure they stick to the script," she said, closing out the conversation. As Ditka left her office, Rebecca leaned back. *One problem solved...a thousand more to go …*

CHAPTER 4

"Hating the government is hating yourself."

University of Virginia
Charlottesville, Virginia

Maddie Steele struggled for several days to find an extracurricular group to join that wouldn't force her to compromise her principles. It proved to be a daunting task. Most groups were easy to rule out. As much as she loved writing, the student newspaper was merely a TRC-driven propaganda tool for the Newmerica administration. She had considered the equestrian team, but remembered they often led student protest marches. There were three book clubs, but looking at their list of books, she cringed. Titles like *Learning to Embrace Your Inner Racist*, or *American Origins—How Slaves Built the United States* were inherently corrupt to her way of thinking. Even the painting group was hijacked from time to time to paint banners and signs for the more militant student groups. It seemed that every aspect of student life had been permeated by politics. *It is like my parents warned me. Wokeism is everywhere.*

Student politics was easy and encouraged by the faculty and administration. Even violent protests were causes for celebration. Students shared 'war stories' of attacking individuals they felt didn't agree with them. They reveled in causing harm to people or businesses that did not align with their beliefs. It made her sick to listen to them talk about attacking locals simply based on rumors that they might be former Republicans. The fact that the faculty not only endorsed but took part in riotous behavior only added to her angst. She saw that the school was forging students into militants, devoid of regret or remorse for their actions.

As much as she hated Doctor Morose's interference and insisting that she join a group, she had come to appreciate what he was doing as a warning. Someone was observing her. They must have suspected that she was not political for a reason.

She had finally settled on a student pottery group. They met weekly, Wednesday nights, for three hours making plates, vases, and sculptures. She cared little for pottery, but she felt that it was safe. If nothing else, she could make some Christmas gifts for family members. While she didn't have a natural aptitude for it, several group members were more than willing to offer assistance. Maddie's was surprised by her first project, a vase that was beautiful after it was glazed. *Even Mom is going to love it.*

Just before her meeting of the group for the third session, she heard a rap at the door of her dorm room at Metcalf Hall. She opened the door to be greeted by a trio of girls, only one of which she knew on sight. Deborah was a beefy girl, who kept her hair short with streaks of pink in it. She wore a nose ring, which didn't help her looks at all. Beside her were two strangers, a young black student who wore a gray hoodie with BLM stitched on it, clearly purchased from the UVA bookstore. The other was a skinny girl wearing a green T-shirt that had stylish tears in several places. "Can I help you?" Maddie asked.

"Yeah," Deborah said. "We were checking student profiles on Facebook. We noticed that you had not put up the logo on your social media for the student ANTIFA rally this weekend. The Chainbreakers expect student support. That includes you."

"I don't do much with my social media accounts," she replied. It was an understatement on her part. She deliberately did not post anything other than occasional updates or non-discreet photos. Her father had warned her that other students would be watching her.

"Well," the young black woman jumped in with a twist of attitude. "Everyone is posting it and you aren't. That got us wondering; is there a reason you are not supporting the rally?"

She tried to keep a poker face but could feel her skin get warmer. "It's not that; I don't keep up with social media. I'm busy with studies."

"It's been pointed out," Deborah weighed in, "That no one has seen you at any of the rallies or protests."

Maddie made the decision then and there to lie—it was the best course of action at that millisecond. "That's not true. I have gone to several rallies!"

"Well no one has seen you there," the girl in the green T-shirt weighed in with an accusatory tone.

"Well I was," she huffed in response, trying to appear offended by their accusation.

The chunky Deborah leaned in slightly. "We haven't seen you; nor can anyone else remember your attending anything."

"You're spying on me?"

"We are watching you," the black female said. "We watch everybody."

Her mind raced. These were essentially strangers, showing up in her room, making accusations. Was this a prelude to something else, something physical? Her mind danced to the small pistol her father had given her, which was hidden in her room. He had told her to keep it. "There's only three things you can count on Maddie—family, Smith and Wesson." He had taken her shooting many times, training her on how to aim and shoot properly. The temptation to grab the weapon was there, but she suppressed it.

"You've got no business in what I do or don't do," Maddie snapped. She had observed students long enough to know that being a victim was respected, so she donned that emotional cloak quickly. "What are you up to, spending your time looking at what I do on social media?"

The two white girls had not expected that response; that was clear from the stunned looks on their faces. The young black girl was unshaken. "Look here, girl. We have eyes on you. People that don't take part in politics—they are suspicious. People that don't do what everyone else does, like promoting protests on Facebook; they might be posers, pretending to be supporters when in reality they are the opposite. We are watching you," she warned. With that, the trio stormed off down the hall. Maddie closed the door and locked it; then with her back against the door, she slowly slid to the floor. Her heart was pounding and she was stunned at the boldness of their confrontation.

They threatened me. They came here to intimidate me, maybe flush me out. Her father had been right about the risks of attending a nonconservative school. For years she had managed to be invisible. But now she knew—people were watching her.

She wondered what to do. It would be easy to post the banner about the protest on her social media accounts. That was not going to be enough. Like the girl had warned, they were watching her. Maddie had known that someone was observing her; Dr. Morose had tipped her off to that. Now it was clear that more than one person was involved. Just putting up a meme on Facebook was not going to suffice; she realized that. She didn't want to do it; it was the same as caving in to their intimidation tactics, which rubbed her the wrong way. *If I could do that and it would end this, I would...but it won't be enough for them.*

The realization hit her hard. *I'm going to have to go to one of those rallies.*

The District

The NSF Secretary had to admit that she liked the bit of subterfuge that Burke Dorne had insisted on for the meeting. It was twilight, and the sun was setting beyond the hills of Arlington and Joint Base Meyer in Virginia, across the Potomac. She walked over to the steps of the Clinton Peace Monument and looked up at the statue of the dead President. Gone were any hints of Thomas Jefferson, whom the memorial had originally been built for. His statue had been melted down and made into Freedom Medallions, awards granted by the Ruling Council to individuals that demonstrated sacrifice for the Newmerica cause.

As much as she was vocal regarding women's rights, she had not been opposed to Bill Clinton replacing Thomas Jefferson. He was a flawed man; there was no arguing that. Then again, toxic masculinity made males inherently flawed. The irony of the word 'peace' as part of the monument was not lost on her either. *Somalia, Bosnia...this is more of a monument as to how we can reshape history when it is convenient.* While far from perfect, his wife had lobbied hard for the monument, burning the last of her political capital in the process. The Secretary had abstained on the final vote rather than support it, something that Hillary Clinton had been scornful of until the day she died. *She was a bitter relic of a failed system anyway.*

Climbing the steps, she saw the figure of Burke Dorne in front of the statue and moved up alongside him. Dorne was nominally in charge of her clandestine group of operatives. The night of the Liberation, he had betrayed his peers in the Secret Service, practically opening the doors of the White House and Treasury to the mob. Dorne had proved his worth, doxing many of his comrades at a critical juncture during the overthrow. He was a true believer in the cause, enough to be responsible for the deaths of numerous Secret Service and Homeland Security staff.

Dorne was more than that to her…he was a fallback plan of sorts. She knew Senator Lewis's witch hunt probe of her agency was going to demand that heads roll. It wasn't personal; it was political. If push came to shove, she fully intended that the person to take the fall would be Burke Dorne. While she hoped it wouldn't come to pass, she had already made preparations—made sure that Caylee Leatrom was connected to Dorne, more so than her. *In the end, who will they likely believe? Someone that was a traitor to his own organization? Or me, a former Congresswoman and member of the Ruling Council.*

If all went as planned, she wouldn't have to throw Dorne under the bus. She had something larger in the works, something that would solve several problems at once. It had taken two operatives to detail out; it was that complex. Men like Senator Lewis were not corruptible. The only way to take them down was to make them into something they weren't. Documents were being created; voice recordings were being forged, and a dozen little details were being worked out. *My whole life people have underestimated me, and that is a mistake they will all regret.*

"We work in the same building, Dorne," she said. "This cloak and dagger stuff is fun and all, but hardly necessary."

"What we have to talk about shouldn't be done in the office," he said. "You can't be sure who might be monitoring what we say."

That made her chuckle. "Burke, the NSA, FBI, Homeland Security—they are all NSF now. They report to me. We are the ones that do the monitoring."

"Are we?" he said, handing her a small device no larger than a pencil eraser. "We found this under a lamp in my office."

"A bug?"

He nodded. "Not a high end one—commercially available."

Someone dared to spy on her? *This is going to cost someone their life.*

"We have surveillance systems in place. Who planted it?"

"Secretary, you specifically asked that your office not be monitored. As I recall, you said, 'I'm not falling into Nixon's trap.'" Dorne hid some of his smugness, but not nearly enough for her taste.

"I want to know. Who did this?" she demanded.

"I have people working that. The range of this device is relatively short."

"So the person monitoring or recording is how far away?"

"Within 500 feet."

Her mind raced through the possibilities. First was the people supporting the Pretender President. *Of course I would be a primary target; I'm leading the fight against them.* The District was a secured place, with checkpoints, street-sweeps, and federal ID required to move about the city-state. *Unless they are using an operative-level person, it can't be them.*

Was it Senator Lewis? His hearings were coming up soon and he had already demonstrated a knack for getting information about her agency. *He's daring, but not this bold. He would not risk pulling a stunt so close to his little circus show. He won't do anything that might damage the credibility of his time in front of the camera. I can deal with him...after all, he's a politician. That means that his morals and his values are subject to change.*

That opened up a more disturbing thought. What if it was someone from the Ruling Council? Or some rogue element within the FedGov that was not loyal to her? Was it possible that some of her people might be turning against her? She wanted to dismiss the thought, but she couldn't. I have stepped on toes—it is a necessary part of my job. Protecting Newmerica meant you had to take extreme measures from time to time. She knew that every action she took was in defense of what she and the others in the Ruling Council had built. *That doesn't mean that some of them wouldn't rejoice about me falling.* The Secretary internally cringed at that thought. Almost all of them had been threatened or blackmailed by her at one time or another. *Just about all of them would rejoice at my downfall, but I doubt any of them have the balls to try such a brazen act of subterfuge.* Still, it was a difficult thought to shake.

"I want polygraphs of everyone that has been in the building in the last thirty days," she said firmly.

“I will handle it personally,” Dorne replied.

“Good,” she said casting a quick glance at the smiling bronze statue of President Clinton, his arm around his wife.

Indianapolis, Indiana

The head of the Secret Service, Charli Kazinski, hated the trips the President was taking. Jack had told her that the visits were necessary for political reasons, but that didn’t make her job any easier. Indianapolis was safer than most cities; it was in the President’s home state. Jack had done well to make sure that his supporters greatly outnumbered the Newmerica protesters. Still, all it took was one determined person to infiltrate the crowd. The warning from Caylee made matters even more tense for Charli.

There were threats everywhere when the President went out in public, now more than ever. Busloads of SEs and BLM protesters tried to come into the state from Illinois and Michigan. They were met at the state borders by loyal NSF troopers and, in two cases, biker gangs that had blockaded the roads in anticipation of their arrival. The Sons of Liberty, the SOL, had shown up as well, armed to the teeth. When they tried to ‘peacefully protest’ being stopped, they were met with overwhelming force and many were arrested, and their weapons were confiscated. Shots had been fired at one biker gang and for several hours, Charli had seen images on the Internet of buses being set ablaze and protesters being rounded up. Big Tech censors had eventually taken them down, but it was reassuring that the majority of the protesters had been intercepted. As for the beatings…*play adult games, win adult prizes. Bullies and thugs are all tough until they face real resistance.*

She knew that didn’t mean the President was safe, not by a long shot. There were local protesters, no doubt fueled by hate and propped up financially by the Ruling Council. The NSF in Indiana had splintered and the majority sided with the Governor and the President. Loyal NSF forces had donned their old uniforms in many cases and were actively working to keep protesters blocks away from where the President was visiting, making the organization disappear in a matter of days. Her advance team had carefully vetted everyone working security, but she knew that was not enough.

Charli knew that the real threat was less likely from a black bloc wearing punk kid than from one of the NSF's covert operatives. She had spent time with Caylee, prying out of her how operatives worked. That was the threat she feared most, the next Caylee Leatrom lurking in the shadows. Operatives were trained killers, ruthless, utterly devoted to protecting the Newmerica cause. Caylee had told her how operatives looked for every crack in security, how they were trained to blend in. They were trained for penetration operations, knew explosives and were adept in long range sniper fire. Charli had posted her new Secret Service agents on the rooftops and in any location that might pose a threat. As much as she liked to believe she had covered all of her bases, she knew Caylee and respected her skills. *A lone operative can do a shitload of damage in a short time.*

She had convinced the new President not to announce some of his schedule. This outing had never been made public; it was a spur of the moment activity. Doing that made it difficult for even an operative to plan an attempt on the President's life. Difficult—but not impossible.

As they moved toward the Soldier's and Sailor's monument in the middle of the city, she worked with the crowd. Most of her new agents were former military men and women that had mustered out after the Joint Chiefs had refused to come to the aid of the former President. They formed a cordon around the President as he moved, a human shell, keeping the onlookers at bay. Charli shifted with them, helping augment the small, trusted team she had put together. Her eyes were everywhere, watching for anything that seemed potentially threatening.

She spied one woman that stood out to her. While most of the crowd was cheering, waving their hands to get the attention of the President, a short, stocky, black female was not smiling—not cheering. As Charli and the security detail moved around the circle of the massive Civil War statue, she angled herself to get a better view of the female.

The woman's arms were at her sides. Where the rest of the crowd looked happy, she had a scowl on her face. "This is Slingshot," she said over the cheers of the crowd. "Possible target. Off to my two o'clock. Black female, short, yellow top."

"This is Ringo," responded agent Kingston. "I've got her. She has her hand on her purse."

"This is Rocket," came the voice of agent Angela Herringer. "I am shifting to intercede."

Charli's eyes darted to the President and then to her team members. Rocket was in civilian attire, a common practice for agents. "Rocket—have you got her?"

"I'm on it, Slingshot," she said. Charli's heart started to pound as it always did when she worked the protection detail. She would have preferred to be in a command van, but her selection process for the newly formed Secret Service was intense, leaving her with a shortage of agents. Rocket slid through the crowd, squeezing past people with hardly anyone noticing. Angling up behind the suspect, she deliberately bumped her, jostling her purse from her shoulder down to her hand. Charli heard her say, "I'm sorry," and Charli reached down to help her with the purse, giving her a chance to double-check it.

"No glory," she called. "Nothing in her purse of any consequence."

Charli wanted to sigh with relief but didn't. There was still fifteen minutes with the crowd and she was hell bent on making sure another President didn't die on her watch.

Later that afternoon she moved into the temporary office that Service had taken over in the Birch Bayh building. Unlike another nearby old federal building, The Joe Donnelly Freedom Center, formerly the Minton-Capehart Building, it had not been forced to change its name after the Fall. Birch Bayh was of the right political party, though the Newmerica government had started to change those old legacy named buildings as well, embracing the new 'inspirational leaders' since the overthrow of the government.

The room was musty and the furniture was old, probably older than Charli herself. The President was secured aboard Air Force One with his transit detail and she was busy packing up. It surprised her to see Jack Desmond walk in. "There are times when I miss the good old days," he said with a wry grin. Jack had been in charge of the defense of the White House during the Fall and had been Charli's boss at the time.

"I figured you would be with Silver Eagle," she said.

"I drew the short stick this time. You know the drill, not all of the cabinet positions on the same plane. I'm hoping to catch a ride back with you."

"Missing your earlier career?" she smirked.

"I never asked for any of this," Jack said. "You know that. They pushed me, hard. So I did what I always do. I am pushing back twice as hard at them."

"Good," she said with a resounding tone in her voice. "They have pushed half of the country around. I like the fact that *they* are nervous for a change. At the same time, it does create some risks for me and my people."

"I saw your message," he said, taking a seat on the old gray desk.

"Colorado is too risky, too blue," she said. "Same with New Jersey."

"I agree," he said.

"Excellent," she replied with relief. The President had provided a list of locations he wanted to visit and Charli had been blunt in her reaction to some of them.

"Don't pat yourself on the back. He's the President and he makes the call. When I spoke to him about it, he suggested Maryland as an alternative."

"Please don't say Baltimore."

Jack's face winced in response. "Like I said, he's the President."

"Jack, he's only the President until someone kills him. The Ruling Council has whipped up a good portion of the country to do just that. Baltimore is 45 minutes from DC. Look, if he insists on Baltimore, push him into Fort McHenry."

"He wants people to see him," Jack countered.

"They will. The local media will cover it and we can arrange for boats to come by and do a little parade of sorts. We can clear a large enough audience for him. It's a patriotic site. My people have scoped it out. Since Francis Scott Key was deemed a racist, the site has been closed for close to five years by the FedGov. He can talk about how they are destroying our nation's history. Most important, it is safe."

Desmond nodded in response. "I'll make it happen, Charli. I have to say, you are becoming quite politically astute. That old Charli never would have backed her argument that way. I'm impressed."

Coming from Jack, his words meant a lot. "I—we have all been through a lot. We've risked everything in supporting him. It's the only way to get back to the way things used to be." Her memories of hiding, pretending to be an NSF officer, and the death of the former President weighed heavy on her. "If I have to adapt to win, then that's what I'm going to do."

Jack nodded knowingly. "Let me help you pack up," he said, sliding off the edge of the desk. Charli watched him grab a camera case and start for the hallway. For a brief moment, it was like the old days…before the Fall. *God I miss my life then.*

CHAPTER 5

"Freedom is selfish."

Philadelphia, Pennsylvania

Deja Jordan had never been to Philadelphia. Her first reaction was that it smelled funny. All cities had a certain stink to them, especially in the early morning hours. It was a mix of garbage, humidity, and sometimes the hint of urine or feces from the Shelter-Dependent People. Philadelphia had that and a hint of rotting wood, a musty stench, and something else, almost a metallic taste, that lingered on the back of her tongue. Minneapolis still had the aroma from the fires that had engulfed the city some mornings during and after the pandemic. Deja wondered if every large city had its own unique bouquet.

Her hotel was near the site of Independence Hall, and she had gone down to that plaza after arriving the night before. After the Liberation, the Liberty Bell had been removed…she had heard plenty of rumors about what had been done with it. Independence Hall had been set on fire during a celebratory protest over the death of the Traitor President. Its destruction made perfect sense to her; the Founding Fathers were all white men, bathed in rich, white privilege. *They could have ended slavery when they formed this country, but they chose to keep my people in chains. Why have a building to celebrate a founding that was based on the sweat and blood of enslaved people?* The burned out building had been dismantled, and the bricks had been turned into paving stones for the new Liberation Plaza. She had walked the almost empty plaza, surrounded by stores that had been burned or abandoned since the riots, admiring the statues of the victims of oppression, men and women murdered by racist police officers. The sculptors did not have the statues look down at those on the plaza, but skyward. It was inspiring for her. *They gave their lives bravely so that we could have Newmerica. They don't have to look down ever again.*

Walking the streets, she arrived at the headquarters for the largest of the Social Enforcement teams that worked the city, Righteous Liberty. The logo for their Chapter was Independence Hall in flames and as she entered, she saw numerous eyes at the main desk focused on her. "I'm Deja Jordan. I'm here to meet with—"

"We know who you are and who you are meeting with," the young white girl at the desk said, tossing her blonde, streaked, pink hair to the side. "He's down the hall, first door on the left." She didn't even gesture with her hands, only a quick darting of her eyes.

Deja understood the attitude. Social Enforcement teams were close knit. Outsiders, even someone like her, a comrade in arms, was viewed with distrust. In this case, there were likely more in play. *They were embarrassed in front of the whole world by the Valley Forge incident. That puts them on the defensive.* As she entered the office in the former police precinct, she saw a tall man sitting at a desk. He clearly did not fit the run down décor of the office. It was newer, modern, sleek…no doubt looted. That was part of being in the SEs, you got first pick of your victim's stuff, and this man had clearly wanted a top-of-the-line desk.

"I'm Deja Jordan," she said, extending her hand.

He rose and shook hers, hard, almost as if he were deliberately attempting to hurt her with his grip. "Trey Phillips," he said. "They told me you was coming. Said you was looking for Raul Lopez. Word is you are some sort of hunter." He gestured to the seat in front of the massive, black desk and she slid into it.

"That's right," she said taking a slight pause. "The word I use is *Digger*. Look, I know this must look like some strange shit. I'm not even from here. I didn't understand it either. But they gave me my orders and tickets and sent me. I don't want to step on any toes or anything. Hell, I'm not sure if I can be much of a help here or not. I'm just doing what the new bosses said to do."

Her words seemed to erase at least two wrinkles on Trey's tall brow.

"Some strange-ass shit has been going down," he said. "Four weeks ago my regional director went on a trip, or so they told me. My regional hated to travel. She was afraid of flying. She was going to meet with me that Monday morning. No phone call, nothing. I tried to reach out to her family; I got nothing. She just up and disappeared. My new NSF manager said she's on extended leave, but no one seems to be able to contact her."

"Four weeks?"

"Yeah."

She paused. "My district manager died right around the same time. Strange circumstances too."

Trey nodded and almost showed a smile. "I've been doing some digging on my own, under the table shit. Right before we got folded into the NSF, all but two of the leadership of the SEs have either died or disappeared."

Deja leaned back in her seat, almost as if his words had pushed her there. "It's not a coincidence," she said slowly.

"Fuck no! It all happened right before the NSF moved in. We got played. The NSF has always hated us. They were never about the cause; hell, most of those cops were the ones trying to crack our skulls for protesting. There's some other shit too. I heard that a few SE teams were killed by the NSF…their black ops fuckers."

It was hard to process. Why would the NSF take out the leadership of Social Enforcement? *It would be easier for them to assume control. We were going to be powerless to respond. Cut off the head and the body dies.* "You've been able to confirm it?"

Trey nodded. "Pretty much. It has taken me weeks to piece it together. They bent us over and fucked us from behind, hard. So you can imagine. I'm a little suspicious when someone from another SE team is shuffled in here from out of state."

"I'm not here for any other reason than they sent me," she replied. "Maybe they want me out of Minneapolis? I don't know. I came because my new NSF boss told me to, nothing more or less."

Trey Phillips paused; his eyes narrowed as he looked at her. "Okay. This whole thing with the shakeup has got a lot of people on edge, including me. I mean almost overnight, we got stabbed in the ass by the

NSF. And for what?"

"I always ask myself one question, 'Who benefits from these actions?'" she said.

"That would be that ice-cold bitch in charge—the Secretary of the NSF. Our new boss."

She nodded. It made sense. The leadership of the SEs is removed, and almost instantly, the surviving organization is reorganized under the NSF. *Would she be that bold? We are talking about the murder of possibly dozens of people. Would she do that just to get control of the SEs?* She paused for a moment thinking it over. *Yes, she would. She started out as a ditzy Congresswoman, and since the Liberation, she is in charge of the largest police force on the planet. If this was planned out, she could have used her operatives to pull it off.* "I am not surprised," she finally said. "That woman is dangerous. We didn't realize how dangerous until she got into real power."

"I'm not shocked either," Trey replied. "She pulled off her own little coup. Kill everyone that might resist her; then simply take us over. That's some seriously cold shit. It makes you wonder what else she has planned."

"I'd rather not go there," Deja replied. Her answer was honest, because it was scary to contemplate. "We should focus on this little SOL fucker that caused all the trouble. So what do you have on this Raul Lopez?"

"We know that it was the Sons of Liberty that hit Valley Forge. Some group calling itself the Order of the Bell or some bullshit like that. I talked to our people there and at least two of the survivors of their raid are pretty sure he was with them. The SOL was thought to be dead; I mean no one had heard from them in years. Suddenly they got up in our shit big time."

"Any ideas of where they are?"

Trey nodded quickly. "A few. Word is they may have been using an old industrial building as a base. It was burned a few days ago…arson according to the NSF and the fire department. That kind of shit happens all of the time in those old buildings; the capitalists that own them torch them for the insurance money. We got a tip though; had to use some knuckle-persuasion to get it, but he talked. Said that there was a bunch of people living there for weeks; they had guns too. It had to be the SOL."

"They must've gotten him out of the city by now," she said.

Trey got slightly defiant. "No fucking way. NSF has cameras and heat scanners on the highways. Even if he was hiding in the trunk, we'd know it. We have put people at all of the checkpoints in and out of the city starting right after the raid. We know that he was filmed after they hit the camp, and he was in the city then. I think he's still here."

"So he's gone deep."

Trey nodded. "Little fucker is hiding somewhere local; he has to be. I think we need to start tossing some neighborhoods; you know, the kinds of places where he might be or his buddies might be holed up. We get our hands on one of these SOL greasers, we will get them all."

She understood the thinking, but Philadelphia seemed too big for such tactics. "What you are talking about would take every SE warrior in three states to pull off."

"You have a better idea?"

As a matter of fact I do. "We need his mother and other family members. NSF has been looking for them. The NSF works one way, and we work another. We have people in Texas. We need to lay hands on his mother. We squeeze her and he will come out of hiding."

"I like the way you think," he said smiling. "If it was any place but Texas. Yeah, we have people down there, but not like up here. Those Texas racist-rednecks have a hard-on for Social Enforcement."

He was right. She couldn't deny it. Deja had watched the slaughter of innocent people in San Antonio years ago on television. It had made recruitment for social justice warriors in the state next to impossible. "Send the word to other states to get our people in there. No matter where this Lopez is, if we get his mom, he will have to come out of hiding. If that doesn't work, we need one of his compatriots, someone he cares about. Get a list of all of the people he was with in the Youth Corps. We find one of them, we might be able to put the hurt on Lopez—get him to make a mistake. "

"Let me place some calls," Trey replied.

"Keep the NSF out of this," she added. "I know we roll up under them, but if our suspicions are right, they can't be trusted."

"Count on it."

The District

Rebecca Clarke stood in Equity Square, formerly Judiciary Square, and looked out at the black, marble monument from the podium with her best mournful face painted on for the cameras. As the Director of the TRC, she knew how to leverage a long pause of silence. With her left hand, she took a tissue and dabbed the corner of her eye, wiping away a tear that did not exist. She sniffled, adding to the sadness of the moment. While she was focused on the speech she was going to give, a part of her was reveling in the limelight.

As she looked out at the crowd, she pretended to muster the courage to go on. "Forgive me. We stand here today to commemorate the dead, those that died at the hands of not only a vicious pandemic, but at the negligence and incompetence of leaders who did not care for the people they were to protect and serve." Her words were chosen as a direct shot at the Pretender President.

"This is the new Biden National Memorial to those that died from the pandemic. He too was a victim of the traitor, dying early as if he were poisoned with the same virus that killed hundreds of thousands of Newmericans. He was a beacon to us all, a new hope, one swept away like the others that died. It is only fitting that he stand here, gracing our honored dead with his perpetual smile…comforting us as he had so many times before." With a nod the covering came down from the statue showing the former President-elect, arms open wide, a big smile on his almost grandfatherly face. Rebecca wiped away another false tear as the crowd applauded. Connecting the dead man to the Traitor President was her handiwork from the very beginning and something that she was proud of.

She let the applause dwindle out before continuing. "It is only fitting that his statue be here, where the National Law Enforcement Officers Memorial once stood. Biden, the President who never was, understood just how corrupt law enforcement had become under his predecessors hands. Part of our national healing was the removal of the old monument of oppression and racism. I am sure Joe would be happy to know that the bronze of his statue came from the hideous and dark lion statues that once stood here." Again the applause came, and she savored every clap. It had been Rebecca's idea to place the monument on this site and to use the material from the statues that were once there for the President-elect's statue. It had taken some wrangling with the remaining Congress, who were constantly playing with the design of the entire park, but she had managed to push her demands through. *We'll have a new Congress and Senate soon. They will be more pliable and less attached to the old ways of doing things.*

"He was a great man, dedicated to equality and equity. He devoted his entire life to serving the old nation. If he had been allowed to take office, he would have no doubt been one of the greatest presidents. But that honor was taken from him by the Traitor. He killed Joe with his handling of the pandemic and the stress he laid at his feet—as if he loaded a gun and shot him. That is why we call him the Martyred President." The labeling of the Presidents was a concept she had come up with, one she was proud of. It depersonalized them, made them objects rather than people. The Traitor, the Martyr, the Pretender…that was all Deborah's wordsmithing.

"Today is not about the President-elect; it is about the loss and the sorrow we carry. The names etched on these marble slabs belong to those that died during the pandemic. It is important that we do not forget them. We must honor them, not only in our hearts, but in our actions.

"An election is looming, and already the oppressors of old are once more marching on the streets, out to take away our rights and crush all that we have accomplished since the Liberation began. They want to take away your reparations, your free education, your health care. They want to impose their racist ideology on you all."

She paused as the crowd began to boo and cry out things like, "Hell no!" and "Screw the Pretender!" The current Newmerica flag, rolled out by the TRC a few days before, was unfurled in the wind behind the protesters for effect. This new one, the eighth so far, was a rainbow of color with a black, up-thrust fist. The cameras would capture it in the background as she and her people had planned and rehearsed.

Rebecca was proud of her speech; she was taking a mournful and sad moment and turning it into righteous anger at the enemies of Newmerica. *Never pass up an opportunity to hurt your foes.* It also helped that a significant portion of the crowd had been hand selected by her advance team. The rehearsals for their indignation had paid off. She was confident that both she and her message would get great press coverage. It helped to have the media in your back pocket.

"Look to the names that surround us in this park, our heroic dead," she said and gestured to the marble slabs all around Equity Square. Painting the victims as heroes was always useful...*no one would dare argue otherwise without looking insensitive and cruel.* "If you loved them, if you remember them, hold those memories dear, but honor them when you go to vote. They should not have died in vain. Don't let them down or tarnish your loss by not voting to keep the people in power. Only you can prevent a surge of corruption, racism, hate, and yes, even death."

The crowd cheered her words vigorously. *For the reparation points we are giving them for attending, I'd hope they would.* Under the applause and cheers, she stepped down.

Tess Ditka met her at the base of the stage where the podium stood. "Excellent speech, Director," she said.

Of course it was. "I'm glad we did not include a flyover. That missing man formation is so old school," she said as the two of them made their way to the waiting black SUV. Jess stood at the door as her security team opened it for her. "This will be in the first five minutes of every news broadcast tonight," she assured Rebecca.

"It had better be," she said as Tess entered the SUV next to her. "Have you arranged for a rebuttal?"

"I have. We have several spokespeople who will claim that the traitor didn't kill all of the victims. One will be a former old school police officer who will be upset at their memorial being destroyed. He will demand that the new statue be torn down and the rest of the monument smashed. Another will be an old white man in a suit and tie. He's going to be labeled as a 'Conservative representative.' He will talk some smack about the martyred President. His rebuttal will claim that the Traitor President wasn't responsible for the COVID deaths; in fact, his actions *saved* lives." That last sentence made Tess chuckle.

It is laughable. They were paid actors, like many of the supporters in the crowd. To create the illusion that the press was fair, it was necessary to put on some dissenting voices. They would intentionally appear radical, if not crazy. They would rant, say things that would have to be bleeped out by her censors, in other words adhere to their scripts. Their presence not only would convince people that the media was unbiased, but that the people that stood against Newmerica were horrible people, riddled with racism and hate, who meant to bring harm down on them. The result would be fear, and fear was a powerful weapon for a communicator.

"I want it covered on the morning news tomorrow as well," Rebecca said. "We need the imagery to dominate the media cycles. Prompt the commentators that anyone who doesn't agree with the speech is soiling the memories of a dead elected President," she commanded, glancing out the tinted window at the new flags fluttering in the background of the memorial she had just dedicated.

We are at war. It is not for the hearts and minds of the people; it is for control of thinking. Only a few on the Ruling Council understood the full gravity of the Newmerica situation, but Rebecca did. The emergence of the Pretender President put not only the nation at risk, but her own life. *Everyone thinks the military wins wars. It isn't. They only know how to kill. It is control of language and control of what people can think that determines ultimate victory. For the first time in history, thanks to Big Tech and the media, we have the ability to manipulate people into thinking what we want out of fear. Control what people are willing to express and victory is assured.*

Philadelphia, Pennsylvania

Caylee angled her beat-up, gas powered sedan through the backstreets of Philadelphia, keeping a watchful eye on her rearview mirrors. The exterior of the vehicle was a battered hot-mess, but she made sure that the engine was in great working order. She wore a fake nose and chin, and a wig of unkempt brown hair with a streak of white that looked as if it were a bleaching mistake. She knew that the NSF was looking for her; their highway and street cameras would be running facial recognition. They had been hampered greatly by the damage Jack Desmond had orchestrated by attacking the Bumblehive data facility and Charli by destroying the NSF building in Virginia, but that didn't mean that she was safe.

She had 'requisitioned' several gas ration cards from two drivers at rest areas before starting her trip. They both had "Newmerica and

Proud!" bumper stickers on their hybrid cars, so from her perspective, they were practically asking to have their asses kicked. *They should have known better that to broadcast that in Tennessee,* a state that had swung solidly behind the new President. She had more than enough to get herself and Raul Lopez back to Tennessee, if not more.

The neighborhood she was driving through was old; the houses almost all looked the same. She was sure that at one time, decades ago, it was quaint. Children probably played in the streets while parents sat on their front porches and carried on conversations in their once lush, green yards. Those days had long passed. *This place looks too scuzzy even for meth-heads to use.* White picket fences had been replaced ages ago with rusty and twisted chain-link material. Garbage had blown into the fencing in the yards and remained there trapped in the rust, decaying as tall weeds poked skyward. Some yards had cars on blocks; other yards were bare ground. For all of its talk of urban renewal projects and breathing life in the old neighborhoods, the Newmerica government had not reached this suburb…and she doubted they had even tried. *A lawn mower hasn't run on this street in years.* Eyeing the address, she pulled the sedan to a stop in the house where she had been told that Lopez was being protected.

Reaching into the duffle on the passenger seat, she pulled out the Ruger-57 and tucked it in her shoulder holster; then she pulled her flannel shirt over it. She had a tactical knife on her left shin, an ankle holster with Springfield XDS on her right. Caylee believed in being prepared for any contingency, and there were few situations that could not be resolved without the proper application of firepower.

As she got out of the car, she eyed the street in both directions. A pit bull barked loudly four yards down, but otherwise the streets were empty. Her trained eyes studied the small porch and the windows with drawn curtains, and she calculated that once she got on the porch, the number of people that could fire on her from the inside was limited. While she did not anticipate an ambush, Caylee never let her guard down. She grabbed a small kit-bag from the floor of the passenger seat and took it with her.

She knocked on the door, chipping off some tiny, dull dirty-green paint flakes in the process. It cracked open, with a chain in place, and an eyeball peered out. "Who are you?"

"I have come for the package."

"Prove it."

She paused, remembering the code phrase Jack had given her. "Rockets' red glare," she sighed, making a mental note to talk to Jack about his choice of code phrases.

The door closed and she heard the chain being fumbled with. It opened and she slid in. The room was dark, despite the fact that it was mid-day. The curtains were pulled shut, allowing the only outside light to get in through the holes and the places where the curtains didn't come together.

"I'm Anthony," the man at the door said, extending his hand. Caylee eyed it but did not return the handshake. "I don't need to know that. Where is Mr. Lopez?"

He emerged from the narrow, dark hallway and she instantly recognized him. He looked young to her. *Too damned young for all of the fuss he's caused. That means he has been through a lot already in his life, and somehow coped with it* Raul rubbed his eyes as he walked out. "I'm Raul."

"I am your escort, Mr. Lopez," she said. "Before you can step out, we need to make changes in your appearance." She glanced to the tiny kitchen out of the corner of her field of vision.

"What do you mean?" he asked.

Caylee started to the kitchen, where she caught a hint of toast in the air. It was easily the cleanest room in the house. The living room/entrance had a couch that possessed the aroma of every human and pet that had made contact with it in the last two decades. Some of the stains on the plaid upholstery appeared more durable than the material itself. The kitchen was cleaner though. The Formica countertops, easily dating back to the 1950s, were chipped, cracked, and burned in several places. The refrigerator was clean though as was the linoleum tile floor. Setting the kit bag on the small table, she gestured to one of the two chairs.

"The FedGov has every camera out there running facial recognition software looking for you. Chances are pretty good they are using IR to check for cars smuggling passengers too. I need to change you enough that you don't show up in their security scans. Otherwise, this is going to be a short trip." She pulled out a prosthetic nose and chin piece, a set of hair trimmers, and a decal sheet dotted with fake tattoos.

Raul eyed the materials suspiciously. "Will this stuff work?"

Caylee pulled back her own fake nose. "It has kept me off their radar for most of my career." She dabbed a piece of cotton and began to wipe down his nose with alcohol. She fitted the nose with contact cement—industrial strength—enough so that the nose wouldn't fall off at an inconvenient time. The color wasn't quite right, so she used a small micro-sprayer to change the tint to match Raul's darker skin. To his credit, he didn't squirm or interrupt, opting to let her do her job.

As she fitted the chin piece, she asked Anthony, who had been standing nearby, to fill a bowl with warm water.

"What are those?" Raul asked as she soaked the tattoo sheet in the bowl.

"Tats. Nothing permanent—but these should last a few weeks, more than enough to get you to safety. Raul seemed to flinch a little at her explanation. "Is there a problem, Mr. Lopez?"

"Not really. My mother—she hates tattoos. I never got them."

"Look," she said in a low tone. "Facial tattoos can play havoc with the cameras trying to scan you. While I grant you, these are far from attractive, they should distort your facial features enough to get you past even a close-up camera shot." Raul nodded and she carefully applied the tiger stripes to his left cheek.

Taking out the trimmer, she narrowed and shortened his eyebrows; then went to work on his hair. She cropped it short, barely visible. "My apologies for the mess," she said as Anthony got a broom and dustpan out to clean up the mess.

Raul rubbed his head, feeling the light stubble there. "I'm bald."

"No," she said curtly. "You are safer because they are looking for someone with a full head of black hair."

Turning to Anthony, the other man grinned. "I wouldn't recognize you if you came up to me on the street, dude." Raul rubbed his new fake chin gently.

"It feels weird."

"You will get used to it," she said, starting to pack up her kit. "We will be traveling a long distance, so you are going to have your face scanned a lot."

"Why not take the back streets?"

"They will expect that. In fact, the SEs have roadblocks on all of the secondary roads. The smart move is to use the highway. It avoids up-front and personal inspections, and they will not expect us to use the freeways. We will beat them by doing what they least expect."

"What happens if they spot me?"

Caylee didn't want to alarm him, but she also knew that the reality might frighten the young man. "Let's say, I am more than able to deal with any problems that might surface."

Raul eyed her and seemed satisfied with her response. "You've done this kind of thing before, haven't you?"

She paused. "I have. I was an NSF operative."

The use of that word, 'operative,' made both Raul and Anthony freeze. Caylee continued. "I *used* to be one, Mr. Lopez. I no longer work for the NSF; I work against them. That was why I was sent here."

"Why would anyone send someone so high level for me?"

She shrugged. "My contacts didn't go into great detail, but I can speculate. You are a hero of sorts. The fact is the NSF wants you badly—it makes you a symbol of the struggle against Newmerica. We live in times when symbols are important. Detroit—Valley Forge—your being labeled an enemy of Newmerica has earned you new friends and allies."

"What happened in Detroit—that was an accident," he quickly reacted to her words.

"I do not care," she assured him. "You are my mission. When I'm done with you, I go on to the next one. For now, it is important for you to do what I say, when I say it, without hesitation. Do that, and we will get through this fine. Understood?"

Raul nodded. "Alright then," Caylee continued. "Let me gather my gear and we will be on our way." She packed her kit and Raul shook hands with Anthony. They moved to the door and Raul hesitated before stepping outside, looking up and down the street. "You have nothing to worry about, Mr. Lopez. Act casual." They moved to her sedan and he got in next to her. When she moved the bag of weapons to the floor, he was clearly surprised at her arsenal. *He would be more shocked at what is in the trunk.*

"I didn't catch your name," Raul said as she started the car.

"I didn't give it to you."

"What do I call you?"

"For now, my name is Ester Flores." She carried a perfectly forged FedGov ID card and papers to support that persona, one of several she had with her.

"That isn't your real name though is it?"

"No," she said, turning onto the street.

"So who are you really?"

She glanced over at Raul Lopez. "When we get through this, I'll tell you."

That seemed to be enough for Lopez as he settled back in his seat.

CHAPTER 6

"Words are more deadly than bullets."

Indiana National Guard Armory, Michigan City, Indiana

Colonel Trip Reager's battalion of the 36th Infantry Division of the Texas National Guard had deployed in Michigan City along the Lake Michigan coastline, right along I-94, which led into Chicago. The Indiana National Guard Armory was filled to capacity with his vehicles and personnel. Despite the packed conditions at the armory, he felt somewhat secure. The Indiana forces maintained checkpoints along I-94 in case the Newmerica government decided to generate some sort of confrontation. The locals brought in real food, which was a step up from MRE's and helped with the morale of his troops.

Now that the troops were billeted, he gathered his officers in a tight conference room. There had not been a lot of time to brief all of them before they had left Texas…the focus had been on the logistics of their deployment more than the mission. Some of the faces around the room were relatively new, where others had served with him since that dark night in San Antonio.

"Alright ladies and gentlemen," he said, instantly silencing the conversations in the room. "It's time for us to talk about our op. Those of you that have not served under me on a deployment before, ask questions if you are unsure. I'm not going to climb down your throats. It's more important for us to be on the same page than worried about our egos.

"The President has ordered us to deploy in Chicago to support a fair and free election. I assume all of you know that Chicago is a hotbed of

Newmerica loyalty. We are going right into the belly of the beast. We will manage three polling places and ensure that the rules are followed and that no one is intimidated by the Newmerica forces.

"We will deploy at Grant Park, Wrigley Field, and Soldier Field."

"Aren't they called something else?" Captain Gerald 'Trigger' DeYoung asked.

He was right. After the Fall, the Newmericans had gone on a spree of renaming things. With Grant being a Republican, there was no way they would leave his name on a park. After Senator Sanders died, they had changed the name of Grant Park to Sanders Park. Soldier Field had been changed to something less militaristic—Sacrifice Field. The Ruling Council had little use for the military, and honoring them was something they strove to avoid. *It'll be a cold day in hell before I use their naming conventions.* "I'll be sticking to their real names, not the shit that the Newmericans want us to use." That brought several supportive nods.

Trip continued. "We will be augmented by three companies of infantry from the Missouri National Guard as well. A number of NSF officers from friendly states have declared allegiance to the American government, and some of them will be coming with us as well, though most are going to be sent to cities that are less hostile than Chicago. I have also been assured that we will get help from the Sons of Liberty too. Together, our job is to ensure the safety of the voters so that the election is free from influence."

"Sir, Chicago is likely an armed camp," Lieutenant Judy Mercury said. "They have a lot of SEs operating there. I went to Chicago before the Fall; those locations are going to have us surrounded by potential hostiles."

Reager appreciated her candor. *Judy never pulls her punches.* "You're right on most accounts. Social Enforcement activity is expected to be high. Chances are they will pull in Chapters from the 'burbs to confront us. The Newmerica folks have a lot to fear with these elections. That is why we are going to plan a defense in depth. Grant Park is a good site because it gives us larger fields of vision; we will see threats coming. Wrigley and Soldier Field can be easily defended on the perimeters, and we will deploy so that the voters have a safe zone around those locations where they can enter and exit freely. It's not going to be easy, but I like to think that we are pretty smart people and can plan this a hell of a lot better than some SE thugs wearing body armor they bought off of Amazon." His last comment got more than one chuckle in the room.

"Colonel," Captain Marc Keller spoke up. "What are our rules of engagement? Things could get out of hand pretty quick. Keller was new to his command structure. Where Lt. Mercury had been with him for years, Keller had not. Colonel Reager knew the real question he was asking. *"Is this going to be like San Antonio?"*

Trip drew a long breath, using that extra moment to gather his thoughts and choose his words carefully. "I've been told to use common sense. So let me be clear. We will go in with the hope that this is a containable riot. I will not tolerate men and women under my command being injured or killed. If the situation merits, I alone will give the order to use live ammunition. I take such responsibility seriously. The thought of Americans firing on fellow Americans disgusts me. It tears at me. The people we are facing, however, have staged the overthrow of our country. They refuse to even call themselves Americans. I do not seek violence; nor will I tolerate anyone under my command initiating violence. However, if people bring the violence to us, we will respond. If we are shot at, we will return fire. If we are physically assaulted, we will use any and all means necessary to end that situation and restore calm."

"I can work with that," Captain Travis "Trigger" DeYoung said, brushing back his short, light blonde hair.

Colonel Reager paused for a moment. "If our enemies come looking for a battle, we will give them a defeat…complete and utter. Understood?"

His words electrified the room; he could see it in the faces of his commanders. Several nodded. Keller's jaw was set forward; Mercury's face went crimson. Anyone that had been on riot duty knew that things could quickly get out of hand. People did get injured or killed. The Social Enforcers were experts at brick and bottle tossing, Molotov Cocktails, and they were not afraid to engage. What Colonel Reager was telling his personnel was simple, "We are not putting up with that shit."

"Understood, sir," came back the chorus of the room after a heartbeat.

"Good," he said, rolling out a large map of Wrigley Field and the surrounding neighborhoods. "Let's get started …"

Columbus, Ohio

"Stop staring at me," 'Ester' said from the driver's seat. Raul snapped his head to look forward, embarrassed slightly at having been caught staring at her. It was hard not to look at her. This was an actual operative. The rumors about them were legendary. They were said to be ninja-like assassins that worked for the NSF.

Raul had been bored so far on the trip. None of that was helped by the flat, almost empty landscape, along I-71 leading to Columbus, Ohio. They had hopped on the highway only because the secondary road was so terrible. The driver, who called herself Ester, was not much of a conversationalist, though Raul had tried. The concrete sound barrier walls that lined the highway as they got closer to the city were broken in many places and covered with spray painted graffiti. Vines snaked up the walls, finding holes and slithering through. In his travel across the country, he had seen similar sights. He remembered when the walls were maintained, like the roads and bridges. The occasional jolt of the sedan on a pothole or damaged pavement was a reminder of how things had changed in the last five years.

"Sorry," he said. "I've never met an operative before."

"Maybe you have," she replied. "Part of what we do is blend in. If you go around looking like a bad ass, it attracts unwanted attention."

"They say you are assassins," he ventured cautiously.

She shrugged slightly, never taking her eyes off the road. "If you're asking me if I have killed people, the answer is *yes*. What I did, I did because I felt it was right at the time. It was my job. Operatives do a lot of the dirty work that has to be done to keep a government functioning. I preferred the law enforcement side of my job, but when push came to shove—I shoved."

"What changed?" Raul said, actually savoring the dialogue as opposed to the last few hours of silence.

"The Secretary used me to stir up problems with the SEs. When I stopped being useful, she hung me out to dry and sent two colleagues to kill me. I came to the quick conclusion that it was better to be on the side of my former targets than to work for a government that had ordered me killed."

There was something in the way she spoke, so quick, so blunt—

it rang with honesty. "I never planned on being part of a resistance movement. I fell into all of this by accident. I thought the Sons of Liberty were gone, wiped out."

"Everyone did," she added. "That was how they were able to come back from the brink, by staying off the radar." She hit the turn signal and took the exit.

"Why are we pulling off here?"

"Food, gas, a chance to stretch. Remember, we're not fleeing; we're just on a trip, two friends, going to see your family."

"Are you expecting trouble?"

Ester grinned. "I always do. Force of habit. It is what keeps me alive."

The exit took them off on the Pickerington exit. Twilight was settling in on Columbus as the sun was obscured by dark clouds clinging to the western horizon. The lights from the plaza were on, showing how many of the businesses were closed. The KFC was open, though someone had shot out the lower portion of the sign. She angled the car into the weed-infested parking lot and parked. Five other cars were parked there, one whose driver had clearly ignored the fading paint stripes on the cracked parking lot surface. Raul watched as Ester pulled a Sig out of the kit bag on the floor and stuffed it in her belt line so that her shirt would obscure it. "Should I have one?" Raul asked.

She nodded. "If you know how to handle it, sure." He took out of a .38 Smith and Wesson revolver and checked to confirm that it was loaded. Sliding it into his pants pocket, he got out of the car as Ester locked the doors.

The KFC had seen better days, but the food was hot and filling. He glanced at her and saw her eyes constantly sweeping the nearly empty restaurant. *Nothing slips past her.* As he went for another piece of chicken, her hand reached out and touched his wrist. "Let's take the rest to go." He was confused until he rose and saw a group of four young men huddled around their sedan. She moved calmly to the door, whispering loud enough for him to hear. "I'll handle this."

Ester walked to the car as if the young weren't there; she stopped two yards away from the car. "Hey," one of them called out. "Look what we have here."

Raul surveyed them. Two already had knives at the ready, keeping them out of her line of sight, but within his. "The two on the left have knives."

"Thank you," she whispered back, and then she turned to the men. "If you don't mind, we need to be moving on."

"What if we do mind?" the tallest dark-skinned man said with a wicked grin. "You and your boyfriend aren't in a position to do much about it."

Raul wanted to reach down into his pants and grab the pistol…it was as if the gun was calling him. He also knew better. Jayden had drilled it into him. "You don't pull a gun unless you are prepared to use it." Ester said she could handle it, but they were outnumbered two to one.

"We don't want trouble," she said calmly.

"Neither do we," a third voice weighed in, deeper, more throaty. He was the heavyset one of the four, easily clocking in at 275 lbs. "You're from out of state. We are part of the local SE here…kinda a welcoming committee. You being a stranger and all, you should know there's a tax for coming to Columbus."

"I was unaware of that," she said calmly.

"Yeah," the first man added. "And we are here to collect; that's all."

Ester nodded slowly, moving slightly to Raul's left, clearly positioning herself in his mind. "And what is this tax?"

"Your car," the beefy man said. "And your dinner." He eyed the bag of chicken that Raul was holding.

The first man weighed in again. "And looking at your fine ass, I think we're entitled to something that is finger licking good." That brought about a chuckle from all of them. The two with knives made theirs visible, as if on cue.

She paused for a moment, looking at the large man. "I don't think we'll oblige," she said coolly. "Now, why don't you step aside and let us get on our way?"

The fat man laughed, along with two of the others. "What makes you fucking think we'd do that?"

Ester eyed him sternly. "What is your name?"

"What?"

"Your name. What is your last name?"

"Jonas," he said. "Why? What's it to you?"

"Well Mr. Jonas, I believe in being courteous. I will explain to you why you will let us go on our way. It is simple, probably simple enough for even you to understand. If you don't let us get in the car and leave, I will beat you up. Given the numbers, I do not have time for niceties, which means a lot of pain; broken bones are likely, perhaps worse. You have chosen the wrong vehicle and travelers to pick on. I get it; mistakes happen. If you try and force this issue, you will regret it. The best course of action is for you to go your way, and we will go ours." There was an eerie professionalism in her voice, a strange calm that made Raul more nervous.

The one that had not spoken pulled out a revolver. He didn't aim it, but waved it around far too casually. "Your boyfriend is pretty quiet. Busy pissing himself? Maybe you can't count bitch, but there are four of us and two of you." He took a step toward her.

Ester moved as if she were a living bolt of lightning. Stepping toward the man with the gun, she hit him in the windpipe with a stab of her fist and with her other hand she grabbed his gun hand. He panicked, choking for air, as she spun his gun around and fired a shot at the tall man, hitting him in the side. He thudded against the sedan under the force of the impact, and the rear side window exploded as the bullet passed through him and into the vehicle.

With a twist of her wrist, she got the gun free and used the man struggling to breathe as a meat shield, tossing him at the others.

Another gun popped and flashed. The fat man had pulled it out and it looked as if he had grabbed the trigger when he reached around to his back waistband to get it. He wailed loudly as the other two lunged at Ester with knives.

The first one stabbed at her, but she deflected him with a chop to his forearm mid-thrust. With her free hand she jammed his elbow from underneath, bending it backwards with a pop as he dropped the knife.

Raul saw the other knife-wielding man—who wore a dark hoodie—lunge at Ester and Raul drew his own pistol. It was not a jerked shot; he squeezed the trigger as he had been taught. The round caught the man in the side of his neck, splattering blood all over the vehicle as Ester fired her liberated gun into the foot of the man that attacked her with the knife.

The bullet made a thwacking sound as it punched through his sneaker, and then it sprayed blood upward as it hit the pavement of the parking lot and ricocheted back up through the foot and into his opposite shin. The spray of gore hit Ester when she wheeled around, gun arm extended and braced, looking for targets.

Raul had been distracted by Ester and didn't see the man he had injured rise and lunge at him. A fist hit his face—really just a glance. Raul staggered back and fired again. The shot sent the man staggering backwards to the car where he slid down, dead.

The chubby man staggered, blood making his running pants wet and dark. "Whoa! Hold off man! I don't want trouble," he stammered, and his hands grabbed the bullet entry wound, which oozed blood.

Ester held the gun leveled at him. "We already have trouble and unfortunately for you, I can ill afford witnesses." He pivoted to run, but the car and the legs of his downed comrades were in the way, making him nearly fall over. It didn't matter. She fired two bullets hitting him in the base of his skull, splattering him all over the vehicle. As he slid down, he left crimson streaks on the side of the car.

She turned and fired a round into the chest of the first knife attacker who was attempting to scramble away on all fours, taking him down. She fired one final shot into the tall man, ensuring he was dead.

For a moment the two of them stood, breathing heavy, over the four dead men. Ester said nothing, but surveyed the rest of the parking lot to make sure there were no other witnesses. Only a nearby barking dog gave any hint of sound. Raul felt his face and could tell that his prosthetics were missing—the victims of the punch he had taken. He looked around but could not see them on the pavement. Slowly he turned to Ester and made eye contact with her.

"Get in," she said, stepping over one of the victims to open the driver's side door.

"The car is covered with blood," Raul said as he maneuvered around the dead and the car to get to his door. Amazed, he glanced down and saw that the KFC bag was still in his trembling hand.

She used the sleeve of her shirt to wipe the blood off of her face. "We need some distance from here. We will have to dispose of the car and get a new ride."

"You killed three of them," Raul said as she turned over the ignition.

"I did what I had to," she replied calmly and they took off. "Thank you for shooting the one in the hoodie. I could have handled him though. I had my block already to go. Your shots did make it much easier though. Stupid SEs. If they had half a brain, they would have ambushed us. Standing out in the open like that, they practically invited getting their asses killed."

"You're right," he said. Touching his face he could feel the tacky spots where the false skin pieces had been. "I lost my disguise," he said.

"I know," she replied. "It wasn't your fault. I have a few other pieces in my kit I might be able to use. For now, lean forward, breathe steady. You're all hopped up on adrenaline."

"Why aren't you excited," he said, obeying her orders.

"I've had experience with this kind of thing," she said.

"I'll say!" Raul said, the adrenaline starting to top off. His heart was thudding in his chest as he spoke, and his entire body felt electrified.

"Still, you showed good decision-making back there," she said, turning down a side street as the street lights flickered on, casting the road in instant shadows. She handed him the weapon she had taken from her would-be attacker. "For now, stuff them in with the rest of the dinner. We will have to wipe them before leaving them someplace where they will be picked up."

"I've never seen anything like that," Raul said. The air roared through the shattered window as the sedan picked up speed. She turned sharply on another street. The houses were nicer in this neighborhood, and there were more streetlights. The way she drove, he wondered if she had a place in mind, or was she simply choosing a route that might throw off the NSF if they came after them. To Raul it didn't matter…all that counted was that they were alive.

"Hand me a biscuit, will you?" she asked. He fumbled with the guns and the leftovers and handed her a biscuit. She chomped down on it and chewed vigorously. She swallowed hard, never lifting her eyes off the road. "KFC makes the best biscuits."

Raul reached in the bag, pulled out a leg and nervously chewed at it. He didn't even know he was hungry again, but somehow eating seemed to calm him. Each bite soothed his nerves more. They finished at the same time and he handed her a napkin.

"Can you teach me how to do that…you know…what you did?" he asked.

Her eyes darted over to him and she smiled. "It takes years of training to do that, Raul," she said. "But, given you shot that guy to save me, I guess I can teach you some moves." A smile rose to his face. *She is fantastic, like something you see in a movie or video game.*

"We have to torch the car," she said with remarkable calm. "The NSF has been struggling with their investigative side, but there's no point in us leaving a spec of DNA for them to find. We will need new prosthetics too. The cameras in that KFC will have our images. We need different faces so the NSF can't tie us to those bodies."

She's done this before ...

"You tell me what to do, and I'll do it, Ester," he managed, stopping to wipe his own hands.

"It's Caylee," she said. "My name. Caylee Leatrom."

Raul smiled. It was going to be a long night, but he knew now that she was more than his escort. She was his friend.

The Hermitage National Park
Nashville, Tennessee

Julius Bernstein wedged himself in the fork of the old hickory tree and used his enhanced binoculars to get a view of the Hermitage. The early autumn air had turned some of the leaves brown already. They would be dropping in the next big wind, but in the meantime, they provided cover. The mornings were cold in Tennessee, outside of Nashville where he was hiding, followed by hot afternoons still, almost as if the state were defying nature as much as it was the Newmerica government. It made his camouflage a sweaty mess after a few hours, but he was used to it.

Tennessee was harboring the Pretender President. *The man did not have the good sense to stay dead after the Liberation*…that thought made him snicker to himself. Everyone thought that he had died in the bombing that destroyed his limo. It turns out that someone had misidentified his DNA…probably another traitor in the NSF. *They will find that technician and ensure that justice is done...our form of justice.* Julius knew that he was in enemy territory. Not as bad as Texas, but still a hostile land. *These right leaning governors were looking for a chance to stab Newmerica in the back. We should have gone farther in the camps—we should have killed them all.*

He knew his family would never approve of such thoughts…not that he spoke to them. They always were so proud that they had come from a family of Holocaust survivors. The concept of wanting to wage a genocide was contrary to his upbringing, but Julius coped easily with that thinking. *We are not the Nazis. Our cause is just—a free society that the world will envy.* As an operative, he had done a lot of horrible things, but he had done them for the right reasons, which made it just and fair.

The Hermitage was an armed camp from what he could see. He remembered right after the Fall, how Social Enforcers had attacked landmarks like the Hermitage. For the most part, they had been successful in erasing the icons of America's racist past. Mount Rushmore had been defaced; Monticello and Montpelier had been burned to the ground, and Mount Vernon lay in ruins. A few sites had managed to survive, and the Hermitage was one of them. It stood defiantly, stark white in the distance, a monument to the man that had lived there in Julius's mind. Seeing the mansion made him angry, frustrated, and ashamed.

Hermitage had been President Andrew Jackson's home and he was one of the worst offenders in the long line of tyrants that had governed America. He had cost thousands of native Americans their lands and lives and had been a slave owner. The SEs that had rallied to destroy the Hermitage had expected to set it ablaze and erase Jackson's physical existence. They had bussed in rioters, as they had done at dozens of other sites around the nation. It should have been easy. The local police, before they had been nationalized into the NSF, were no match for the numbers they were facing. *It's an embarrassment that the stupid ANTIFA morons had botched it.*

The Governor of Tennessee had not relied only on the police and the Park Service for order. Unlike many of his peers, he had taken swift action with the news of the Traitor President's apprehension. The Governor had deployed several companies of the Tennessee National Guard at the site. The battle that followed had been vicious, with armed locals, no doubt alt-right militia, turning out to support the guardsmen in the rioting that followed. While they had successfully wrecked and vandalized Jackson's tomb on the site, his home was left intact. It had been a bloody affair, not as bad as what had gone down in San Antonio, but it had left a lot of people hospitalized and a few dead. Seeing the building, a monument to a failed government and a flawed leader, made Bernstein's stomach knot.

Since the return of the Pretender President, the Hermitage had been his home. They called the Estes Kefauver Federal building in Nashville the Southern White House, but it was mostly where the administrative work of the American government was headquartered. The Hermitage was where the false President lived. His press releases said it was not chosen in support of racism or slavery, but it was chosen because it was the home of a 'great American.' It was a lie to Julius, one he refused to embrace. *This is additional evidence as to how corrupt America really is. That nation is dead and gone. All that remains is a few stubborn people and a pretender to the throne.*

His mission had been to assassinate the Pretender, but that was proving to be a challenge. The Federal building in downtown Nashville was heavily guarded. Two blocks around the building had been cleared and were covered heavily by his DHS and Secret Service. Julius had come up with a few ways to penetrate the defenses, including a hang gliding landing on the roof, but none of the options seemed to have a chance of success. Hitting the President inside the Southern White House was not feasible, not with a high margin of success. He needed to be sure he would be successful. *If I don't take him out, it will backfire on me and on the Newmerica government.* If he were killed or captured in the attempt, there would be no way for Ruling Council to deflect the blame for the assassination. *It would be impossible for anyone to believe that Russia or China was responsible if they had me in custody.* Julius had no intention of being anyone's pawn. *I need to kill him and get away with no evidence linking the attack to Newmerica.*

He adjusted his ghillie suit slightly as he shifted on the hickory branch. With the White House building proper ruled out, he was hoping to be able to pull off an attack at the Hermitage. For several days he had been surveying the Pretender's home and found it far too secure for his liking. He was almost a mile out sitting in the tree making his observations, and even from there it was hard to find gaps he could leverage. When the Pretender got into his limo, there was no good line of sight on him. The grounds had electronic surveillance, IR, and heavily armed troops. Out of fear of a military strike by Newmerica, a contingent of anti-aircraft vehicles and even a few tanks and APCs patrolled the perimeter. He begrudgingly admitted that whoever was in charge of protecting the would-be President had done a remarkable job.

His mind turned over the options. He used Arnold Air Force Base for his travels, and that place was also well protected. He could attempt a sniper attack at one of his public appearances, but those introduced a lot of random factors including a limited period of time to plan an attack. *I need to find a better way.*

Julius's list of venues for an assassination was dwindling each day. It did not deter him. If anything, he savored the challenge. There was something more with this mission. By killing the last link to the Traitor President, he would be an unsung hero for the new nation. He knew that his identity would be secret, known only to a handful of people—but he would be a hero. In generations to come, when the truth came out, they would name high schools in his honor…there would even be statues.

I will single-handedly decapitate this American resurgence!

CHAPTER 7

"Being afraid is being vigilant."

Washington DC
FIVE YEARS EARLIER ...

The Capitol and DC Police had been overwhelmed by the assault on Capitol Hill, which was evident to everyone there. Shots were fired, rubber bullets at first, spraying the front row of the protesters as they swarmed up the steps in a black-clad wave. One such round had nicked the underside of Becky's forearm and it still throbbed…but she ignored the pain. Too much was at stake. *We are so close to victory!* Like everyone else, she understood that there was no turning back.

She nearly fell, stumbling over a uniformed body of some officer that she presumed was unconscious or dead. There was no remorse from him, regardless. It did not bother her in the least. Everyone knew that the police, even the Capitol Hill police, were racist and corrupt. The fallen officer was little more than a doormat to be walked on by her.

"We should burn it all!" one youth cried out. He was carrying a flag with the fist of ANTIFA.

"No!" she screamed back. "The building is a symbol. Burning it makes us look more violent. Get to your targets and secure them!" she commanded. The young, redheaded man with the flag nodded, understanding, and yet looking disappointed. *This will play out on the Internet and on TV. We need to control the images we allow. That is why Daniel sent me here.* Her entire college education had trained her for these moments, and she was not going to squander them.

The crowd seemed to pause for a moment, flooding into the hall, unsure what to do next. She could sense the confusion. No doubt some of them were surprised they had gotten as far as they had. A small subgroup toppled a statue onto the floor, crushing the foot of one of the protesters who wailed in agony as the marble of the edifice cracked and shattered, caving in some of the marble floor in the process. *This has the potential of getting out of control.* "Where's the Speaker's office?" someone called.

She had studied the maps, apparently more than those that were confused. "This way! Follow me!" she called, pointing down the hall where the blue velvet rope marked the office door of the Speaker of the House. On her words, the crowd surged toward it as if the mass of people were a single, living entity. The locked door was battered several times. Someone picked up one of the poles used for the roping outside the door and turned it into a battering ram. It took four solid hits to shatter the dark wood door near the handle and lock—no easy task as the crowd pressed forward like a surging wave. It crunched and cracked under the assault and the noise level rose.

Becky angled herself in the front of the crowd as the mass squeezed through the doorway and into the outer office. She heard breaking glass somewhere off to her right but ignored it. *They can't kill the speaker, not now.* Having been in many protests during the summer of 'The 'vid,' she knew that things could get out of hand fast and it was her job to make sure they didn't. *We need her for now.*

The wall of people hit the Speaker's interior office door in unison, breaking it down with a moan and snapping sound as it collapsed under the assault. Inside, the Speaker of the House sat behind her desk, her eyes wide open and red, her hair disheveled and mussed. She went erect in her seat as the group reached out for her across the desk, not quite able to reach her. To Becky, she looked like a confused grandmother, frightened, dazed by the audacity of the crowd. Someone moved around the desk and grabbed her forearms, holding her tight. She struggled, but it was a lost cause. Not only were the numbers against her, but so was her age. Someone in the crowd spit on her pristine blue dress prompting others to do the same. Becky understood their feelings. The Speaker represented a corrupt government, one that worked against the people it was supposed to protect.

"Kill the bitch!" someone said and there were angry cries in support.

Becky clawed her way to the desk and fumbled with her taser, hitting one large man in front of her. His body quaked under the jolt she delivered, sending him dropping to his knees. Using him as a footstool, she stood on top of the Speaker's desk, putting herself in command of the room. "No harm comes to her!" she commanded. The eyes in the room fixated on her. "We need her cooperation. We have to be sure that the rest of the leaders are taken as well. She's a prisoner of the people!" The sound of the crowd dropped by decimals as she spoke, and in that instant she had complete control of the room.

"We need to move her," said a burly man at the side of the big desk. "We'll take her to the tunnels with the others." That had been the plan all along. Rebecca, however, had an agenda of her own.

"Wait," she commanded. "We need her here, for a few minutes. Get the camera crew from CNN here," she barked. The burly one nodded, not only at her words, but at her leadership of the moment. She climbed down from the desk and moved next to the Speaker, putting her hands on one of her elbows. The stink of alcohol greeted her as she helped the older woman to her feet.

"Thank you," the Speaker said. "I understand why you are here and I want you to know…I can help you. We are on the same side, you know. We want the same thing."

Becky shook her head. "No, we are not on the same side, Madam Speaker. We were *never* on the same side. But you have something that needs to be communicated—to ensure a smooth transition of power."

The face of the Speaker sagged with the harsh words and her jaw dropped.

FOUR YEARS EARLIER ...

College Station, Texas

Trip Reager stood with Jake Hill at the end of the counter at Slice of Heaven and asked for clarification. "How many buses?"

"Four," Jake said. "The leader was some woman named Angel Jones. They have signs and clubs and such. They aim to misbehave; that's for sure."

Trip had been expecting some trouble, but he thought it would be a legal challenge. The Newmerica government had ordered him to shut down the Slice of Heaven, but he had refused. His lawyer had done her job well, filing blocking motions, demanding proof that he was polluting in the form of environmental studies, etc. "Bury them in their own red tape." That was what she said and he hoped it would work.

Texas had not hopped aboard the bandwagon with the so-called Ruling Council and the Newmerica government. That didn't mean there wasn't support for it in the state, but they had been mostly subdued. In recent months there had been some trouble—rioters bussed in from other states causing trouble—but the local authorities had handled those incidents well. He never expected this kind of thing to happen in College Station, though, and certainly not targeting him.

"There's more," Jake said. "Jessie's with them."

"What in the hell are you talking about?" he snarled. Jessie was in Austin, at the University of Texas.

"Sorry to say it Trip. I saw her with my own two eyes, carrying a sign like the rest of them," Jake said.

The words hit Trip hard. *How could she turn on her own family like this? We are her parents. This restaurant is paying for her education!* He wanted to call Jake a liar, but he knew better. Both of them were veterans; they had spilled blood on the same sand. "God damn it!" he spat as his face went hot with anger. His mind shifted from being a father with a rebellious daughter to facing the threat at hand. "Alright Jake. Clearly they have come looking for a confrontation. Get the word out to the VFW and everybody we know. Tell them to come down here. Tell them to come armed."

"Roger that old buddy," Jake said.

"And before things get out of hand, get Jessie out of there. I'll deal with her later."

An hour later the protesters came. Calling them protesters was a fallacy; Trip knew that. Some had guns, though by the way they held them, they didn't know much about firearms. They were more of a threat to their own people than the locals that had gathered to defend the Slice of Heaven. There were a lot of baseball bats, frozen water bottles, the kind of stuff to provoke a bloody confrontation.

Trip's friends who gathered were locals, conservatives that had little tolerance for outsiders telling a local business owner what to do. They were armed and many were veterans. Some took up positions on top of his restaurant and the BP gas station across the street. They knew how to set up fields of fire if matters got out of hand. Law enforcement was there as well, though they represented the smallest number. Most of them stood on the side of Trip and his defenders, staring out over the parking lot at the black-clad mass waving signs and repeatedly chanting, "Close him down!"

Trip picked up his walkie-talkie. "They are coming up the middle of Texas Avenue. Sheriff, you got your teams in place?"

Sheriff Daniel Rodriguez's firm voice came back fast, "Roger that Trip. We'll come in on them hard. No shooting, we could have a hell of crossfire if this gets out of control."

"Affirmative," he replied. The last thing he wanted was bloodshed… not with his daughter in the middle of it all.

Angel Jones, still arrogant, stepped out in front of her black bloc clad force, a snarky grin painted on her face. For a few moments, everyone froze in place; both sides faced each other across the parking lot. "Mr. Reager. You are hereby ordered to close your establishment."

Trip stepped out with the AR 15 in his hands. "Our Governor doesn't recognize your authority, and I sure as hell don't."

"It doesn't matter if you recognize the government or not; the law is the law and you are in violation of it."

*Keep pushing lady…*A part of him wanted matters to spill out of hand, as long as Jessie got clear of it. "As I see it, no one elected you or the people you represent. Your laws have no meaning here. You're a bunch of punks in Amazon.com riot gear. My business will stay open. I suggest you turn around, get on your buses and go back where you came from," he said loudly, so that everyone could hear.

"And if we choose not to?" she taunted.

"Play adult games. Win adult prizes," he snapped back.

That was when the first brick flew from the rioters. Whoever had thrown it was aiming for his restaurant but fell short, hitting a car and bouncing into Tolbrook Harper, a friend of his. It was followed by a salvo of glass bottles filled with frozen water. "Hold your fire!" he barked in his best command voice, moving for cover next to a parked, white Bronco. He felt a tug on his right shoulder and saw a stain of red where a .22 had clipped him.

Combat instincts, long suppressed, resurfaced in an instant. It took a great deal not to give the order to return fire. "Surge! Break them up," he said. He toggled on the walkie-talkie. "Sheriff, we are mixing it up here."

"Roger that. Here comes the pain," Rodriguez replied.

The defenders of the Slice of Heaven rushed forward into the front line of the rioters. They held up homemade Plexiglas shields which shattered under the first strikes of the clubs that the Texans were swinging. Where the college students were armed with bats and small pieces of cheap pine, Trip's people carried thick hardwood clubs, some with spikes hurriedly driven into them.

The rioters were unprepared for a full-on frontal assault. It was obvious that they were used to groups holding back, playing defense. Trip's friends were on the offense. Shouldering his rifle, he rushed forward, pulling out a riot baton, aiming for the largest of the protesters. He brought his baton down on his head, which had been protected by a knit black hat, hardly protection from the hit. The big kid staggered back, then turned and ran.

That was when the Sheriff's two teams hit their flanks. The black-clad mob seemed to instantly tense even more, realizing they had been out-maneuvered. Trip was hit by a glancing blow from a baseball bat, one he returned with a jab from his baton, right in the solar plexus, leaving him toppling to the blacktop, gasping for air.

Several Molotov cocktails were thrown, one hitting a Prius and setting it ablaze, another splashing two of Trip's neighbors who had come to help him. They dropped and rolled and others rushed over finally managing to smother the flames on their pant legs. One rock hit the front door of the Slice of Heaven, shattering the glass. Trip ignored the fires and continued to swing his baton with controlled fury. *For people so worried about the environment, they sure as hell love setting fires and burning gas.*

Groups of rioters shifted to the right flank—despite the deputies there—breaking the windows at the nearby 7-Eleven and clamoring through the shattered glass, grabbing at displays, clearly looting. Erratic pops from small arms rang out in the haze of the twilight darkness, punching through the wails and moans of the wounded on both sides. A baseball bat, thrown in his direction, clattered on the parking lot pavement, coming to rest at Trip's feet.

"Hold your fire," he barked, not sure who was doing the shooting in the melee. The rioters began to retrograde, falling back half a block as he and his people continued to press forward.

The light evening breeze shifted, and he caught a hint of tear gas in the air. It wasn't at all like the stuff he had trained with in the army, but it still made his eyes water slightly. Turning slightly away from the breeze, Trip paused for a moment to check his own wound, a graze. It didn't hurt until he saw it; then it felt like a hot poker being pushed into his upper arm. *Damn I hope that Jake found Jessie.*

The sheriff used the walkie talkie to order everyone to hold their fire as Trip tried to move out toward the wounded. A crack from the protesters slapped into a deputy off to the right, hitting his Kevlar tactical vest and knocking the portly officer to the ground. Another volley of fire from a half-dozen guns rang out in response as law enforcement and the locals dropped another handful of protesters. *Shit!* The last thing he wanted was gunfire.

Thankfully, the effects of the return volley were instantaneous. The black wall of rioters broke into a run for their buses. Signs were dropped in the panic and several people tripped over each other, forming small clusters of stumbling and clawing protesters. A trio stumbled out of the 7-Eleven with hands full of food. One bumped the shattered glass window, breaking off a piece that sliced his arm; the youth spilled his looting spoils on the ground in a splatter of blood and he cried out in pain. An officer moved in quickly, taking him into custody. Several of Trip's friends moved over to the deputy that had been shot and dragged him back, away from the fleeing protesters.

The Sheriff grabbed a handful of Trip's friends and supporters and deputized them on the spot. They headed off towards the buses, out to apprehend the rioters. Trip's heart was pounding in his ears as he surveyed the dead and wounded, worried that his daughter may be in the number. *Please God, don't let Jessie be hurt!* Out of the corner of his eye, he spotted Jake, who held Jessie at his side, half-dragging the resisting youth by her elbow. In a millisecond he was awash with relief, replaced instantly by anger at his daughter. He slid the baton into the holder on his belt and marched over to her. Jake released her as her green eyes locked with her father's. Her face was partially covered with a black scarf, but he could see the anger as she looked at him. It was like looking in a mirror.

"What in the name of hell are you doing, Jessie?"

"This restaurant is a polluter," she fired back as the scarf fell from her face. "I'm doing what's right for the world."

"This restaurant pays for your schooling. It puts food in your stomach and a roof over your head."

"Tuition is free now, Dad," she sneered back. "The people pay for my school."

He wanted to slap her but held himself in check. *Nothing the government ever provides is really free—taxpayers foot the bill.* "You're being a fool. OK, so Newmerica pays your tuition. Who do you think pays for your room and board? For your books? For your shoes? This business—that's what!"

"I don't care," she fired back. Her anger was enough that even Jake backed away, leaving Trip to cope with her alone. "What you are doing is against the planet," she yelled at him.

In his entire life his daughter had rarely talked back to him. Trip had told himself it was because of respect and love. Now what he saw in his daughter's bright green eyes was the opposite of those emotions. It was hate mixed with anger, with a twist of rage thrown in. He wanted to hug her, to soothe her, but he could tell that the young woman before him would have none of that.

"Get your ass home," he finally replied. "We will sit down with your mother and talk about it."

"I won't!" she fired back. "And you can't make me!" Jessie Reager stepped back from her father, out of his reach.

What has that college done to her? Brainwashing...that's it. Trip's instincts were to fix the problem. Take her out of the school, and try to get back the little girl that he and Nancy had raised. *Is that person even in there?* The raw anger on Jessie's face felt as if he were facing a total stranger, someone that happened to look like his daughter. "Jessie, come home. Talk to your mother—"

She cut him off. "I don't need to talk to her or you! Who do you think turned you in, Dad? It was me!" That too was something new for him.

Trip drew a long breath and tried to curb his own frustration. *They got into her head...they've corrupted her. They took my little girl from me.* The frustration was that he didn't know where to channel his rage. He didn't know who personally was responsible, but certainly Angel Jones had played a part.

What hurt deepest, the cut that dug deep into his soul, was Jessie's confession that she had turned him in. It was one thing to talk back to her father; it was another to betray her family. "This business is our lives, Jessie. It is what puts food on the table."

"Spoken like a true capitalist! All you care about is money. You don't care about the environment. I worked for free for you, Trip," she said, using his name for the first time in his life. "You exploit the proletariat like every other corrupt conservative." The rhetoric flowed from her lips with conviction. *She really believes that bullshit.*

The betrayal was complete; he felt it. In Iraq, he had been wounded twice in battle. Those hits, and the grazing shot he took that night—all hurt physically. That pain could be treated, suppressed with drugs, and the wound would heal. This was far worse. It was an emotional wound, something that an enemy across the world could never have delivered. His pride and joy, his beloved daughter, had been taken from him. She no longer existed. What stood before him was a stranger wearing his daughter's skin.

What will Nancy say? Thoughts of telling his wife made him more afraid than he'd been on any patrol he had ever been a part of. Dread came along with guilt for allowing the professors to twist his daughter against him...against the family that had raised her. "You get your ass home, right now!"

"I won't!" she wailed. "You can't make me. I'm not like the people you exploit!"

The words washed over him. *What have they done with my little girl?*

"Go," he said almost wearily. "Get the hell out of here."

For the first time that night, she seemed surprised by his words. Trip continued his verbal counterattack. "You hate us so much—the people that raised you—go. Get your ass back to that school. Let them feed and clothe you, because I sure as hell won't. How *dare* you talk to me this way? How *dare* you turn on your family—the people that brought you into this world and love you? Go. Don't even think about coming back."

Jessie's eyes were wet, but he was no longer sure if emotions were tugging at her or if she had caught some of the tear gas. He also no longer cared. She turned and ran across the parking lot and into the night.

Jake, who had been a witness to it, stepped forward. "Trip—she's your daughter. Don't let her go like this."

Trip turned to his friend. "I have no daughter, Jake." Then he turned back to his restaurant so he could begin the cleanup.

CHAPTER 8

"The greatest threats to our nation are those that refuse to accept their inherent flaws."

University of Virginia
Charlottesville, Virginia

Maddie Steele chose not to carry a sign in the march. It was humiliating enough to be coerced into taking part. The protest was organized by the Chainbreakers, the largest of the ANTIFA groups on campus. The theme of the protest was not fully understood. Based on their signs and banners, it seemed like the students were asking for a half-dozen possible demands. Everything from "LGBTQFM—now and forever!" to "No Fascism" and "Kill the Pretender!" was prevalent. The messaging seemed angry and convoluted. For Maddie, one thought kept going through her head...*How did these people ever topple the most powerful nation on the planet?*

She knew the answer—they had help from the Deep State and sympathetic members of Congress. *That didn't work out well for most of them.* Many were killed by the end of the Liberation, and those that weren't were either jailed or sent to quarantine. A very small number rose to power, some in the Ruling Council, some as leading parts of the Newmerica regime. The most dominant one was of course the Secretary of the NSF. Before the Fall she had been written off as a fringe looney. Now she controlled a nationalized police force. *There's some sort of joke in all of that, but for the life of me I can't think of it.*

Maddie struggled to keep an expression of grim solitude on her face. She didn't want to be there in the first place. She found most of the Chainbreaker causes to be appalling. The urge to turn 90 degrees and walk out of the rally was constant and nagging.

She couldn't. People were watching her. They wanted to find a crack in her façade and as much as they were probing for it, she was not going to surrender to her emotions and give them the satisfaction. They want me to be like them, and I will appear to do that. When people chanted, she mouthed the words without saying them out loud. When they held their fists skyward in defiance, she did the same.

The hardest part was the shame she felt. Her family had been in hiding since the Fall, living under assumed names to avoid detection. As much as her father had been a conservative, he kept his leanings in check so that no one would make a move against them. In a nation where the citizens were encouraged and rewarded for reporting on each other, the illusions of compliance were vital.

The protest went down West Main Street, packed tight by a hillside and the buildings. A lot of the small businesses were closed, their windows boarded up with plywood, all adorned with layers of graffiti. She remembered coming to Charlottesville before the Fall; it had been a vibrant and thriving community. The regular protests, the looting, and the economy had crippled most of the businesses. The few that were open closed up quickly at the first sign of the marchers, not wanting to be targets for looting.

She met the gaze of her roommate, Pris, who had been attending more marches than classes since they shared a room. She gave Maddie a wave, which she returned. She didn't know much about her roommate; nor did she try and learn about her. They were cordial, and Pris seemed to value her privacy almost as much as Maddie did. For Maddie, it was the perfect kind of relationship.

As the wave of protesters passed under the railroad bridge and emerged out of the blackness into the dim streetlights, she caught a glimpse of one of the girls that had confronted her, the chunky girl, Deborah. Maddie locked gazes with her and Deborah lifted her hand and made a V shape with her fingers; she then pointed them at her eyes, then at Maddie. *I've got my eyes on you.* Maddie simply turned away, walking a side step to put a few individuals between her and Deborah.

The threat was there, unspoken, but as real to her as if the words had been spoken between them. Maddie felt her face go hot, not from embarrassment for being in a march she had no interest in, but from anger. *They use threats and intimidation to force you to do what they want.* It wasn't that she was against any of the things they were marching for. *I think everyone should be treated with the same respect. I think fascism in any form is bad. But aren't they the fascists?*

They had forced her family to adopt a new name under the risk of her father being arrested or sent to Social Quarantine. He had given up a successful career to start over *again.* They lived under constant fear of being exposed. Now they were making Maddie march in a protest that she didn't believe in, and forcing her to do something against her will. And despite her doing so, Deborah made it clear that they were watching her, intimidating her. *Haven't we been through enough? All I want to do is finish school, but they won't let me do that. They want me to compromise what little I have left...what I believe in.*

The march continued to Ridge Road where the protesters blocked off traffic. Maddie was shoved up against an SUV; a mother and two small children, one an infant, were inside. There was a look of stark fear on the mother's face. The press of the crowd held her in place, making it impossible to get away. The vehicle could not move because of the swarming crowd; instead it swayed from side to side as the protesters rocked it. Two young men—one an Asian American she recognized from a class, another a thick-around-the-waist white student—climbed onto the hood of the Nissan and began jumping up and down. The hood of the vehicle crumbled as the heavy student moved to the roof, and his bulk bent the roof inward.

Maddie was pushed into the vehicle, and her face was pressed against the driver's side rear window. In the back seat, she could see the young child, in a car seat, screaming...its cries were drowned out by the myriad of chants of the crowd. *This is wrong! These poor people.* A horror washed over her. *I am part of this simply by being here.* She could not claim she was entirely innocent—her body was part of the mass pushing into the vehicle, despite her wishes. In that moment, she could smell body odor, a hint of smoked pot, and something that smelled like licorice. Maddie could not understand how, in that moment of repulsion, she had noticed the aromas. It made no sense; then again, nothing she was experiencing made sense.

A mix of nausea, anger, fear and icy resolve came to her as she stared in horror inside the vehicle. She finally twisted and shifted enough to get away from the vehicle, pushing back into the crowd of protesters. The feeling of being surrounded chewed at her nerves.

Speeches blared over bullhorns in the intersection; some overlapped each other, making listening to any specific message nearly impossible. The chants of the crowd were a low, indistinguishable roar. Their messages and calls for imaginary justice were unimportant to her; she tuned them out with sheer anger and concentration. When she finally reached the edge of the protest, she broke out of the mass of sweaty students and into the darkness.

The walk back to Metcalf Hall was akin to the walk of shame for her—like a young woman slinking back after a shameful one-night stand. She hung her head, avoiding eye contact with other students that were beginning to drift back from the protest. While they were laughing and happy, she was the exact opposite.

When she got back to her room, she sat at the edge of her bed for long, silent minutes. A part of her felt that she had betrayed her family on top of betraying her beliefs. She struggled with the guilt and indignity she had brought on herself by attending the protest. As she wrestled with her conscience, she began to feel dirty. She knew that some of it was from the mass of students that had pressed into her, but much of the feeling was in the back of her mind.

She stripped, tossed her clothes into the hamper and stepped into the shower. She left the water on almost scalding hot as she turned slowly, letting it wash over her. *Do I tell my parents?* Not over the phone. Her father had warned her not to discuss anything about her political leanings on her cell phone. The NSF was constantly looking for 'extremists,' i.e. conservatives. The wrong words or phrases would unravel what her father had worked so hard to put in place to protect them all. *No, I won't tell them about it until I see them when they visit.*

Maddie stepped out of the shower, using one towel for her curly hair, the other wrapped around her body. The hot water had helped, though she could not quite shake the image of the child crying in the back seat of the car. She dressed, putting on clean panties, bra, T-shirt and running shorts. She knew she should go and get something to eat, but the thought of interacting with other students, people that supported such events, made her stomach knot up.

As she walked over to turn on the TV, she saw a piece of paper at her front door, folded twice, with her name on it. Someone must have slid it under the door while she was in the shower. Picking it up, she opened it slowly, as if it possessed bad news. Instead, she saw a simple message: "You're not alone. We will reach out to you. GBA."

Her heart pounded in her chest as she looked at the handwritten message. GBA. That graffiti was rare, but had been televised as being from radical conservative extremists. The NSF had put out warnings that it was a banned slogan, one of hate and divisiveness. *God Bless America.*

She clutched the note so tightly that it wrinkled in her hands. Suddenly the fear was gone, replaced by something new, something she had not felt since coming to college. Hope.

Philadelphia, Pennsylvania

Deja Jordan looked at the camera footage from Columbus, Ohio. Recorded the previous night, it appeared on a large monitor. It had come in overnight, a lucky hit by a search algorithm, downloaded from the NSFCloud. Around the young man, a red circle was flashing, imprinted by the NSA team that had tagged the footage of the attack on an SE squad. The video image zoomed in on the face and showed that it was a 78 percent match to Raul Lopez. "Got your ass!" she said with a grin.

"That doesn't look much like him," Trey said from over her shoulder.

"Don't let the bald head fool you. NSA says it is probably him," she replied, not lifting her eyes from the video. She backed it up to the point where he has punched and zoomed on the image. "Look, he was wearing some sort of makeup or device to hide his appearance."

Deja stared intently at the image. The picture quality was not outstanding, even with the enhancements that the NSA/NSF had applied. She then adjusted the image with her mouse, angling in on the female that was with him. Advancing the video, she was surprised at the speed and deadliness of the woman. There was eerie grace about how the female moved. It wasn't only because of training; there was a hint of art in her actions. This was obviously not a bodyguard of some sort. *This was a professional.*

"And the car?"

"Columbus NSF found a burned out car of the same make and model an hour ago, about thirty minutes away. They are sweeping it for DNA and prints," Trey said.

Her head shook as she pried herself away from the monitor. "They won't find any."

"How can you be sure?" Trey Phillips asked.

"You watch this," she countered, replaying the video of the attack. "That woman is a pro. She's not going to make a mistake like leaving trace evidence. NSF, I mean *we*, will spend a lot of time picking through the ashes, but it won't help." Deja caught herself. She was still referring to the NSF as a separate entity. *We are part of them now. It's hard to shake old habits.*

"She made a mistake tangling with the local Social Enforcers. Not exactly a brilliant move."

"I watched the full vid," she said. "Those SEs were fucking with her. We don't have audio, but I bet she was trying to talk her way out of the entire confrontation."

"Why engage? They were two-to-one odds. Not the best move."

Deja ran the video again from start to finish. "The odds were always in her favor," she said when it came to an end. "She killed three of them—Raul only killed one. Those asshats never stood a chance."

Standing up, she closed her eyes slowly in thought. *They are on foot, for now. They'll need a car.* She opened her eyes and pulled up Google for a map of the states around Columbus. She looked at the roads in and out of the city. *They came from here to there—so where are they going?* To her, it seemed obvious. *Tennessee. He's going to safe ground, a red state, where the Pretender has set up camp.*

"Get me the Special Agent in charge of this in NSF. We need to talk."

Trey nodded and checked his phone; then he used the landline to place a call. It took three minutes for him to get through. "Detective Gallagher," he said, handing the phone to her.

"Hello, Detective," she said. "I am Deja Jordan—"

He cut her off fast. "I know who you are Ms. Jordan," the voice replied.

She felt the tension through the phone line. "I was just looking at the video that the NSA processed."

"We already analyzed it on our end," the curt voice responded.

"Well then," she said, reeling in her desire to snap back. "I think it would be prudent to establish roadblocks on all roads heading out of Ohio to the south."

"Why is that?"

"He's fled Philadelphia. Lopez will want to go to a safe place. That means the south—probably Tennessee."

"That's a lot of resources to pull," he replied. "And on a hunch."

"Where else can he go? His escort is clearly a professional. He knows we are going to be expecting him to move to Texas—that's too damn risky. Going to Tennessee makes the most sense," she said.

This time she was not interrupted. She hoped the silence wasn't a prelude to being hung up on. "You know, that's not a bad idea. We were focusing our efforts on Columbus and all roads south. Block them from reaching safe ground." The definition of safe ground meant Kentucky. The Governor there was liberal, but was unwilling to put his head in a noose when it came to going against a legitimately sworn President. *He should be a lot more worried about what we are going to do with him once this whole 'America-thing' goes away.* His hedging his bets had resulted in the state turning traitor on Newmerica after days of fence-sitting and hand-wringing, siding with the Pretender President's administration. Their law enforcement had cut ties with the NSF, further complicating matters. *We can still catch them there, but it's not as much under our control as it was a few weeks ago.*

"Like I said, the person he's with, she's a pro," Deja said. "You won't get her sweeping neighborhoods."

"Maybe we need to do both," Detective Gallagher said.

"They'll need wheels," Deja said. "They won't buy them; they'll take them."

"I'm ahead of you on that front. I've got a query in the NSFCloud for any and all vehicle thefts in a four-county area around the city."

"If your people feed stolen vehicle data to the roadblocks and checkpoints, you will save yourself some time," she said, impressed that the detective had thought about their mode of transportation.

"Good idea," Gallagher said in a much more relaxed tone. "Listen, we are going to need a lot of feet on the ground to implement what you are suggesting. I'm in Cincinnati. Why don't you head this way? NSF can cover a lot of ground, but getting the SEs to cooperate is proving a little *challenging.*"

The offer caught her off guard. "Alright. I'm not doing any good here in Philly."

"Great. I will shoot you where our CP is. I look forward to meeting you."

He hung up and Deja turned to Trey, handing him the receiver. "Well?" he prodded.

"I need a ride to the airport," she said.

"Where you heading?"

Deja drew a deep breath. "I'm going to help the NSF catch this little bastard," she said, glancing at the monitor one more time. *And I want to meet whoever this bitch is that's protecting him.*

The District
Truth Reconciliation Committee Headquarters

The National Secretary of the NSF stood in front of the long row of glass windows that overlooked the reconcilers. There were hundreds, if not thousands of people, in a sea of cubicles below her, all with multiple monitors, all buried deeply in their work. From her perch, she surveyed them analyzing images, blocking inappropriate images, flagging those that might be subversive, rewriting news posts on the web. The dull hum of the air conditioning and the cool blast of air didn't shake her concentration as she marveled at the work happening under her.

For decades, the facility had been the National Building Museum. It was one of the museums in The District that garnered few visitors and closed up after the Liberation. There had been talk of demolishing the antiquated structure, but the Truth Reconciliation Committee needed a home, so major revamping and updating had been done. While the outside of the building still loomed with its stoic red brick, the interior had been gutted and refurbished, complete with the underground structure to hold the massive data warehouse that the TRC required.

She heard footsteps and knew who it was before she looked up. When she slowly lifted her gaze from the workers below, she saw

Rebecca Clarke, the Director of the organization she stood in the heart of. Rebecca was always dressed in crisp, professional, dark colors, an almost manly suit. She flashed a grin as she approached, a false indication of friendship. While both of them sat on the Ruling Council, their relationship had been tenacious at times. Part of the problem was ego. Rebecca saw herself as an equal, only because she controlled the messaging for Newmerica. *There's always a little lack of respect when it comes to the work I do...and she will someday pay for that arrogance.*

"I had no idea you were coming, Alex," she said politely.

"I tried to schedule time with you," the Secretary replied. "I was told it would take two weeks."

"So you thought you'd show up?"

The Secretary grinned. "And here we are."

"I'm not given to cloak and dagger meetings," Rebecca replied. "I heard you were in the building on an unscheduled tour and I came down. My schedule has been packed lately, especially with the election coming up."

"I've found that sometimes a little subterfuge is necessary," she said, crossing the arms of her Bergdorf Goodman black blazer.

"What can I help you with?"

"The upcoming congressional hearing is scheduled to start soon. I want to ensure that the coverage is appropriate to what is discussed. I am, after all, Daniel's running mate. Smearing me, even in a small way, hurts all of us."

Rebecca was smart; even she had to give her that much. "If you are asking whether we are going to cover it, the answer is *yes*. The leak of the information on the net was not contained because of the terror attacks on the Big Tech companies. Some of the accusations in that data are fairly severe, as I'm sure you know. Several documents claim you arranged for the assassination of the top levels of the SE organization, among other things. The genie is out of bottle and a lot of people want to know the truth. So yes, we are going to cover the hearings."

"Of course you are, Becky," she said curtly.

"I don't go by Becky anymore. Rebecca has a better ring to it."

"Of course," she replied. "Rebecca I would never suggest that you shouldn't cover them. By the same token, I strongly believe that the coverage of these pointless interrogations needs to be minimal."

Rebecca said nothing for a moment, staring at her in icy silence. "Are you worried, Alex?" The Secretary heard the unspoken subtext of the question...*do you have a reason to be worried? Did you actually order these killings?* The Secretary felt it was an insulting question. I am the only one that could have given those orders. *Who are you to question my motives? I won't give her the satisfaction of specifics. Besides, she fits perfectly into my plans.* "Worried? I don't get paid to worry," she said with confidence ringing clearly. "Some of what I will talk about is bound to cross into the realm of national security. Also, every second that you broadcast gives our enemies material that they can twist against us. I was hoping that you understood the implications of that."

Before Rebecca could respond, the Secretary cut her off. "Let's also remember that it is possible, however unlikely, that we might lose in a general election. I am the VP on the party ticket. Damaging me, damages us all. We all had a part in the Liberation Rebecca, you included. If this Pretender gets elected, we will face all out civil war or worse; we may find ourselves in the hands of our enemies. While there are those that might want to see me taken down a notch or two, they also would find themselves facing repercussions." Her words were careful, weighed, and loaded with implied threats...threats that were very real. *I saw what you did with the Speaker of the House that night. We both have blood on our hands in one form or another.*

The tint of red that rose on Rebecca's face told her that her verbal salvo had hit home. "I understand fully. By the same token, we are at a critical juncture for our nation. Newmerica is being threatened as it has not been since we founded it. What the people want is a feeling of legitimacy in what we do, which means a measured bit of transparency. As I said, the information that this rouge operative—"

"*Alleged* operative," she corrected. "I think you'll find that much of what has been put on the web is disinformation spread by the Pretender's camp to destabilize us at this critical time. Proof that this Caylee Leatrom even exists is tenuous at best. The operative program is a myth, spread by our enemies. From where I sit, it would be far wiser for us to simply bury this entire witch hunt that Senator Lewis is waging rather than give it a hint of authenticity or credibility."

"It would be convenient for you if I did that, wouldn't it?"

What are you getting at Becky? "I'm not sure what you mean?"

"If I don't cover this, any dings on your career are never made public."

"I assure you that everything I am doing is in the best interest of Newmerica. With these elections coming up and several states shifting away from our government, this is simply not the time for us to show weakness. Our enemies are watching."

"Dissemination of the truth is my responsibility," Rebecca replied. "I will do my duty."

"Spare me the party line. We both know the truth is what we make it. You've been doing that for quite a while. You and I were in the Capitol the day of the Liberation. We both know what decisions were made and by whom. I know what I did that day. I also know what you did." *Two can play this game Becky.*

Rebecca was silent for a moment, clearly pondering what the Secretary had said. "I will do what is right," she said in response through half-gritted teeth, clearly trying to curb her anger. That pleased the Secretary; it meant that she had gotten to her.

"That's all I could ask for," she said, turning to walk way. She took one step and then turned back. "You know, I have been meaning to ask you. Do you have a lot of contact with your parents? Do they still have that house on Beacon Hill?" Her words were loaded and coy. *That's right, I am keeping tabs on Mommy and Daddy. I want you to know that. I want that nibbling at the back of your mind when you are making decisions that impact me.*

Rebecca scowled at the hint, giving the Secretary a bit more satisfaction…*the icing on the proverbial cake.* "I haven't spoken to my parents in years," she snapped. "We don't exactly see eye-to-eye."

"I know," she said. "Yet somehow neither of them ever ended up being interviewed about their capitalist ties. Both of them seem to have escaped spending a few months in Social Quarantine."

Rebecca's dark brown eyes narrowed as she looked at her. "If that is a threat, you're wasting it Alex. Go ahead; toss them in quarantine. I don't care."

"Threats are beneath me," the Secretary replied. "But sometimes happy coincidences happen."

Rebecca's mouth opened to offer a rebuttal, but the Secretary finished and turned to the door. "Thank you for your time old friend."

As she reached the door from the glass-walled, interior hallway, she allowed herself to smile. It didn't matter that the threat had little weight with Becky. What mattered was that Becky knew she was *willing* to make the threat to begin with. *It reminds her of the forces I have at my disposal.* The members of the Ruling Council vied for power and position with each other. Becky was not immune to the power plays. Planting the seed of a threat served to remind her so-called peer of her reach and authority. Becky was one of the few people that might try to leverage this crisis against her. Now she had given her something to think about, to cause worry. *Let her mull that over.* As she left the building a few minutes later, she was confident that she had mitigated much of the coverage she might be facing.

CHAPTER 9

"Victims are symbols of hope."

The Southern White House
Nashville, Tennessee

Jack Desmond cradled the warm cup of coffee in his hands as if he could draw the caffeine from its contents through the touch of his palms. When he saw Charli Kazinski enter the break room, he could not help but smile. Memories of their time in the Secret Service, before everything that had transpired in the last five years, were still there, wanting to surge forward. Charli was very good at her job; she had even taken a bullet for the last President. Working daily with politicians made him squeamish at times, even those loyal to the cause. His former subordinate was different; her values didn't waver. *She has remained true to herself—despite all that has happened.*

Charli brushed back her short cropped hair and got herself a cup of coffee. "Hiding in here, Jack?"

"The whole nation is up in arms. Half of the population would like to see everyone in this building swinging from a rope, including you. Our supporters love squabbling with each other. Our enemies abroad get stronger every day we are in turmoil. I'm trying to coordinate a fair election in a nation that hasn't had one in a long time. I have a military that is unsure where it stands, a rebel government already fighting a war with us, and you are asking me if I'm hiding? Hell yes I'm hiding" Jack chuckled, but it was forced.

Charli didn't dilute her coffee; she simply sipped it slowly. "They wouldn't have given you the job if you weren't up to it."

Jack shook his head, glancing at his own coffee in search of solace. "I got the job by default. Nothing can prepare you for a civil war. And don't kid yourself. We are at war."

"You served in the Army, so you have some experience," she reminded him.

Those years were far behind him, a blurred series of memories. "I was a Lieutenant—ROTC, the Royal Order of Trained Cowards…that's what we joked about—the name. I never saw action though. Now I am making decisions to send a lot of young men and women into harm's way. I know that a lot of them are going to be injured or killed before this is over. It keeps me up at night."

"Jack," Charli said slowly. "You started this; now we have to see it through. Rekindling the Sons of Liberty…that was you. There can't be a moment of hesitation or concern. Our enemy is ruthless and entrenched. They know what will happen to them if they fail…the same thing that will happen to us if we fail. They will see every one of us hang if we falter in the least."

"I know," he said, taking another sip of his coffee. "That's why I don't take this job lightly. The Newmericans are a brutal regime cloaked in the guise of being open and friendly. You have seen what they are capable of."

Before she could answer, Andy Forest entered the break room, earning him a sly and rare grin from Charli. Jack knew they had been dating, if that was what you called it. Andy went to the vending machine and got a Diet Pepsi, and then moved over next to Charli. "I hope I'm not interrupting."

Charli glanced at him, and then looked back at Jack. "Fearless leader was conveying his concerns about what is coming…how bad the bad guys are."

Andy nodded. "They are weaker than anyone thinks, in my humble opinion," he offered.

Andy was not a politician. Before his father's death, he was a consultant. Jack understood one thing about him; he was not burdened with the political implications of the current state of affairs. If anything, Andy offered his opinion based on facts. The President admired him, and Jack had nothing but respect for him. "What makes you say that?"

Andy shifted on his feet. "My father and I talked about it a lot before he died. First, they have become complacent. They took down the country so fast, rounded up all the opposition…it left them with fewer targets. The fervor that got them to overthrow the government is gone. Even with us now as a target, they will squabble among themselves about how to do it. They have built a huge government, massive layers of administration and diluted authority. It's big, but lumbering.

"Second, they are following the path of all revolutions. Once revolutionaries get in power, they turn on each other. Stalin had Kerensky killed, along with millions of his own people. Mao turned himself into a cult figure and went after capitalists, and, eventually, his own political opposition. Castro didn't just kill Batista supporters; he murdered anyone that posed a threat to him after coming into power. Now, look at what happened just a few weeks ago. The Secretary of the NSF organized the assassination of almost 200 people to seize control of Social Enforcement."

"She's dangerous," Jack said.

"She's Robespierre—from the French Revolution. My dad drilled it into me when I sat with him in the hospital and I did my own research on it. Robespierre was an architect of the revolution, but in the end, his allies all turned on him. That will happen with her as well. I am willing to bet that there are people in the Newmerican government right now that are plotting her downfall. She's a true believer and that makes her dangerous; but so is everyone on their Ruling Council. When you build a nation on hate and distrust, it eventually bites you in the ass. It is the nature of revolts in history. We have given them a good reason to unite, a common enemy, but that doesn't allow them to escape destiny. They will turn on each other…they already have. Look at that coup where NSF killed off the SE leadership and absorbed them, almost overnight."

Jack said nothing for a long moment before Charli broke the silence. "That's why I like him; he knows his stuff." Jack saw the side-glance she gave him, the way her eyes opened wider. *I'll be damned—Chari and Jack are a thing!*

His mind raced as he tried to process what Andy had said. *We need to foster dissent in their ranks. Keep them at each other's throats.* "Your father was a brilliant man."

Andy nodded. "The Ruling Council is scared. You saw the news, that tiny little blurb about a Congressional Hearing on the material that Caylee put out. While I doubt little will come of it, it is clear that as much as the Secretary consolidated power by absorbing the SEs, now people are questioning how she did it. Think about it. We haven't seen even a hint of oversight into the Ruling Council until now. Their façade is cracking."

Jack found himself smiling. He knew that some of the Newmerica leadership were turning on each other, but how to leverage that information had not clicked with him until Andy had spoken. *A good disinformation campaign can help spread their distrust of each other. We can force them to flip on each other, stab each other in the back. This is not just about waging military operations; it needs to be more complex.* He took another long drink of his coffee, its warmth renewing his own energy. "You've given me a lot to think about," he said, walking to the small stainless steel sink and dumping the rest of the coffee.

Ripley, Ohio

US-62 ran along the north bank of the Ohio River; the two-lane highway snaked and twisted along the trees that had already dropped their leaves. From the abandoned Marathon Gas station where Caylee had parked their stolen pickup truck, she had good visibility of the bridge to Kentucky. It had been the William H. Harsha Bridge, but as she surveyed the sign with her binoculars, she could see that the name had been spray painted over. In Newmerica, there were no memorials to dead conservatives, regardless of their accomplishments. No doubt they would dredge up someone to name the bridge for some time soon. The only reason they probably hadn't was that southern Ohio, despite their best efforts, still had strong conservative ties.

They had walked nearly three miles the night of the attack at the KFC, finally hot-wiring a beat-up old Chevy Silverado. She knew that stealing a vehicle might tip off the NSF or the SEs, so she took one that was not likely to be quickly reported—from in front of a crack house. Chances are the vehicle had already been stolen, based on the meth-head that got out of it and went inside to make his buy.

She had applied makeshift makeup and prosthetics to Raul to try and make his face less likely to be scanned. They had slept in the vehicle, making their way to Cincinnati first thing in the morning to cross over into Kentucky. Like its neighbor, Tennessee, the state Governor there had recognized the President and the new American government—much to the chagrin of the Newmerican government. The state still had a strong presence of Newmerica, SEs and the NSF, but they were gradually beginning to flip over to the American side of the fence. It wasn't entirely safe, but it was better than Ohio at the moment.

Caylee had come to like Raul. She asked him about Valley Forge and he told her the facts—not embellishing his role or getting into his feelings. That was something she could respect. If anything, Raul played down his role…she could hear it in his voice. Years of training taught her to spot when someone was lying, but Raul was forthright in his tale. He told her about the priest that had been killed and how he had shot the men in Detroit.

She began to see him as a person caught up by circumstances. There was an innocence about him that she found oddly appealing. She showed him how to improve his weapons handling and a few other little tricks. *The kid knows his stuff. He's a victim of the law of averages…in the wrong place at the wrong time.* It made her even more protective of him. *He's so innocent; it makes me* want *to guard him.*

The bridge was barricaded on the Ohio side of the river and manned by six visible Social Enforcers. From what Caylee could tell, every car was being stopped and searched. She studied the banner that they had put on the bridge and noted that it was an SE troop out of Pennsylvania. *I liked it better when they weren't part of the NSF…when they didn't coordinate their efforts.*

"How's it look?" he asked.

She did not break her gaze with the binoculars. "Not good. Another SE roadblock, armed sentries."

"You think they are looking for us?"

She lowered the binoculars and gave him a twisted grin in response. "I think it's a safe bet. We took a big piss in their pool with those thugs at the KFC."

"Can't we drive further on down the road, cross somewhere else?"

She shook her head. "Sorry kid. They had Cincinnati bottled up and this bridge too. Chances are whoever's running this op is wanting to block us from heading south. That means they are smarter than the average Enforcers."

Raul looked dejected as she spoke. "I learned in my time in the Army and the Agency that traps like this either have to be circumvented, or you spring them and blast your way through. The way they have their cars parked, we can drive across the bridge, *if* we get past their guards."

"How do we do that?"

Caylee's mind went through a myriad of scenarios. Trying to cross in broad daylight was going to be problematic, even with the false IDs she had. If they had managed to get videos of them at KFC, even with the cosmetic changes, chances are they would get caught. A part of her liked it, but to be effective, she would have to deal with the SEs or risk the truck getting shot to bits. The key was to overpower the defenders, to strike so fast they were unable to respond.

"We wait until it's dark. It makes identification more difficult," she said settling on a plan. "I will sneak up on the checkpoint. You'll drive up, armed and ready. I will whittle down the guards and you will blast whoever sides up to your window. I'll jump in and you drive like hell across the bridge."

"They'll catch me before that!" Raul said.

She shook her head. "They are looking for a man and woman. You'll be alone, which will likely have them relax at least a little. As long as you remain calm and don't fire until they are next to the truck, we should be OK." Experience told her otherwise. *We were fortunate with the SEs in the parking lot. They were not prepared for us to strike. They weren't looking for us. This situation is different. They are prepared, guns ready.* Caylee knew she could whittle the odds down, but it was going to be close. *Unfortunately, we don't have much in the way of options. At this time of the year, the river is cold and fast. We need to cross at a bridge and this one is fairly isolated.*

For the next few hours, she prepped Raul. She pulled a sawed off shotgun out of her bag and instructed him on how to use it. There was less chance of missing with a shotgun; pellets have no friends at close range. Caylee showed him how to fire it cross-body, warning him about the kick. He didn't question her; instead he seemed to be intensely focused.

Twilight came and with it a chill in the autumn air. Clouds came in from the west and darkness blanketed the Marathon station and the road earlier than usual. She had put on a black sweatshirt, old and torn in a few places. Caylee reached into her bag and pulled out several knives, pistols, and magazines for reloading. Opening the door of the old Silverado, she checked her gear and then leaned in. "We don't have radios. I need some time. I have a lighter. Watch for it. When you see it come on and off twice, you start down the road to the bridge."

Raul nodded nervously. He's afraid, which is good. Fear heightens the senses. "You'll do fine Raul; do what I told you." She even offered him a thin smile of support. She closed the door slowly, leaning into it to latch it, and then she crept across the road and onto the embankment leading down to the Ohio River.

The progress was slow. Saplings and briars covered the embankment, along with garbage that had washed up there or had been tossed by motorists. The dull, yellow lights from the bridge provided her with plenty of shadows. Walking on dead leaves was tricky, but done slowly and methodically, she knew she would not generate a lot of noise or attention.

It took the better part of an hour to reach a position below the guard rail at the roadblock. She rose enough to get a good view of the guards. Decked out in their black bloc, they didn't strike her as intimidating beyond the weapons they carried. The myriad of gun bans had the ATF rounding up registered weapons, but they left them in the hands of the true criminals—the Social Enforcers. Two of the people held their weapons as if they had been trained, probably ex-military from the look of it. The other four—they were rank amateurs. Two had their holsters on for cross-body drawing, which took far too much time for her taste. One female joined the group from her car, an Enterprise rental according to the sticker on the bumper. She was a young black woman, well dressed, clearly someone in leadership. Speaking with the other SEs, she showed her credentials and they seemed to respect her. *Great...that makes seven baddies.*

A car turned from the road to the bridge, and she ducked down before the headlights hit her face. Listening to the conversation, it was clear that the people guarding the bridge were tired.

"I gotta piss," one said as the car was cleared to cross.

"Then piss," snapped a chubby Enforcer.

The man made his way along the road, past Caylee, moving into the darkness so his friends wouldn't watch him. She followed him, stealthily creeping along. When he got some thirty yards down the road, he dropped his pants and unleashed his stream.

Caylee slid over the rail and pulled a KA-BAR knife from the sheath on her leg. The rush of adrenaline roared through her body, but she drew a long breath of cool air and controlled it. That was one of the things that professionals did; they made sure that the adrenaline was not in control of their bodies; that *they* were in control. Moving behind him as he urinated over the rail, she slid the knife along his throat so fast and smooth that it barely made a sound beyond his last gurgle for air. Grasping his shirt collar, she gently lowered his body over the rail and let him slide down the embankment. Following him over the rail, she checked his pockets for anything of use; she came back with his wallet, which she tucked into her pocket.

The body dropping made a rustling sound that none of the others seemed to pay attention to. They were joking, talking about how they were stuck in the middle of nowhere. She moved closer to them, knowing that sooner or later they would come to look for their missing comrade.

"Hey Bee," the chubby one called out after five minutes. "Where are you at man?" All he got in response was a distant owl hooting.

Chubby motioned to another lean, white kid and the two of them started down the road along the rail. "Come on Bee; you taking a dump or what?"

Two at once would be harder. She went through her options. Arming herself with a fighting knife in both hands, she once more climbed over the rail. As she delicately and deliberately moved in behind them, one turned, somehow alerted to her. "Hey," he said in a low tone, just before the blade cut his throat. As his body dropped, his friend turned. "What the—" he stammered, desperately reaching across his body for his pistol.

Caylee buried the knife in his throat hitting his neck bones hard, and then she pulled it across, nearly decapitating him. His body fell on top of Chubby's with a dull thump. A cold night breeze had kicked in, stirring the leaves, muffling the body's fall. *I knew he had that holster badly positioned …*

She knew time was of the essence now. Three of the seven were down. Using one hand to shield the lighter's flame from the group at the bridge, she flicked it on and off twice. A mile or so down the road, at the Marathon station, the headlights of the Silverado came on.

Turning back to the blockade, she went over the guard rail and started to make her way to the bridge again.

The District

Rebecca looked at the web page posting and felt like pounding her fists on the desk. The headline read, "Progressives trailing in key battleground states." Across from her sat one of her TRC managers, Jamison Holly, whose face was already red from having been summoned to her office. *He has a good reason to be fearful.*

"How in the hell did that story make it to the web?" she demanded.

"Our people are overloaded. Somehow it slipped through the cracks," Jamison said. "It is an honest mistake."

"You think that's acceptable, Jamison?" she asked. "Because if you do, you are out of a job. And if I fire you, I assure you, you won't be getting benefits." Unemployment in Newmerica had no stigma and little risk. Since the pandemic, being unemployed simply meant you made as much as you did while working with none of the effort.

"No, Director," he said nervously. "The reality is that we are overloaded. The opposition has spun up additional news agencies, and their reporters are generation stories that support their views at a record rate. We've never seen it on this scale."

Rebecca remembered the early years of the Great Reformation, when she had formed the TRC. The conservative news outlets had cried in outrage at the Liberation and demanded justice. She had maneuvered to silence them, thanks to assistance from the technology companies on the West Coast. Those reporters and editors who had defied her became targets for social justice. Within a few months, there had been no opposing viewpoint—only the perspective of the Ruling Council. *My actions then brought us calm and peace. Without the rogue media giving people reasons to be upset.* Now, that was being challenged again.

"I have assurances from their hosting provider that the site will be down in a matter of an hour or so…'technical difficulties,'" Jamison said. "It will be like it never existed."

"How many people will have read it by then?" she asked. *How many of them will start to question what we have been telling them—that we are overwhelmingly popular in those swing states?*

Rebecca was one of the few people who understood the *real* truth—not the truth that she and the TRC put out. She had overseen the running of polls in various states. In the urban areas, the current administration was viewed favorably. In many parts of the country, however, support for the Pretender was not only growing, but it was solid. That information had to remain buried.

"I have been assured that we have the IP addresses of everyone that accessed the site," Jamison said firmly. "I intend to hand that list over to Social Enforcement. Those people will get the message—that they shouldn't be reading subversive material."

She looked at the story one more time. "This looks like our polling data," she said with disbelief.

"Is it?"

Jamison would not have seen the real polling data; no one was supposed to have. *I thought I buried those results.* "Someone has taken our data and smuggled it to this reporter," she said.

Just saying it, she could see the mix of emotions wash over Jamison's face. *He's figuring out that we are stopping the story because it is true.* "We need to contact the NSF. This reporter needs to be brought in so we can find out who has betrayed us," he finally said.

Rebecca thought carefully about responding. *Alex would love that—she would use it as leverage against me in the Council. Knowing her, she might even turn her goons loose on me.* Most people didn't know the Secretary of the NSF the way that Rebecca did. Memories of what happened under the Capitol the night of the Liberation came back to her. There was ruthlessness then, far beyond that of a normal politician. *She would not hesitate to use this against me.* "No. We need to conduct our own investigation into this. Do you understand Jamison?"

"Yes ma'am," he replied.

"Find out who had access to that polling data. Launch an internal investigation; let's do our own digging. Someone has to be held accountable for leaking our information." She worded her response carefully. *If not the guilty party, then Jamison might have to be the fall person for this.*

"Don't worry," he assured her nervously. "I will find the guilty party."

"You'd better," she warned.

Ripley, Ohio

Deja saw the headlights approaching the bridge slowly and her hand drifted down to the pistol at her side. She had been in Cincinnati, overseeing the checkpoints, but she knew that the two targets were not going to try to cross to the south there. Simply put, there was too much force on those bridges. *It will require them to try a crossing somewhere else, like this wide-ass spot in the middle of the road.*

During the twilight drive out to the bridge in Ripley, Ohio, she had time to think about Raul Lopez. She had studied what information the NSF had shared on him, which was damned little. He didn't seem like the type to turn traitor, but he had. If it was him at the KFC, he had gone from being in the Youth Corp to sparking riots, to being involved in an op to release political prisoners from a camp, to being a killer…all in a relatively short period of time. *What would turn a young kid from Texas into a terrorist so fast?* That question ate at her. She had posed the question to her NSF contact, Detective Gallagher, when she had gotten to Cincinnati. He told her it didn't matter. But to Deja it did. It bothered her. *If they can turn a kid like that, how many others are they flipping?*

Distrust was something she understood. Newmerica had prospered because of it. They had convinced citizens to monitor and report on each other. Margaret's mysterious death, and deaths of the rest of the Social Enforcement leadership made her wonder whom she could truly trust. The only people that seemed to benefit from the decapitation of the SEs was the Secretary of the NSF. Before she had arrived at the bridge, she wondered if she was being played in some way, if she was somehow a target. *They must have had other reasons, things above my pay grade.* That was something that Deja wanted desperately to believe in, but it was hard. Margaret, for all of her quirks, was a good person. She didn't deserve to be murdered. The thought that leaders of the Newmerica government might be killing innocents to seize power was dangerous to contemplate. She suppressed those thoughts and focused more on Lopez and his dangerous sidekick.

The woman he was traveling with was a pro, no doubt about that. *I wish I had that bitch's moves. Is she the one that turned this kid?* The video had shown her moves to be lightning fast, with precision. *Whoever did her training created a killing machine.*

Across the river were officers of the NSF, though they had pulled off those patches and had sewn on the old Kentucky State Police replacements. Kentucky had become a hotbed of rebellious activity since the Pretender President had emerged from hiding. Deja understood why they were there—a show of force. She had seen similar shows of force across the Ohio in Cincinnati. It was disturbing to her. *Why would anyone want to go back to the way things were? Why would anyone want to follow that man...someone who had propped up the Traitor President?* The only answer she could come to was the one that the TRC offered—they were racists and separatists who wanted to impose their horrific will on the good people of Newmerica.

Deja had watched the online video of the Pretender being sworn in before Big Tech managed to take it down almost a week after the event. Seeing his face, alive, had been infuriating. *We were told he was dead.* Rumors abounded that he was a fake, someone pretending to be the former Vice President. She didn't buy into that. *You can fake a face; you can't fake a voice.* It was him alright. A part of her admired his daring, getting sworn in for the whole country to see. The respect ended there. *He's as bad as the man he is trying to replace.* The TRC summed it up best—he is willing to plunge the nation into civil war to fulfill his own desire for power and to set the Great Reformation back decades.

She blocked the glare of the headlights of the approaching vehicle with one hand as the SE sentries shifted. Deja glanced over for a moment and noticed a few of them were missing. *That's weird...one guy went to take a leak, and now we're short what...three guys?*

"Looks like we have a new customer," the leader of the SEs. 'Ranger' Thorton, a stocky college-aged kid, was far too young to have taken part in the Liberation.

Deja turned her focus to the approaching vehicle, a truck from the look and sound of it. Stepping off of the roadway, she nodded to another of the SEs, Alice, to approach the vehicle from the passenger side. The group she was visiting knew what they were doing; she had seen that much. The truck made the turn off the road running along the river, and slowly drove toward the bridge.

She followed Ranger to the vehicle, coming up on the back side of the cab. She pulled out her Maglite and turned it on, flashing it in the back of the open bed of the truck. There were a few pieces of wood back there, graying two-by-four pieces, and rust—a lot of it.

Ranger stood next to the driver's side door and flashed his light through the dirty and smeared door window. "Roll it down," he commanded, "I need to see your face." Alice moved along the passenger side; her flashlight flickered on and off until she banged it on the side of the truck bed. The other two guards stood off in the distance, on the opposite side of the road; they stood casually with Ranger between them and the driver.

"Ms. Jordan," she said, her face going taunt. "Big bag on the floor." Instantly there was tension in the air. Deja moved closer to Ranger. As she looked in at the Hispanic youth, the realization hit her. *That's him... that's Raul Lopez!* Someone had put makeup on him, disguised him, but she could tell it was him. "Put your hands where I can—"

Alice suddenly jerked backward, into the dark, her flashlight flying in the air, its beam swirling in the darkness. It was as if an invisible hand had grabbed her and pulled her into the darkness. Deja aimed her flashlight at Alice in time to see her body drop to the ground. There was a blur she barely saw, another figure. Deja transferred the Maglite to her left hand and reached for his pistol. Mid-move, there was a flash and bang. The figure that had taken Alice down fired a weapon.

The gunfire in the dark temporarily made her eyes lose focus as she pulled the weapon. Behind her, one of the two SEs opposite of the truck cried out, no doubt hit by the shot. She instinctively crouched next to Ranger.

Suddenly the driver's side door erupted with a massive roar that made her ears pop. Her left arm jerked as Ranger flew back, doubled over, almost blown in half by a shotgun blast from the driver. Something wet hit her face, part of the blast. From her crouched position, she toppled over backwards, searing hot pain coming from her left arm. All around her sounds were muffled; there were other flashes, and then the truck spun out, racing across the bridge. The blast from the exhaust washed over her as she rolled onto her right side to get out of the way of the vehicle. She felt the crunch of glass under her, grinding into her arm and leg, no doubt from a shotgun blast through the door, and the rolled down window.

Goddamn it! Deja glanced at her left arm and saw blood. *I've been hit!* The driver's side door of the Chevy was a massive gaping hole, illuminated in the dim lights on the bridge. A figure leapt into the bed of the truck, clad like her in black. Deja held her gun out in front of her and opened fire wildly at the vehicle as it raced across the bridge. She could barely hear her own M1911 pistol as she fired. Each kick of the gun made her upper left arm throb.

The rear window of the fleeing truck exploded after one squeeze of the trigger causing a bit of satisfaction. She emptied the magazine, hitting the tailgate of the truck as well, as it swerved from side to side trying to dodge the shots. Someone in the back of the vehicle popped up and unleashed a number of shots in her direction, close enough for her to flatten on the roadway for a moment. *Ricochets! Too fucking close for comfort.*

Those shots were joined by gunfire flashing from the Kentucky side of the river in response. A flicker off to her left caught her attention. *Those assholes are firing at us!* As the truck reached the far end of the bridge, she adjusted her aim, now targeting the flashes from the former NSF officers of the Kentucky State Police. The remaining SEs followed her actions, firing across the river. *You fuckers want a fight...you got it!*

CHAPTER 10

"Hurt feelings are a form of abuse."

Whiting, Indiana

Poised at the norther Indiana/Illinois border, Whiting Indiana was more of a distant suburb of Chicago than it was a city in its own right. It sat at the southern edge of Lake Michigan and in the autumn, the wind coming off of the lake made the air feel much colder than it was. Colonel Reager came up on the forward position where his forward platoon was poised on US20. The three M1 A1 Abrams were situated behind cover. One was parked in an abandoned Oldsmobile dealership, where it had driven into the old brick building and was using its lobby for cover. Across the street the other two tanks were positioned in the burned out hulk of a Dollar General, no doubt looted during the riots five years earlier. As he glanced at the lead tank, he could see that the paint was chipped in several areas, revealing some desert tan paint underneath. Like much of the National Guard, it had seen battle many times before. The Texas tanks were equipped with Tank Urban Survival Kits (TUSKs) to up-armor them for urban combat.

Captain "Trigger" DeYoung moved alongside him as was about to walk across the street. Before he could take a step, DeYoung put his hand on Trip's shoulder. "You don't want to do that sir," he said.

Trip Reager paused and surveyed the street more cautiously. "So the report is true. They have a sniper over there?"

"Snipers Colonel, plural. None of them have hit shit yet," Captain DeYoung said. "They take mostly pot shots at us when we are exposed. I'm willing to bet there is more than one shooter. They aren't professionals, but they are getting better. Sooner or later one of us is going to catch a round."

Not on my watch. "Where are they?" Trip asked.

DeYoung pulled out his iPad. "This is our position," he said, pointing at the map. "They are using an old apartment building around the corner and two blocks up on the right. It gives them a good field of fire of the street."

Trip studied the map intently for a few moments, and then slowly made his way to the corner of the building to see if he could get a quick glimpse of the enemy's position. As he slid his head around the corner, a crack sounded and a bullet ricocheted off of a brick about a foot over his head. A mist of concrete bits rained on him as he jerked his face back to cover. Wiping the bits of gray material off of his face, he frowned. "What is the composition of the enemy and how many are we talking about?"

Captain DeYoung set the iPad down and rested his hands on his hips. "I deployed scouts on the rooftops of some buildings that painted us a fairly good picture. IR signatures and visual sightings believe that roughly two squads are covering the street. We have had visuals on one more squad with three Technicals a half block back."

"What are the Technicals armed with?"

"Nissan and Ford trucks with bed-mounted machine guns, 50 cals. One has what looks like a recoilless...probably something left lying around in the armory. From what we can tell, these are Social Enforcers, but they have been outfitted with additional firepower, probably from the Illinois National Guard."

"Punk-ass kids with firepower," he growled.

"Yes sir, Colonel," DeYoung replied. "Nothing strong enough to take out our tanks, at least not anything we've seen."

"That's always the rub," he said, shaking his head. *I'm more worried about what we haven't seen yet.* "If they gave them these kinds of toys, you have to wonder what other kinds of shit they may have waiting for us." In a few days he would be deploying into Chicago, and I-20 was one of the routes he planned to use to penetrate the city. The Newmericans were simply not going to let that happen. They were deliberately positioning troops like this to hold him at bay. *They are operating under the assumption that I won't respond vigorously with the full force at my disposal.* Trip knew they would be prepared for him to react, with footage being filmed that, once edited, would make him look like the aggressor. *One thing that Newmerica does well is package fear.*

Chief of Staff Jack Desmond was no fool. He had learned from their example. As a result he had directed Trip to have all incidents filmed as well, so that there would be a counter to the disinformation that the enemy propagandists of the TRC would push out.

The Colonel knew he could try and ignored the sniping attacks that hit the building the day they made their push into the city. *If I wait, I run the risk of one of my personnel getting wounded or killed.* That thought made him angry. Memories of San Antonio came back to him, dark memories. That night he had made the choice to protect his personnel, and the cost had been high on both sides. Now he found himself facing the same kind of decision. *I waited last time. Probably longer than I should have. I won't make the same mistake...not this time.*

"Captain," he spoke slowly, deliberately choosing the right words. "Would you agree that the enemy snipers present a clear danger to us at this time?"

"I do sir."

"As do I. As such, I order you to use your squadron to eliminate that threat."

"A few rounds of HE should do the job, sir," DeYoung replied.

"I concur. Make sure we get camera footage of guns. Let them shoot at the tanks first; make sure it is a response to their aggressive action."

"They will deploy those Technicals the minute we make our move."

"It's a dumbfuck move if they do, but you are probably right," Trip said. "If and when they do, take them out as well." The words weighed heavy on him. He knew he was firing on citizens of the United States, even if they didn't agree that they were part of that nation any longer. In the back of his mind, he tried to justify this as a defense. *After all, they are the ones that have opened up on us...they brought this down on themselves.* Embracing that line of thinking was the only thing that made it palatable to engage the enemy. Adding to that was the broad discretion of his orders from the President. "You are authorized to take whatever measures are necessary to secure fair and free elections and to minimize the risks to your troops." The open-ended nature of the orders gave him wide latitude.

"We will make short work of them, Colonel," DeYoung said, his southern Texas drawl creeping into his voice.

"I would prefer not to fight, but I cannot sit by and risk our people's lives," Trip replied. "I'm going to assume a position back around the corner. The moment you come under fire, you are authorized to eliminate that threat with all force necessary."

"Understood," the Captain said, climbing up onto the point tank. He put on his helmet and adjusted the mic as he squeezed into the right side of the turret. Trip quickly moved to his position, sliding in the foam earplugs he always carried. The lead tank's engine roared to life, kicking up exhaust and sending light litter flying. The M1 Abrams tank roared to life and exuded a sense of raw power. Even from a distance of thirty yards, it was something to be both feared and respected.

The tank turned, its treads grinding on the bricks and rubble, pulverizing much of what it went over. The turret elevated slowly in anticipation of moving out of cover. As it came through what was left of the wall of the old car dealership, multiple pops of gunfire rang out, laughingly hitting the armor with no threat.

The tank would draw fire, so Trip felt safe sticking his head out. He saw a flash in one of the third story windows in the apartment building where the enemy was. There was a whooshing sound and he saw a missile streak in. *A Javelin!* The missile darted down fast, hitting the front armor near the top. The blast knocked Trip back and down on his butt, hard. Dust and debris rained around him and his right ear popped from the blast.

As he scrambled to his feet, a part of him half-wondered if the tank had been destroyed. Javelin anti-tank missiles usually needed around one hundred yards to properly lock and elevate for the kill shot. Whoever had fired the missile had not been trained on it, or he would have given himself greater distance. Still, there was a chance that the tank crew might already be dead.

Through the haze of smoke, the turret turned slightly and the 105mm gun returned the favor with a resounding blast of its own—proof that the tank was still operational. *Goddamn it, yes!* The apartment building's third floor erupted as the high explosive round went off, raining red brick and sending out a momentary plume of smoke and dust. Suddenly, the two floors above it disappeared, dropping straight down. The entire structure collapsed in less than a heartbeat, sending a mushroom cloud of smoke and dust rising into the air and marking the grave of the building.

The tank traversed to another building down the block and fired a round of high explosives into it. The front of that structure blew out, but the building managed to remain upright, though fires broke out as soon as the smoke and debris fell away.

The Technicals, converted tricks with weapons mounted in the beds, came down the street pouring fire at the tank, swerving and squealing as they charged at Trip's position. Another one of the Abrams tanks in the squadron moved out as DeYoung's lead tank turned to face them. The trucks had tack-welded armor plates—crude and ineffective but welded into place. The machine gun fire hitting the tank was a joke, sad and in vain. Both tanks fired, their massive guns making the ground throb around Trip and making his ears ache.

Leaning out further, he saw the lead Technical explode in a ball of flames, almost imploding on itself in a ball of orange fire. The other turned sharp at the last moment as the shell exploded in front of it, tossing the Ford truck end over end and sending the gunnery crew flying in the air. The last one, equipped with a recoilless rifle, fired at the second tank. A round hit with a loud blast, making Trip crouch for cover. One bit of shrapnel tugged at his uniform pants, tearing them slightly. It was too close for comfort, but he did not fall back.

The M1's machine guns hit the Nissan with the recoilless gun on the back. The big bullets chewed apart the silver-gray truck. It skidded sideways into a long-abandoned Walgreens, plowing into the graffiti-painted plywood covering the windows. The second tank maintained its fire for a full second to make sure there were no survivors. Trip understood the overkill. When shot at, troops responded with extreme violence. As the Nissan came to a grinding halt, smoke rolled from its riddled engine compartment, now reduced to worthless scrap metal.

For a full two minutes, there was silence beyond the engines of the tanks. The Newmerican forces were no longer firing. Trip wondered if any were still alive. He wanted to muster pity for them, but it was proving impossible.

The lead M1 reversed, returning to the partial cover of the smashed Olds Dealership, and the second tank backed up, taking a new position behind another cinderblock structure. They crunched and ground their way into position, still covering the roadway, but out of line of sight of any potential return fire.

Trip moved up to the lead tank to inspect where the anti-tank missile had hit. The armor was splayed out and blackened from the hit. It had nearly penetrated and if it had, it would have surely killed the crew in a millisecond. The metal was so hot that it was still smoking at the edges from the hit. The Colonel pulled his earplugs out, closed his mouth and blew hard to re-pop his ear.

The turret hatch opened and Captain DeYoung emerged, staring down at the damage. "We were lucky," he said, shaking his head at the hit.

"Luck…and they were handling weapons without experience. It's obvious they have been picking up toys out of the armory," Trip replied coolly. "It's good for us to know. Chances are when we move into Chicago, we are going to face more surprises."

DeYoung pulled himself through the narrow hatch and started to climb down as Trip moved to the rear of the tank. The engine shut down and he found himself patting the tank's side, the way one might do with a pet dog. It was an unconscious gesture he doubted he could ever fully understand.

There was a time when I didn't want to do anything other than make good pizzas and enjoy my family. The Newmericans had taken all that away from him—daughter, wife, family, home, and his business. *They did this to me; pushed me back to my old life. They made me be a warrior again. And they will regret it before this is over.*

Nashville, Tennessee

Operative Julius Bernstein sat in the Starbucks across the street from the auto accident that had taken place some fifteen minutes earlier. Two old gas guzzlers had slammed into each other on Demonbreun Street three blocks from the Estes Kefauver Federal Building, the so-called

Southern White House. The two drivers were out of their vehicles, yelling at each other, and the traffic was already backing up.

They put on a convincing show of mock road rage. The crash was no surprise to Julius, since he had arranged it. As much as Tennessee had recently sided with the Pretender President, there were plenty of Newmerica supporters in the state. He had hired the two SE participants in the fender-bender, and they had been more than happy to accept the wad of Barack Obama twenties.

Julius glanced down the street where the Presidential motorcade was coming up on the traffic jam. He observed the procession divert from the wreck and their destination, heading down busy 10th Ave South. As he watched, he sipped his coffee and winced. Three days earlier he had staged a stalled vehicle in the same general area, and the motorcade had gone down a different path.

Killing the President was proving challenging. Getting into the Southern White House was possible; he had come up with several ways to do so. Getting out, however, was problematic. Julius had a burning desire to complete his mission, but not get caught or killed in the process. Assassins were a liability, and he was sure that if he fell into the hands of the enemy, the Secretary would ensure that he would never implicate the Newmerican government. He needed the means of killing his target and not being close enough to get captured himself.

Striking at the daily motorcade seemed to be the best option. The problem was that the changing motorcade routes proved frustratingly random. He was hoping that they would follow the same plan when confronted with obstacles. Whoever was running the Secret Service knew their stuff though. *This means I can't block the limo in traffic and take it out easily.* Speeding by on a motorcycle, he had hoped to pass next to the limo and attach an explosive charge, drive a block up, and detonate it. If the explosives were shaped and set correctly, it would punch through the vehicle before the Secret Service could remove it—killing the occupants. That had been his initial plan. Now he was going to have to scrap it. *Too much variability for me to stage this properly.* As an operative, he knew planning would be essential. It wasn't enough to have a good plan; you needed contingency plans.

Explosives had been used the night of the Liberation when they thought they had killed the then-Vice President. Somehow he had either survived the blast or had not been in the limousine when it had blown up. Further complicating matters, his body had been misidentified in the wreckage. Julius knew that whoever made that mistake was probably being visited by his counterparts or was already dead.

Bombs could be very effective as assassination tools, but if they weren't done right, they sometimes failed to kill their targets. The key was to make the bomb big enough so that failure was impossible. Julius knew what he was going to use as the transport—but it was now a matter of getting it close enough to the Pretender.

Studying the maps around the Estes Kefauver Federal Building, he noted the new surveillance cameras that had been installed on several lampposts and on private buildings. The White House back in The District had a perimeter of nearly eight blocks around it that was under full surveillance at the time of the Liberation. The only reason the defenses had been breached was that the massive crowd that had disabled many of them was so large that the Secret Service had not been able to kill enough of them to force them back. Whoever was protecting this President was tightening that protective circle around the building, which was going to complicate matters even more. He spotted undercover security walking the streets more frequently. One had gone over to the crash, pretending to be a helpful bystander—standard procedure. That excited him, the presence of the enemy. It made it a game, him vs. the Secret Service. Julius loved games of strategy in his youth and now he was playing one for real. Could he get close enough to kill the Pretender without getting caught? The operative was sure that he could, but the longer it took to plan, the less likely he was of having success.

He rose with his coffee in hand and started to walk away. He passed a dull white Grumman Postal Delivery Truck that had been repainted back to white with red and blue trim. When Newmerica had been formed, all postal trucks had been painted flat black. Now that Tennessee had sided with the Pretender, the trucks had been returned to their former tyrannical colors.

The truck rounded the corner and drove to a parking spot in front of a card shop. The carrier got out, mail in hand. He was unsure why it caught his attention, but he was fixated on it. Then it came to him. *No one pays attention to the US Mail.* They are expected every day at the same time at the same place. Security would be less likely to check the vehicle, because they expected it. Then there was the size of the truck. That was a bomb that could very well fit his purpose.

Julius Bernstein smiled and took a long sip of his coffee. *Yes, this will do just fine ...*

Moranburg, Kentucky

Raul jerked the steering wheel a hard right to left as bullets shattered the window of the truck. He could barely hear, having fired the shotgun through the driver's side door of the vehicle. Muffled cries from Caylee in the back confirmed that she was still there. The flashes of gunfire in front of him did not seem to bring a hail of lead with them, so he assumed they were firing back across the Ohio River.

One officer stood and pointed to where he was supposed to come through the barricade. He was going too fast, and what was left of his passenger side door caught the concrete divider and was torn off. He drove back nearly 200 feet before slamming on the brakes.

His left ear popped painfully as he stepped out of the truck and looked in the back. Caylee was there, reloading, rising just enough to check whether she had a shot before bounding out of the truck. The tailgate was riddled with holes, at least six of them; the lights from the bridge marked where the bullets had hit. Glancing at the cab as he ducked for cover in front of the truck, he saw another half dozen holes there as well. *How did we not get killed?*

His protector came around the vehicle to his side, weapon at the ready. "Are you OK?"

"Fine," he stammered. His adrenaline was pumping exactly like it had that night at Valley Forge. In his departure from the truck, he had hardly noticed that his protector had a pistol in his hand as he crouched down. The popping of gunfire continued but seemed to fall off. A policeman, wearing Kentucky State Police shirt, not the garb of the NSF, came over to them. "Are you both alright? Is anyone hurt?"

"We're good," Caylee said.

"Cease fire!" called a voice from the barricade they had run. The last gunshot came from the far side of the river, hitting nothing that he could see.

Another older officer trotted over, still keeping low in case the bullets started flying again. "Are you OK?"

"We're fine," Raul said.

"You mind telling me what this was all about?" the older officer asked. Raul saw his name badge, "Captain James Rinks." Raul started to open his mouth, but Caylee cut him off.

"Federal business," she said, pulling out an ID and flashing it.

"You're going to have to tell me more than that, ma'am," he said, taking a moment to study the ID. "Ohio just fired shots at my people here in Kentucky because of you."

She drew a calming breath. Raul watched her as she wrestled with her composure. "My apologies for that Captain Rinks," she replied in a startlingly professional tone of voice. "I was escorting this individual to Tennessee at the behest of Jack Desmond. Those SEs back there tried to apprehend us. We did what we had to do to get over here to safety."

Captain Rinks eyed her suspiciously. "Jack Desmond, the President's Chief of Staff?"

"Yes," she replied. "This man is Raul Lopez." She jerked her head toward Raul.

Rinks stared at him as Raul removed the prosthetics from his face. "This is the hero of Valley Forge?" He had never heard that title and even with his blood pounding in his ears, he could not resist smiling. Coming from her, it was a deep and sincere compliment. "Yes sir," he said. "She was protecting me."

Rinks looked back at Caylee. "I'll be damned. Don't go anywhere. I need to get confirmation on this." He turned to one of his troopers. "Dickerson, get these people some water." The Captain walked off and the trooper handed them bottles of water. Raul fumbled with the top, his hands still shaking from the excitement.

"You did good back there," Caylee said to him as Raul's right ear finally popped. "That shot through the door was perfect."

Raul took a sip of water and it oddly made him feel a little calmer. "Thanks. I was scared I'd mess it up."

"Most people would have," she said, taking a sip from her water bottle. "You drove across that bridge like a pro. It's a miracle we were not both hit." Coming from her, the words had extra meaning.

He glanced at the truck with its missing door and the shattered glass. "I think the truck is toast."

Caylee smiled. "We will get a new ride and get you somewhere safe," she replied confidently.

Raul glanced over toward the river. "They won't stop, will they?" he said sitting and resting his back against the bumper of the battered truck and tucking the gun into this waistband. "They will keep coming."

She did the same, sitting next to him, putting her gun on her lap. "It is tempting to lie to you Raul, but I won't. This isn't over yet. Newmerica doesn't like people that stand up against them. You represent that. Over here, you're a hero. Over there, you are the villain. You are a symbol they can't tolerate—someone that believed in them and then turned against them. That rescue you did, it exposed their dirty little secret about the Social Quarantine Camps. The masses all thought it was propaganda that the camps were torture sites. You showed them the truth and they hate that—trust me, I know. I did the same thing. The truth, the *real* truth, is something they can't tolerate." As she spoke Raul felt a strange connection between the two of them. He somehow knew that she felt it too. *Whatever she has done has also made her a target of these people.*

Caylee continued as she cleared her weapon and checked the magazine, replacing it with a fresh one. "Their whole system is a house of cards built on carefully crafted lies and threats. It is sturdy as long as there is no dissenting opinion. They have had it that way for years now. You, my friend, were like a stiff breeze blowing in with the truth. They will pump out information saying you are wrong, but too many people believe in what you exposed at Valley Forge. So, they will resort to the one thing that can make this go away, taking you out of the equation."

Raul frowned; then he took out his gun, performing the same steps that Caylee did, as she had taught him. "I didn't want to be a symbol of anything. I wanted to help those people."

"No one wants to be a symbol except the narcissists of the world. If you wanted to be some sort of icon, I still would have tried to protect you, but maybe not so hard." Her words forced a smile to his face.

Caylee continued, "The states behind the President are far from safe zones. SEs operate there, but not as openly. And some operatives out there might get sent for you. So yes, they will come at you again." It wasn't the news he wanted to hear…it was what he needed to hear. *She's confirming what I already knew.*

"So what do I do?" he asked.

"They are going to come and I will be there when it happens," she assured him. "If they want to get to you, they will have to go through me."

Caylee's words swept away the last throb of adrenaline pumping through his body. The quaking disappeared. It was a commitment that tied their fates together and was calming all on its own.

CHAPTER 11

"When everyone cheers, watch for the handful that doesn't. They are the enemies."

University of Virginia
Charlottesville, Virginia

Two days had passed since the mysterious note had slid under Maddie Steele's door. She could not help but watch for another note to appear. Every time she heard someone walk past her door, she could not resist looking to see if a scrap of paper appeared in the thin gap under the door. There was a feeling of excitement about it, that others at the university felt the same way she did—that they were somehow looking out for her.

The other aspect of it was the spy-like nature of the message. She didn't dare talk about it with anyone; to do so might reveal her true feelings and that was dangerous. While walking across campus, she made eye contact with Deborah from the protest, who only scowled in her direction. *She doesn't believe my efforts were sincere—I can see it in her face.* That bothered her deep inside. *What else do I have to do to get off of their radar? Is that even possible?*

Going to class was the only thing that gave her focus. The distractions that gnawed at her thoughts were easy to purge in a classroom. Even so, her eyes darted around the classroom, looking at her peers, wondering if the person that had secreted her the note was sitting across the classroom. Sometimes she made a flashing moment of eye contact. In her mind, she could not picture any of them as the culprit though she couldn't be sure why.

Maddie got her dinner to go, as she always did, taking it up to her dorm room for privacy. When she returned to her room, another note was on the floor, this time on yellow legal pad paper. "Rotunda, North Oval Room, 7:30 tonight. GBA" It was the same handwritten scrawl she had seen on the previous note.

Slumping into her tiny couch, she sat with her bagged sandwich on her lap, staring at the note. She tried to process the feeling of dread that suddenly descended. The first note simply made her feel good, that she was not alone. This was different. Whoever was writing the notes was now asking for a meeting, and a clandestine one at that.

Maddie would have loved to talk to her father about it, though in her mind and heart she already knew what his words would be. "Don't go. You risk exposing yourself." The urge was to call there, but she knew she couldn't discuss something like that on the phone. The Newmerican government listened in on calls; it was widely known. Most people accepted the practice. After all, if you were not a traitor, you had nothing to fear in their minds. Maddie knew she was not a traitor, but her political beliefs were against those of the government—and that was all it would take. Placing the call and talking about it would put her at risk and her parents as well. It was also violating her father's rules, and those rules had allowed their family to blend in and embrace their new identities.

As she nibbled at her sandwich, she wavered between ignoring the message and waiting for several minutes. What if this was some sort of trap, designed to expose her? The memory of Deborah pointing at her, indicating that they were watching her during the protest, came to the forefront. Internally she countered it with thinking that there had to be other students like her who had the same values and beliefs. Maybe this was someone reaching out to her as a kindred spirit? Perhaps this had nothing to do with politics? The GBA signature negated that somewhat, but it could be someone's initials rather than a statement.

She glanced at her iPhone and saw the time. *If I'm going to go, I need to leave now.* Standing, she remembered that her father had given her a gun that she kept in her room. If there was ever a time for me to carry one, it is now. She went in and pulled out the weapon, putting it in her backpack. Maddie knew how to shoot and handle it well enough, but she did not want to contemplate the circumstances where she would be forced to use it. Still, carrying it gave her a greater sense of confidence.

She gathered her resolve and started off to the Rotunda. When she came in sight of the once majestic structure, she felt a bit of sadness. Thomas Jefferson had modeled the structure, which had been its downfall. During the first year of the Fall, the students had vandalized the building. It wasn't only the graffiti; one of the massive pillars had been pulled down by a particularly aggressive protest group. All the windows had been broken and were now covered with faded plywood. The lower doors had been broken open so many times that the university had stopped trying to chain them shut. The west wing of the structure had been set ablaze and was marked with charred brick and decay. The college leadership had said there were plans to reopen the Rotunda, but that never seemed to happen. It didn't matter that it was a United Nations Educational, Scientific and Cultural Organization site. Thomas Jefferson carried the taint of having owned slaves, so anything attributed to him was considered fair game for the radically woke campus population.

Maddie looked around to make sure no one was watching her as she went up the stairs and slid between the doors to get inside. Light trickled in around the edges of the plywood and joined with the lone light bulb that was on, barely illuminating the once grand structure's interior. The graffiti was so layered that much of what was there could not be read. The wood floor was painted, torn up in some areas, and from what she could smell, defecated on. She navigated the debris and made her way to the North Oval room on the second floor, which had light coming out of it. Her hand unconsciously drifted to her backpack and the gun she had there.

The North Oval room had been used for dissertations. The great table was there still, and sitting in the room were two students—male and female. He was tall, well over six feet, with blonde hair and blue eyes. The female looked generic to her, wearing a dull gray canvas material coat and a knit cap that covered her black hair. The female had a piercing above her right eyebrow, a safety pin that looked more uncomfortable than fashionable. Maddie poked her head in and said nothing. What light filled the room came from a missing piece of plywood that had covered the window. A light breeze fluttered the tattered drapery.

"You came," the female said. "I told him I didn't think you would."

"I'm sorry," she said, feigning innocence. "I was walking through."

The male cracked a smile and shook his head. "You don't need to pretend Maddie; you're with friends."

His words sounded sincere, but she was unsure of the true nature of the meeting, and her heart was pounding hard in her chest. Before she could respond, the male continued. "You don't have to worry. This is one place on campus that they don't come to. I guess they think they've damaged it enough already," he said gesturing with one hand around the room. "I'm Brad. This is Tina."

"Hi," Maddie managed.

"She's scared," Tina said to Brad. She then turned back to Maddie. "We're not with the people trying to intimidate you. We're the good guys."

The concepts of good and bad were fluid; the law had taught her that much. "Look, I was curious. I got your notes. I wasn't sure who was trying to contact me."

Brad took a step closer to her, with the narrow end of the big oval table between them. "Maddie, we know they are targeting you. They made you go to that protest. Our people have infiltrated them. They think you are a closet conservative. You aren't entirely safe. That's why we reached out to you."

"What do you mean I'm not safe?" The future lawyer in her knew to avoid the conservative issue entirely.

"Look, I can't explain everything to you. We have to be careful that we don't expose our people. Let's say they weren't convinced of your performance in the last protest. We found out and thought it might be a good time to offer you our protection."

"Who is this 'we'?"

Tina spoke up, taking one of the chairs around the table, turning it around backwards and straddling it. "There are a lot more of us on campus than they know about…people that don't buy into their social equity shit."

Maddie was glad to hear those words, but at the same time cautious. "I'm just a law student."

Brad reeled in the conversation. "A law student who has only attended a single protest since she got here. Good grades, but zero involvement in campus political groups until you were blackmailed into attending a march. Yeah, you joined a pottery group, but only because your counselor recommended it." He paused and she drank in the depth of how much they knew about her.

Brad continued, "You think you're alone? You aren't. We are like you," he said, his voice straining slightly. "They have done the same thing to us."

"I don't know either of you," she countered.

Brad pressed on, "Look, we're not asking you to do anything—not yet. You need to know that we are 'like-minded.' We have our own little group, one that they don't know about. We protect students like you, the ones that don't think the way that most of the campus does. Tina here was tracking them tracking you, and that's what brought you to our attention."

Maddie glanced over at Tina who nodded once. "Listen Madison," she said using her formal name. "They weren't fooled by your participation in that march. They are going to come after you, this time a little more forcefully. We call it, 'the squeeze.' They will rough you up a little bit, try and get you to confess your crimes."

"I haven't committed any crimes," she protested.

"You are thinking too much like a lawyer," Brad said. "They are Social Enforcers. They determine what is and isn't a crime. Maybe it's you being ardent or arrogant enough in your protesting; maybe it is only the suspicion that they think you are hiding something…it doesn't matter. They make it up as they go along and deal out justice as they see fit."

The fact that she was being targeted hit her hard. "Thanks for the heads up."

Brad crossed his arms and put one foot on a chair seat. "It's more than that. We have eyes and ears in their camp. If we get advance notice that they are planning something, we will let you know. You cannot be there when they show up. Tina will send you a note if we catch wind of trouble." Tina nodded once heavily in response.

For a long few seconds, Maddie said nothing. It felt like things were escalating, and she had hoped her performance at the protest had produced the opposite effect. It was strangely comforting that a student group out there was on her side; they understood her. At the same time she had not said anything to expose herself, and she was content with that.

"I appreciate it," she finally said.

Brad maneuvered across the oval table from her and extended his hand. She shook it, gripping hard. "We protect our own," he said. Then, lowering his voice, he muttered, "God Bless America." Tina repeated it, and to Maddie's surprise, she did the same after Tina.

The District

Room J was the Secretary of the NSF's private 'war room' tucked away in the bowels of the National Security Force's headquarters. When she entered, everyone looked up—the two operatives and three technicians working in the dim light of the room. She could feel their eyes on her as well as the respect mixed with fear that she generated. *They know what I am doing...and what I am capable of doing.* Some liked their assignment on her special project because they hoped rewards would be tied to its successful completion. Both of the operatives she had chosen were true believers in the cause, dedicated to the continuance of Newmerica. *I learned my lesson with Caylee Leatrom. It's not enough to have someone with the skills; you need someone who believes wholeheartedly in what they are doing.*

She closed the soundproof door behind her and moved to the central table. Power and network cables covered the table top like layers of snakes. Piles of papers filled the few clear areas. Laptop computers were set up with external monitors, one of which was massive. Surveying the tabletop, she stood before them. "I would like a progress report," she announced, casually wiping dandruff from her lapel where a bell-shaped bronze pin was worn.

Operative Ramses Ossege stood rigidly; his massive ebony body was built like a professional body builder, only larger. "Madam Secretary, if I may. We have created a wealth of material to support the program. We have generated false text message transcripts, complete with supporting digital correspondence between Senator Lewis and the Pretender's government. With a little help from the NSA, we have even created false cell tower traffic that supports the message transmissions."

The problem with Senator Lewis was that he lacked vices or weaknesses that could be exploited. That forced her to create some... ties to the Pretender's government in a plot, a deadly scheme that she would use to take him down. That part of the plan was simple for her to conceive, but she knew that was not enough. *He would go down fighting; he would level claims of forgery at me. Taking him on alone would look like a vendetta for his investigation.*

The solution was to think bigger, to make his plotting to be something unforgivable that tied in others that were potential threats against her. On top of that, she had to make it all unfold in an event that would garner public support. Planning that part took time, but in the Secretary's mind, it was all worth it.

"What of our secondary targets?" she asked.

Operative Naomi Yates spoke up from her seat. "Madam Secretary, we found a gap in their calendars and generated a false meeting, complete with video support. We inserted the meetings in their Outlook calendars in the past, so they never even noticed it" Naomi punched up the image and turned her display over so she could see it. The images were far from perfect; the camera angle was off slightly, but it looked very much like Senator Lewis, the Treasury Secretary Barbara Collingsworth, and Director Becky Clarke of the Truth Reconciliation Committee were present. The Senator spoke first. "You've all reviewed the plan?"

"I did, and I have some concerns," the actor playing Collingsworth said. "This is messy—*very* messy. One wrong misstep and we will fry."

"Or worse," the actor playing Becky said.

The Collingsworth character continued. "The election is going to split this country further. Our own estimates show that our people are complacent about voting, and the American administration stands a good chance of winning enough states to lead to civil war. This is our best shot at reconciliation."

Senator Lewis stirred from his seat. "I have coordinated this directly with the top levels of the American administration. Once the Ruling Council is eliminated, they assure us protection from prosecution as long as we make the transition peaceful and orderly." As he finished, the image blurred, then went blank.

She could not hide her joy at the video and beamed for a moment at the brilliance of it all. *In one fell swoop, I will take out all opposition. Best of all it makes the Americans look like the villains of this entire scheme.* "The images are good and I already agreed with the script—so I have no changes. It seems awfully pristine. Almost too good."

One of the technicians spoke up. "It is our intent to corrupt bits of it. The story will be that one of them clearly attempted to delete the file and we were able to restore only portions of the meeting. Combine this with fake security footage of them entering the Senate Office building and some tweaks to the security logs to show they were there, and it will pass almost any test."

"Good," she replied. They were thorough, but she expected nothing less of operatives who were running the program. "And the package?"

"We have it prepared," Operative Ossege replied in his deep, almost rolling voice. "It will do significant damage. We even planted the triggering phone code on the Senator's phone, so any post investigation will further tie him to it."

They are thorough, which is needed. It was hard for her to not feel a swell of pride. *I picked my team well.* "What else do you have?"

The operatives told her of transcripts of conversations, fake audio recordings, cell phone calls, a myriad of supporting information. They had created gaps that were deliberately placed to make the material appear reconstructed and authentic. There were hints that people in the administration were party to the cover-up, giving her ample rope for any follow-on arrests that had to be done. Their presentation lasted over an hour.

When they were done, she complimented them. Then she pulled a small box from her suit pocket. "I can't tell you how important this work is. As you all know, the security for this program is critical. I had some of our people put these together." She opened the box and extended it to them. Inside were small chest pins, much like the one she wore, but they were black and a bit larger and thicker. "There's one for each of you. Because of the nature of this op, I need you to wear this at all times while in this building on your left lapel. Only you will have these pins. They are tied to the security system, so that your presence here is blanked out on all monitors and records. There are no exceptions. They must be worn. Anyone that worked on this with you is to get a pin as well." Each of them took the pin and put it on as instructed…as she knew they would. *Good soldiers always follow orders.*

She thanked them and exited the war room, letting her smile finally broaden to its full extent. I will need to coordinate this with Operative Bernstein's mission. As she marched down the hall to her office, she couldn't help but beam. *This program will cement Newmerica in the hearts and minds of the people and will erode trust in this upstart United States, right before the election. My opposition—all of them—will be taken down and I will finally have what I deserve...the unified love and respect of the people.*

This is my masterpiece...My mother would be so proud!

The Southern White House
Nashville, Tennessee

"They actually fired on one of our tanks?" the President asked in dismay. Jack nodded, "Colonel Reager was there personally when it happened. He eliminated the threat. They had weapons they must have taken from one of the armories." Jack was glad that Reager had not been injured. His actions at San Antonio years earlier had made him an icon for resistance. *Then again, Texas has been a thorn in the ass of the Ruling Council ever since the Fall.*

"And this business on the Ohio border—what was that over?" he asked.

"That was one of our operatives bringing Raul Lopez across the border to safety. I got the call on that a few hours ago." Caylee had a certain style about her that often resulted in gunplay.

His answer seemed to satisfy the President for the moment. "And that incident in Virginia—is that under control?"

"Yes sir. We suffered some casualties, however." Those words made the President shake his head. Jack understood all too well. Every life lost on either side was American in his eyes. Virginia's Governor had mobilized the National Guard in Northern Virginia in an effort to block troops coming in. A handful of Guard units, mostly from rural Virginia, refused to follow those orders. The Governor sent his loyal Newmerican forces to seize and apprehend the arsenals and armories of the units that refused, which had led to battles breaking out. Following Jack's suggestion, the beleaguered Guardsmen were reinforced with National Guard from West Virginia, forcing the Governor's troops to break off and fall back. They took what they could from the arsenal and fell back into West Virginia. *This is a sign of what we will be facing—the level of resistance that they are going to throw at us.*

"Jack, I want you to get me a list of those that were killed and wounded. I want to talk to their families."

"I will make it happen, sir," he said.

The President sifted through the papers on his desk, pulling out one report in particular. "I saw that Minnesota's Governor says she won't be allowing our forces in to ensure a fair and safe election."

Jack nodded. "Not entirely unexpected, sir." A number of states had voiced the same demands to the American President. The states fell into categories. There were states that had pledged themselves already in support of the President and fair elections. Those didn't require intervention. There were states that had been on the fence, political battlegrounds like Ohio, Virginia, Michigan, Pennsylvania, and others that were noncommittal but leaning hard left when it came to supporting the election. Michigan had already agreed to two of Newmerica's Voting Sanctuary Cities—Ann Arbor and Detroit. Virginia had imposed four. Fairfax, Norfolk, Richmond and Charlottesville. Both states had drawn the dividing line as the urban areas vs. the rural communities. Some states were tagged as Red States; these states openly refused to acknowledge the President and demanded he not intervene.

That last bucket of states was tricky to deal with. Some, like Illinois, had already been targeted for intervention. Hence the positioning of Colonel Reager's unit near Chicago. Oregon and Washington states were also on the list of those that would find American troops coming in whether their Governors liked it or not. "You know what really frosts me, Jack? I knew some of these people. Hell, I've had the Governor of Minnesota over for dinner when I was VP. I trusted her and the other damned politicians like her. I thought we were friendly rivals. I had no idea that they would not only lead a coup and try to kill me, but then they would openly stand against the rule of law."

Jack understood the deep burning feeling of betrayal. The Secret Service had a radical mole in their ranks that had doxed him and most of the senior leadership during the Fall. "That's why the election is so important, sir. If they win, they will toss out our entire body of laws, our Bill of Rights, and replace it with something new, something that will validate what they've done. If they score a decisive victory, they will cement themselves in place as a legitimate government."

"Even if we win decisively, some pockets of Newmerica are not going to recognize us," the President said.

"We've known that all along," Jack said. "That's why we have contingency plans." His years in the military and Secret Service had taught him that you needed fallback plans, and those plans needed fallback plans. *Even then, it could be iffy.*

"I know there are voices here in Nashville that want me to take the states loyal to me and let Newmerica have the rest. That's the easy path to walk and some days it is damned tempting. I cannot sit back and be the President that presided over the division of our nation. I'm the President of the *United* States, not the friendly states. Those people that seized Washington DC and the country for the last five years have zero authority to do what they did. Millions have suffered under their heels."

"Their propaganda machine is doing a good job," Jack offered. "They are telling people they will lose their reparations, their health care, all of the freebies they were given."

"They might. Those so-called 'rights' have no authority in law. They gave out those things to do one thing, buy votes. Most people have been living in fear for years now and are sick of it. We all know it. Social Enforcement is another name for Stormtroopers. They have beaten and killed people, intimidated them, run amok in many neighborhoods. The average American is sick and tired of having to look over his shoulder, worrying about armed thugs or that their neighbor will turn them in for some made-up infraction. I trust you that our messaging is addressing and countering those claims?"

"We are, sir," Jack said. "Our campaign manager is doing a good job. It isn't easy. The social media companies take down stuff fairly fast. It is better immediately after the attacks on their headquarters—that shook them up and forced a lot of the snowflakes into counseling. We have enlisted thousands of people to post our messages constantly—so things are getting through." Jack knew that the President did not like the bombing attacks the day of his inauguration, but he also recognized the duplicity and corruption in Big Tech. *Like our attacks on the NSF, the attacks have given us breathing room.*

The President leaned back in his chair and said nothing for a full half minute of deep thought. "There isn't a person who has held my office that doesn't think at one time or another about Abraham Lincoln. The South went to war with the North, not because of something he did, but out of the *fear* that he might abolish slavery. We never did anything to the progressives to hinder their rights—but they followed suit with history and took us down out of fear of what my predecessor might do."

"Nations built on fear always fail," Jack offered.

"Yes, but it can take decades for that to happen. And like Lincoln, I have no intention of sitting back and waiting. This house will not be divided, not on my watch."

Jack understood the line all too clearly. Splitting the nation—letting Newmerica and America exist side by side—had been debated in the cabinet meetings. The President had been adamant about his stand on that solution. His words were burned into Jack's memory. 'It is a compromise, so the progressives would love it. We would give up a piece of the country for some return to normalcy in the rest. That is where we have failed as conservatives. We constantly compromise with our opposition. We give up something and they hold firm. Bit by bit it erodes our position until you end up where we are now, under siege and living in fear. I am President of the United States—not just the loyal states. We will be whole again, no matter how long it takes, but we are not giving ground.'

While the words came back to him, Jack knew that some of the reality was that even if they won at the ballot box, there was no guarantee that the Ruling Council would accept the results. That was why there were plans, and contingency plans, and other 'initiatives.' "Sir, if I were on the Ruling Council, I'd never concede. They have committed a lot of crimes that they will be held accountable for if we win."

"I know. The election is a step down the road to reunification of the country. It's a big step though, and they know it. That's why they are also agreeing to elections. I'm no fool Jack. I know the people we are up against. They will intimidate, lie, and cheat to win. We have to stop them. And if they don't, we will go after them—hard."

Jack drew a long breath. His mind went to the plans he had a part in developing. *We need to be prepared for the worst case scenario, that they cheat to win or refuse to accept the results. God help us all if they decide to slug it out.* Memories of the deaths he had already ordered to get this far tugged at him…Quantico, Falls Church, the Big Tech bombings. Civil War had already started.

"Shall I prep the Razorback Initiative, sir?"

The President nodded grimly.

CHAPTER 12

"Questioning authority is a form of insurrection."

Cincinnati, Ohio

Deja Jordan stared at Detective Dale Gallagher and could not suppress her shame. "He ran the checkpoint you were at?" he asked, amazement hanging with each word.

She looked around the mobile command post and tried not to roll her eyes at his insinuation that she had somehow messed up. "He wasn't alone," she countered. "He had protection—a professional," she said, rubbing her left arm where a shotgun pellet had torn her flesh. "It wasn't like we didn't fight. The prick hit me with that sawed off shotgun. When we fired at him on the bridge, the state police returned fire as well. He didn't just run the checkpoint; he started a firefight."

The detective seemed to catch himself. "My apologies," he replied. "It pisses me off that we practically had him in our hands and now he's in Kentucky." He walked over to the Keurig and pulled out the fresh cup of coffee, handing it to her. It felt good in her hands and got her to crack her first grin since the incident on the river, if only for a moment.

"Thanks," she said, bringing it up to her nose and drawing in the aroma. She had been tempted to rush across the bridge toward Raul Lopez after the gun battle, but the Kentucky State Troopers were ample dissuasion. The coffee helped her forget that Gallagher was a cop, old-school looking, with a hint of gray in his dark hair. He was old enough to be her father, which didn't help her deal with him. While they were both technically NSF, he was a blue-school cop. Even his deep voice rang with authority and experience. While she knew she should respect him, there was that ever-present shadow of how police were before the Liberation. Her father had drilled it into her, 'Cops are all racists.' It was a memory that was hard to shake despite the courtesy he had shown her.

"Look Deja," he said, taking a seat next to her at the map-covered table. "My gut tells me to pursue this perp," he said.

"Me too. Kentucky has thrown in with the Pretender President… hell, most of the fucking south has. Their police have cut ties to the NSF and are going old school. I doubt that it is going to be as easy as heading south looking for him."

"You're right about that," Gallagher replied, taking a sip from his own cup of coffee. "We have a few advantages though. They don't know who we are, so getting across the border should be easy. We know who our target is. While the state governors have thrown in with the Pretender, there are plenty of your people, you know, Social Enforcement teams, that are still operating down there. While most of my former brothers in blue have thrown in with the Governor and left the NSF, your people haven't been rounded up."

The news of defections from the NSF was new to Deja, and disturbing. "Most of the SEs are laying low since the state flipped," Deja said, taking a sip of coffee. She had only gotten a few hours' sleep, courtesy of the pain killers for her gunshot wound. "I already reached out for them to look for Lopez and his accomplice. I think it's safe to guess where they are going."

"Tennessee," Gallagher said.

"Damn right." Tennessee was more of a stronghold state for the Pretender President. Their Governor had been far more aggressive in going after the Social Enforcers in the state, leveling criminal charges against them. Once they faced the fear of prosecution, many of them fled the state. It was understandable—what the SEs achieved, they did by not following the laws. *That is why we were so successful. The legal system is bullshit…it's racist and unfair. Our justice has always been swift.* She knew that once Raul was in Tennessee, which he may already be by now, it was going to be trickier to locate and extract him. "I can put out feelers, but a lot of my people scattered when that old prick took the oath of office."

"It causes a quandary for everyone," Gallagher replied, shifting in his seat. "Say what you will, the man has a legitimate claim for the office of President. A lot of my people are, shall I say, hesitant, to stand up against his followers."

There was no hesitancy for Deja. The Ruling Council had done exactly what it had to—erased the old, corrupt United States and provided a newer, better society. Big business was finally being held to pay for its crimes against the people. Racism was being erased. The people that had illegitimately profited at the expense of others were being put in their rightful place. Businesses were being stripped of their profits, and the money was given back to the workers. Everyone had an equal voice. The only people that didn't like it were the immoral and corrupt, who had held down the *real* people of the nation. "The SEs don't waver. We brought justice to the streets. We give the nation order by rooting out the last bits of exploitation."

Detective Gallagher nodded. "If you didn't do anything wrong, then why are some of your people flipping sides? It's not just the NSF that is deserting. There are a lot of reports of SE's running and hiding."

She opened her mouth to respond, but the words couldn't form. She felt her face get hot, and her eyes narrowed at the detective sitting across from her. For a moment, she felt anger that he had asked the question; then she realized that what she really felt was anger at herself for not being able to answer immediately. The detective seemed to understand he had crossed her, and continued on. "Sorry, I didn't mean to throw that out. My mouth gets me into trouble at times."

"Yeah," she said slowly, almost suspiciously. Gathering her composure, she finally turned the subject back to Raul Lopez. "I intend to go after Lopez and whoever this person was with him. That bitch killed a number of my people. I want a piece of her ass."

"We have multiple warrants for his arrest already on Federal charges after that stunt at Valley Forge. I filed the paperwork on the murders at your checkpoint a few hours ago and for the murders at the KFC, so he has multiple murder and assorted gun charges pending here—solid felony charges."

"That's paperwork," she said. "I want him and that woman." Paperwork was never an issue with Social Enforcement. If anything, it would leave a nasty trail.

"I understand. And a few weeks ago, heading down there would not have raised an eyebrow. Because we set up checkpoints, so did the Kentucky State Police and the local sheriffs. And your team did trade shots with them, so tensions are elevated at the moment."

"I don't care. I want them." The ache in her left arm only served to remind her that this was very personal. *I could have been cut in half by that shotgun. Nobody does that to me...nobody!*

"I think we need a team. I can assemble two of my best people, and I will come along as well," Gallagher said.

"A team will slow us down and attract attention. Not my style," she countered, still not fully trusting anyone in the NSF. Despite his attempts to be supportive, she could not shake the memories of the events in the last few weeks where the senior leadership of the SE simply disappeared or outright died. To Deja, Gallagher represented a source for help, and a possible threat.

"We can arrange a rendezvous point across the border and go across individually so we don't attract attention." He could sense her resistance and pressed on. "Deja, the two of them shot you and killed a number of your team, and ran your blockade. This isn't the work of amateurs, regardless of Lopez's background. You go in by yourself, you might get your ass handed to you on a silver plate. You are going to need help."

To Deja, hearing his words felt like an insult. *I'm more than capable of handling myself!* But then she remembered the previous night and felt another throb of pain from her gunshot wound. Two people had basically trashed her checkpoint, the one she was visiting. They had killed several, wounded others, and had driven right on through. Lopez was a kid to her, but he had been one of the domestic terrorists that had taken people from a Social Quarantine Camp. *I need to stop thinking of him as some kid but more as what he really is, a terrorist.* "You might be right," she finally said. "That bitch that was with him had some skills, icy skills. She was a pro." *And I want a piece of her before this is over.* "You have some people in mind for this?"

Her concession made the older man smile. "I do. Ex-mil. SWAT teamers."

Deja hated working with the old school NSFers, but it was a way to bring Lopez and his accomplice to justice. Detective Gallagher turned to the maps on the table and began to trace road networks with his fingers, trying to find a place where they could rendezvous once they were in Kentucky. A few minutes later his cell phone rang and he took the call. His body went rigid as he spoke with the person on the other end. “Really? Have you gotten them out of the state?” Excitement was there; Deja could not deny it.

When he hung up, he looked down at her. “Good news?” she asked.

“Damn straight. The NSA guy picked up Lopez’s mother’s voice on a call. A Sons of Liberty cell had her hidden away in Kansas. Someone slipped up on their end and let her use a phone. They sent in a strike team and got her and his sister. It got messy with the SOL shitheads guarding them, but, as we used to say, ‘dead men don’t talk.’ They are extracting Mamma Lopez and sis right now, heading for California and safe territory.”

She could not hold back the smile. “Shit…that’s great.”

Gallagher nodded. “It is. If we have them, we have leverage. All we have to do is put the squeeze on them. Lopez will know we have them; he will assume they are in danger. And we will give him the only lifeline open to help them.”

She drew another long sip of coffee. “And if he doesn’t nibble, we are still going after his ass.”

The Southern White House
Nashville, Tennessee

Charli Kazinski sat with the presidential detail and listened intently to the report. One of her people, Agent Stephanie Rollings, had raised an issue that caught her attention. “So what you are telling me is that the motorcade in the last two weeks has encountered, what, four auto accidents that have required rerouting?”

“Yes,” Stephanie replied. “It caught our attention as being a little odd. All were within three blocks of this building.”

It is beyond odd. It is more than that. “What do we know about the people involved in the accidents.”

Agent Bines spoke up, glancing at his report. “That was what seemed weird. Only about half of those were locals. We did some digging into the others and it's clear that some had fake IDs because they are not popping up on any of the systems we have access to. Two of the occupants have ties to SE groups, one in Tennessee, one in Maryland."

"It makes you wonder," Charli said in half thought, "Why would someone be traveling now, with the country in such turmoil? Have we had any luck in tracking these folks down?"

Rollings weighed in. "Following on our hunch we did find one Jacob Markowski of Spring Hill—member of the SE group, Thunder Mountain. He's still hanging here in Nashville, holed up in a Motel 6. I have a team shadowing him right now. So far, all he's been doing is partying with some of the locals. All of the others seem to have vanished."

Charli felt edgy at the implications of the information. Her years in the Secret Service had trained her to be wary of strange coincidences, things that broke the normal pattern. The accidents fell into that category. Some of her people were new to the Secret Service, and she was impressed that they had spotted a pattern that might be easily overlooked. This is a learning moment that I need to reinforce.

"Alright, this is outstanding work. Fantastic analysis, Rollings. A lot of senior people might have overlooked that. Based on what I have seen and heard, I believe someone is testing us, watching how we react to obstructions."

"Ma'am," spoke up Agent Jackson, one of the more junior people. "What makes you think that?"

"When I was on the detail in Washington DC, you might get one accident every month or two that requires a change of route. We've had four in a lot tighter timeframe. On top of that, traffic here is a hell of a lot less than in DC. From what Agent Rollings reported, these accidents occurred just prior to the motorcade's arrival. Toss in that known Social Enforcers are potentially involved in this and it smacks of someone watching us, measuring our response, attempting to figure out our patterns and behaviors." She could see that the team was absorbing her words intensely. She was tempted to tell them about the warning that Caylee had given her weeks earlier of a possible assassination attempt—but held back. *Everyone already knows that those assholes in The District will do anything to hold onto power. They already tried to kill him once before, when he was VP.*

"To what end?" Agent Ferris asked. "All they are seeing is how we react. Our plans change daily, as do our routes. Not to mention that the motorcade is basically an armored convoy." *Ferris needs to learn that no matter what, the President is never truly safe.*

"No matter what, our motorcade ends up here, in this building," Charli said. "Someone is trying to find a pattern in how we respond. There's only one reason for them to do that—and that is to assassinate the President." Her words seemed to suck the air out of the room, if only for a few moments. She could see the resolve on their faces, the subtle changes to their expressions. *Good, they understand the gravity of the threat and are reacting to it.*

Charli leaned on the table, planting her elbows in front of her and using her hands to gesture as she spoke. "We know a few things about this person. He is staging accidents and monitoring the results. That means he is in the area when this happens, that or he has an accomplice in the area. If he is a professional, chances are he will be doing the observation himself. We need to start pulling video footage from everywhere around the sites of those accidents to see if we spot anyone showing up at more than one scene. I want the cell phone towers checked as to who was pinging off of them at the time of the accidents. And as for this Jacob Markowski, let's keep him under surveillance. Under no circumstance is he to be allowed to leave the state though." Everyone was nodding or jotting down notes.

She continued. "Whoever is behind this is smart. The lone crazies, they don't plan things out. They don't stake out the target. If this is a potential threat, they are pros and trying to play us, feel us out for gaps that he can exploit." She immediately thought of Caylee Leatrom. She was an operative. *I wonder if we are facing the same sort of skills, or the same kind of person?* Charli made a mental note that she needed to talk to Caylee and perhaps gain information that might help her deal with this faceless foe.

"I am upping the threat level a notch," Charli continued. "That will put more eyes and ears on the street." She found herself yearning for Washington DC before the Fall. The Secret Service had video coverage that was incredible, surrounding the White House for eight blocks. From some of the angles, they could even read smart phone screens. Cell traffic was monitored constantly around the old White House. With the ground sensors, infrared, motion tracking—it was all but impossible for a lone gunman to take a shot at the President.

The Southern White House, as the Estes Kefauver Federal Building was called, was still being beefed up in terms of surveillance and security. She had a solid, one-block perimeter, but beyond that it was spotty. Charli also lacked the number of boots on the ground that she was used to in the old days. Vetting new agents took time and getting them up to speed on procedures was making it difficult in terms of ready resources. *I wish I had more time, more people, more tech.* Years of living incognito on the run had taught her it was best not to bemoan what you don't have, but to play with the cards you have been dealt.

She also knew that her people needed as much confidence as she could afford to share with them. "We have one thing going for us now. This person doesn't know that we are aware of their activities. They think they are operating in the shadows still. We can find whoever they are because they don't know they need to be watching for us watching for them. It might not sound like a leg up, but trust me. It is."

Charli paused for a moment. "Understand this. I lost one President on my watch. I took a bullet for him, but in the end it wasn't enough to save his life. I want to assure you that I have no intention of losing another. We need to find whoever is pulling these strings before he does real damage."

Arnold Air Force Base, Tullahoma, Tennessee

It had taken two days to get Raul to his new home at Arnold Air Force Base. One of those days was spent clearing up matters with the Kentucky State Police and getting a replacement vehicle. The KSP had been courteous enough to provide escort to the Tennessee border. When they arrived there they faced a three-hour wait while their IDs were checked and their vehicle was checked. She was glad that she had the Kentucky State Police with her given the firepower that she and Raul had in the Kia Seltos they were driving. They had even been given a chance to shower and a change of clothing, NSF sweatshirts and pants—now no longer of use by the Kentucky State Police. Raul had winced when he saw the logo on them, but Caylee didn't. She happened to have clean clothing after crawling through the brush and rolling around in the back of the truck bed.

The checkpoint on the state boarder was new—a hint of the heightened security of the upcoming elections. While most of the drivers ahead of her in the queue were complaining about it, Caylee embraced it. *We can't afford to have open borders, not with the threat of Newmerican retaliation.*

Raul seemed relieved to be in Tennessee, but she couldn't afford that kind of relaxation. *We shot up an SE checkpoint, killed a few of them in the process. That is going to piss them off. Add in that Raul is being called their top domestic terrorist, everyone will want a piece of him.* Radio broadcasts told a wicked lie about how he and an accomplice had ambushed a peaceful SE team on neighborhood patrol, killing three in cold blood before they shot their way through another team to flee into Kentucky. Raul winced when he heard the stories, clearly ashamed of how they were portraying him. She shut off the radio after an hour or so and tried to ease his frustration. "Don't take it personal, Raul. They lie. Hell, their entire nation is built on lies. They hand out mistrust like it was candy on Halloween. Don't worry over the things they say about you. The people that know you know the kind of person you are." Her words seemed to help, at least for the time being.

When they arrived at Arnold Air Force Base, south of Nashville, they were escorted to the base housing where he was going to live. Caylee thought Jack had done well in picking a place that was secure. She would have preferred a safe house in a nondescript neighborhood, but they understood the concerns for Raul's safety.

The airman that drove them to the house gave her a key and assured them that the base was secure. As she had driven in, she had spotted at least three ways to penetrate the perimeter. That was part of who she was; the operative in her was always looking at ways to kill people in the room, places for emergency egress, or gaps in security. She had been doing it for almost five years and before that with the CIA. Her agency experience had been in wet work, assassinations and kidnappings—the kind of business where constant surveillance of your surroundings could be the difference between life and death. *At some point I need to settle down, step away from this shit.* She had to concede to herself that it was nearly impossible to imagine what that kind of life would be like.

While it was clear that the Air Force base gave Raul a sense of security, that was less true of her. The military had straddled the fence when it came to supporting the newly sworn President. Some commanders, posts, bases, and troops had whole-heartedly followed their oaths and committed to the President over the Ruling Council. Many others had refused to acknowledge him.

The problem ran deep in the military. They had refused to follow orders from the prior President, the so-called traitor, when Washington DC was being overrun during the Fall. Following that had come a systematic purge of 'extremists,' i.e., anyone that was conservative. Many in the military kept quiet, hid their political allegiance, simply to keep their jobs, which they loved. The military began a pilot program of social metering, tracking their people's use of social media using a Big Tech solution that looked for radicalized content. This had driven more conservatives deeper underground. The result was a split military, one openly embracing progressive reforms, and a large underground contingent that was hiding in plain sight, waiting for a change…like a new President.

While the commanding officer of Arnold Air Force Base had openly embraced the new President and had claimed to have removed the supporters of the Ruling Council, there was no way to be sure. Even though the base personnel were supposedly behind the President and what he represented, Caylee couldn't help but wonder if some in their ranks might be moles for the Ruling Council.

The house was only sparsely furnished but a step up from many of the places she had been staying. She paced each room, closed drapes, checked every door, and secured all entrances. Raul flopped down on the couch, watching her. "You are always on, aren't you?" he asked as she returned to the family room.

"Yes. In my line of work, it is often necessary," she replied.

"How did you become what you are?"

It was a question no one had ever asked her. "I was a Ranger in the Army, did a stint in the MPs, then got out. When the Fall happened, I was in the Agency doing contract work. A sleaze-ass named Burke Dorne recruited me for 'special operations.'"

"But how did you get like you are?" he pressed. The question impressed her.

"Raul, my line of work was a mix of brute force and brains. People don't always react well to that combo. There were always people out there trying to get me before I got them. Eventually you start to do things without even thinking about them...like me securing this place."

"You've killed a lot of people," he said carefully.

"Yes, I have. At the time I thought I was doing the right thing for the right reasons," she conceded. For Caylee it was one of the few times she had reflected on her past. For her, it had always been easier not to talk about it—to bury those memories. Raul's questions poked at that, and it made her slightly uncomfortable. "I don't enjoy killing or hurting people. I lied to myself a lot, telling myself that it was part of the job. In reality, I liked the feeling of control it gave me."

"Control?"

She nodded. "In so much of our lives, we don't have control over what happens. We allow others to pull the strings and we dance to their tune. A lot of women I know are in shitty relationships simply because they don't have control. I saw it with my mom when I was a kid. I promised myself no matter what I did with my life, I would be in charge of what I did and how I did it. As an operative, people often misjudged me, thinking that because I was a female, I wasn't a threat. A lot of times I did what I did simply because I wanted control of the situation. Of course now I look back at it and realize that the Secretary was pulling my strings all along. I guess control is a matter of perception ..." Raul's question had made her reflect in ways she had not anticipated.

"Do you have a home?"

She cast a quasi-humorous glare at him. "You ask a lot of hard questions, Raul."

"You saved my life up there. I want to know who you are."

Who am I really? Who is anyone? In a world where she adopted disguises and identities and shed them like dirty underwear, it was often hard to remember who she really was. "I don't have a home. My mother is dead and I didn't know my father. I have a half sister out there, but we don't talk—too many years and shit between us. I live wherever I plop my head down at night. Less burden that way." In her line of work, a material lifestyle was dangerous. Having things was not as important as having experiences.

"That must be hard on you. Home is very important. I think about mine all of the time. We didn't have much, but what we had was ours."

"I don't think about it too much," she said, dropping on the couch next to him. "In fairness, it's easier to *not* think about it. There are times I wish I had a house or apartment somewhere, but I am always on the move. Having a place would tie me down, and as an operative, that can be dangerous."

"You're not an operative anymore," Raul pressed.

"No, but I'm still doing that kind of work. Jack is keeping me busy because some of the same people looking for you are looking for me. Now I have something different. I have a reason to do what I do." *I have a cause.*

"If you could settle down, where would it be? Where would you like to live?"

It was something she had never fully contemplated, so it took a few moments to formulate her answer. "I always liked the mountains. Maybe South Dakota or someplace like that. I enjoyed skiing when I was in high school."

"I would like to see the mountains someday too. I miss my family in Texas."

"Being on the run isn't easy," she offered. "I know better than most. We were fortunate to get you out of Pennsylvania. If they had gotten ahold of you, it would have been a show trial. You never would have had a chance in their legal system. Newmerica is willing to take extraordinary steps to protect itself." The voice of experience rang in each word she said.

"So much has happened," Raul said, shaking his head several times. "The riots, Valley Forge; I never wanted any of this. It all got dumped on me."

Caylee understood how he felt. At the same time, he needed a hard dose of reality. "I read your profile, Raul. I know all about you and what went down. The biggest thing that you have to wrap your hands around is that for a lot of your life, you *believed* in Newmerica—hook, line, and sinker. You joined the Youth Corps and I'm willing to bet you liked it. Like so many people in the country, you knew what was going on but chose to look the other way. You'd heard of the Social Quarantine camps, but convinced yourself to believe what the TRC told you…that it was for those people's own good. It was easy for you to simply accept the bullshit they were serving up. I don't fault you for it. Most of the country is the same way, comfortable with the little lies because it fits their own thinking. People prefer to think of their government as benevolent, even if they know otherwise." *I was the same way…I ignored the impacts of my own actions in the belief that it was for the greater good.*

"What changed for you was when the reality of this socialist nightmare hit home—when it impacted you. Most people are like that. Until things happen to them, they look the other way; they play the game. When you became the target; that was when your eyes were opened for the first time. I'm right, aren't I?"

He nodded. "I was fooled."

"You were lied to, like everyone else. The media, Big Tech, the FedGov, all of them twisted your thinking. When the real world showed up with a gun, you came to realize how fucked up it all was."

Tears welled in the corners of his eyes, but he held them in check. Raul didn't sob. He was caught in the web of her words. He had made her face reality, and she was doing the same back to him. "Does that make me a bad person?"

She chuckled. "Hell no. If anything, you are…what's the word? Enlightened! You were like everyone else; you did what you were told to do, believed what they told you to believe. That's how most of the country lives their lives, with blinders on. Now you are free from the burden of all that. You see the country for what it is, warts and all. I would have never even noticed Raul before the riots. This Raul, well, he's got character. He's not a cog in the machine; he stands on his own. The stuff you and the Order of the Bell did—that took guts and courage. This Raul is someone I can respect."

It took a few long seconds for Lopez to regain his composure. "What happens to you now?"

"Mr. Desmond has another assignment for me. That means a lot of planning and prep." Jack had wanted her to take down the TRC after getting Raul to safety. It was no small order, but one she was looking forward to tackling.

"Why don't you stay here," he offered, sweeping his hand around the sparsely furnished house. "There's plenty of room. Besides, I want you to keep teaching me some of your moves."

Caylee opened her mouth to protest, but the words didn't come out. *I could do a lot of planning here.* The thought of another motel room had little appeal to her. Jack would approve it. *If anything, it allows me to keep an eye on Raul.* "I have to go into Nashville to get some data. Let me check with Mr. Desmond. Staying here will save bucks. Besides, I can use the peace and quiet for a change." *The odds of something happening while we are in the middle of an Air Force Base are fairly low.*

Raul broke into a broad smile and Caylee surveyed the room; she was thinking less about defense and more about the room as a temporary place to live and work.

INTERLUDE

"There's a fine line between rhetoric and reality, one best defined by your leaders."

FOUR YEARS EARLIER ...
San Antonio, Texas

Major Trip Reager watched as his battalion snaked through the streets of San Antonio, breaking off on side streets and spreading out. What stuck in his mind was that their camouflage looked wrong. His tanks and fighting vehicles were still painted the tan and splotched brown of their desert pattern. A few were a green and brown forest pattern. They were almost all hand-me-downs, given to the Texas National Guard by the Army, courtesy of their service in Iraq and Afghanistan. *It's the wrong camo pattern for urban fighting.*

His command Humvee stopped at the command post at East Crockett and Elm Street. Sandbags and concrete road barriers had been put up around the tents, a sure sign that trouble was expected. He climbed down from the vehicle and entered, taking off his helmet. Colonel Caine saw him and Reager gave him a salute. "Reporting as ordered, Colonel."

"Major," Caine acknowledged, gesturing to the table that held a blown up map of the city of San Antonio. "Any issues on the way in?"

"None, sir," he said. "We are forming a perimeter four blocks out, per your instructions. We will link up with the second battalion to the north."

"Good. Sorry we had to pull you in on short notice, but a shitstorm is heading our way."

"I didn't have other plans, sir," Trip replied. There was a ring of painful truth in that. His divorce had been finalized the week before.

Nancy blamed him for the split with his daughter. The pizzeria had become a popular place after the fighting there months earlier, but he had sold it. His heart was no longer in the business and half of the proceeds went to Nancy in the divorce settlement. When the Texas National Guard had offered him a full-time opportunity, he had taken it—less out of patriotism than the need for something to do with his life. Trip had lost his wife, his daughter, his house, and his business, all in a matter of months. It had started that night in College Park when Jessie had betrayed him.

Nancy had tried to get him to meet with Jessie, but he couldn't. In his mind, she had turned on her parents, their livelihood—hell—everything. He tried to bring himself to accept her political views, but she wouldn't respond to him at all. Phone calls and emails were unanswered. Nancy had tried to visit her, but Jessie wouldn't even see her. Trip had spent long, lonely hours wondering where he had gone wrong in her upbringing, but he'd never found the answers he wanted. Her college professors and friends had corrupted her thinking to the point where her family could no longer reason with her. She didn't see him as family—but rather as the enemy.

All he had left in life was his service in the National Guard. What few belongings he had after the divorce were in a storage unit in College Park.

"What kind of shitstorm are we looking at, sir?"

Colonel Caine rubbed his chin as he spoke, as if to ease his stress. "These Social Enforcers have formed caravans and are heading this way. Some prick of a historian has tagged the Alamo as, and I quote here, 'A symbol of white privilege' if you can believe that shit. Thousands of snot nosed college pukes want to tear the place down."

"How in the hell can the Alamo be a symbol of white privilege?"

"They state that Jim Bowie owned a slave. That the battle was not really significant. It was all about white people taking land from the Mexicans and the Indians. Their usual bullshit."

Trip shook his head. "You go pissing on the Alamo in Texas, it is going to stir up more than a shitstorm." *It's more like a shit-hurricane.*

"You can say that. Our state has been highly resistant to this Newmerica crap, and apparently they want to make an example with this 'peaceful protest' they have planned. The libtard mayor has committed the police to protecting the protesters on top of that. They've been nationalized into this damned National Security Force. They have buses of police from other states coming in with them. It's safe to say that this is going to be anything other than peaceful."

Great. We have thousands of rioters coming in and the police are going to protect them! What in the hell is the country coming to? "Sir, three battalions are more than enough to form a perimeter, but if they are bringing in police and weapons, this is likely to end up being a bloodbath."

"Which is exactly what the Governor doesn't want," Caine said. "Imagine how they will play that up in the media. They love painting us as a bunch of redneck, gun-loving nuts. You throw in dead teenagers in the street, and it only makes their outrageous claims seem more valid."

"With all due respect, sir, the Governor might not get what he wants," Trip said. *It seems like we are getting the dirty end of the stick on this assignment.* "Is it just us, or are we getting help?"

"Well, we are getting a few thousand of the Texas State Militia, though they are arriving in a slow dribble. We didn't have a lot of time to respond to this. We had to figure out what they were up to and what the target is, and to realize that a lot of other groups are coming. The Texas Freedom Group is sending in some folks, as is the Order of the Golden Triangle, and the Light Foot Militia. The Texit group has 150 volunteers committed to help. We are also pulling in SWAT teams that have not folded up under the NSF. Over a hundred Texas Rangers have shown up as well."

The Captain in command of the Rangers had heard of the orders to fold his personnel into the newly formed NSF. His response had made all of the local papers, "You can tell the Ruling Council they can kiss my pale ass!" It was oddly reassuring that the Rangers were helping with the defense. "You know this is going to be a riot, sir. There's no way around it."

Caine nodded. "It is my intent to form a perimeter four blocks out. We will use non-lethal responses. If pressed, we will collapse to a two-block perimeter around the Alamo. We have positioned barricades here, here, and here to funnel them onto the main streets only," he said, stabbing his finger at the map.

"We might be using riot-control munitions, but there is no guarantee that these kids will do the same. What are the rules regarding the use of lethal force?"

Colonel Caine hesitated for a moment before responding. "We haven't been given any."

That figures—none of the politicians want to get their hands dirty. "Sir, my people are going to want to know what they can and can't do. What is *your* guidance?"

"Major, I cannot have our personnel get shot at, wounded, and killed without returning fire. No one is to use lethal force without my expressed orders."

"Understood, sir," he replied. "We will need a way to coordinate with the various groups coming in."

"Already handled," the Colonel replied.

Trip stared at the map intently. "Sir, if I may. We are set up like a bubble, one that can collapse if possible—but a bubble. We know when they took down the White House and Capitol, the rioters used homemade mortars. I have to believe that they will do the same with us. The tighter our defense, the easier it is to shell us."

"What are your thoughts, Major?"

Trip looked at the map for a second more, then back to his CO. "We should establish some groups, hidden, out past the perimeter. They can act as mobile response forces. If they start lobbing mortars or rockets at us, we can hit them from their own rear—take those things out. Also, having a force appear out of some buildings to their rear might make them fall back—taking the pressure off of us in the center."

The Colonel looked longingly at the map. "That's a damned fine idea. We can use some of the militia to help in that capacity. It's your idea, Major. Go ahead and make it happen."

"Yes, sir," Trip replied. The briefing continued for nearly an hour, with the Colonel showing where he wanted forces deployed, where barriers and fencing were position, etc. Trip studied the map intently.

As he stepped out, he glanced back at the gnarled oak trees that surrounded the Alamo plaza. Concrete barricades were poised before the low wall. He could only catch a glimpse of the Alamo itself, the sunlight shining on it.

The last time I came here was with Jessie's class trip. For Texans, the Alamo was sacred ground. It never had dawned on him that it would serve as a target for the ire of the Newmerica government. *They want it destroyed...they have to have it destroyed. Take that down and you tell the rest of Texas who's in charge.* It was no longer only a symbol of Texan independence; it was about the defiance of Texas toward the Ruling Council.

We can't lose the Alamo to these rioters. It can't happen on my watch ...

FIVE YEARS EARLIER...
Washington DC

Becky Clarke helped the Speaker of the House into her chair while two of her comrades cleared her desk. The swift seizure of the Capitol had caught most of Congress and the Senate off guard from what she could tell. The Capitol Police had tried riot control tactics, but ANTIFA was not playing around and had gunned down many of the officers.

Now, in the Speaker's office, Becky had a role to fulfill that required the ancient woman who was trembling next to her. "Madam Speaker, I need you to focus."

"It's just…this is all happening so fast," she stammered. For a moment, she reminded Becky of her grandmother. Old, confused, somewhat dazed by world events. With her grandmother, she had a bit of pity, but there was none for the Speaker. *She is part of the problem, the old ways of thinking. She and her kind have run this country into the ground.*

Becky extended the prepared speech, a single, folded piece of paper. "All we need you to do is read this," she said. The speaker's quaking hands unfolded it, and she began to read the typed page. Becky saw her mouth drop open as she attempted to digest the words. "What—is this true?"

"Yes, it is," he said, relishing the moment.

"What about the President and Vice President?" she said. "They won't stand for this.

"Madam Speaker, at this time the President and Vice President are dead."

The color drained from her face. Becky knew that a part of the old woman was no doubt happy at the news, while at the same time being fearful for her own life. Clarke continued in a calming tone. "If they aren't yet, they will be shortly," she said with a hint of pride in her voice. "We have overrun the White House, the Treasury…DC is ours. It is in the hands of the people—as it should be." It was hard to contain the pride she felt. Tears welled up in her eyes.

"This—" the Speaker said, holding the shaking piece of paper, "This isn't how the succession is handled. "If they are dead, then the role of President goes to me."

Even now she is attempting to cling to power. "You need to understand Madam Speaker; these are extraordinary times. This body will take over during an interim period…not for long. Just until we can sort things out, that's all." It was a lie, but Becky understood the Speaker of the House far too well. *She needs to believe that she is part of the transition for this to happen.*

"I'm—I'm saying that this is not how we do things," the old woman stammered, struggling to find the words fast enough for her sentences to make sense.

"I know," Becky replied in a soothing tone. "But it is important for the people to understand that you support this change. You've fought hard against this administration. We merely did what you would have done if you had the ability to. The Traitor that sat in the Oval Office is gone. This is the will of the people."

"This," she said, glancing at the document. "This is not how we do it though, dear."

"It is tonight, Madam Speaker," she said. One of the men at the door ushered in a CNN camera crew. Like the ANTIFA people, they were dressed in black bloc attire, right down to their tactical vests that had nicely stitched, "Press" over their hearts.

Becky faced the camera crew. "I'm in charge here," she assured them. "I need you to set up in front of her desk." The CNN crew set up their tripod and camera. "Let's get those flags adjusted," she ordered, and two of the protesters followed her commands, moving the flags in behind the Speaker's desk. Becky moved next to the camera. While much of the office was in disarray from their entry, the image that the camera would film seemed perfect to her—as if nothing out of the ordinary was happening. She knew that this would be in stark contrast to the riots that Americans were going to be watching on TV, but that was deliberate on her part. The confusion will only make any potential resisters hesitate. *Once they hear her speech, it will make them pause, wondering what is really happening.*

Becky turned to the camera crew. "This is not for live broadcast. You'll send it only when I permit it. Understood?" They nodded with the complete and oblivious obedience she and her people had come to expect.

"Maybe we can get you something to drink?" Becky offered to the Speaker. She nodded and pointed to the credenza in the office. One of the ANTIFA team there opened it and was stunned by the alcohol. "Damn woman!" he said with a grin. "You could have a hell of a party with all of this shit. And this is the good stuff." He took out a bottle of vodka and poured some into a glass, handing it to Becky, who offered it to the Speaker.

There was no hesitation; she swallowed it like a professional drinker, without flinching. She straightened in her seat slightly, attempting to muster a degree of composure. Then, she looked up at Becky. "Okay, I think I am ready," she said in a somewhat unsteady voice.

"You will do fine, Madam Speaker. The American people are counting on you to be the voice of reason, to help them understand what is happening. You can do this."

She nodded and Becky tapped the cameraman on the shoulder. He moved in behind the camera and held up his hand. "We're recording," he said.

"Good evening," the Speaker said. "Unparalleled events are unfolding across our nation's capital as you no doubt have seen. The recent election showed that the traitor sitting in the White House was not the people's choice. His call for new elections, after the tragic deaths of the President and Vice President-elect, were unconstitutional and clearly an illegal grab for power on his part. Most of our great nation saw his corruption and thirst for power for what it really was.

"What you are witnessing is something historic—oppressed and marginalized people rising up and taking back what is rightfully theirs.

This is not a coup or an overthrow of the government. The people, who have long felt their voices were unheard, are merely asserting themselves to bring sanity and order to our great nation.

"With the President and Vice President unable to perform their duties, I am utilizing the powers vested in me by our Constitution and I am calling for the formation of a Ruling Council to help govern our nation during this peaceful transition of power. We need to ensure that the people who have been harassed, trodden down, and treated unfairly have a voice in our country.

"To our friends and allies abroad, I want to assure you: The United States is well, strong, and despite what you may see on TV, quite stable. I assure you, our nation is well tonight as we all witness these glorious and historic events unfolding. This is not chaos…this is the face of true democracy in action. Tonight, our nation emerges from the darkness, stronger than ever—and filled with a deep resolve to lift those that have been marginalized for so long.

"Thank you."

As she finished, the Speaker's body seemed to slightly sag in her seat. Becky handed the glass back to the ANTIFA person near the credenza. That person refilled the glass and Becky slid it in front of the Speaker, who took a long drink and cradled the crystal glass in her skinny, trembling fingers as if it were the only thing keeping her upright.

"That was well written," the older woman said. "Did you do it?"

"I did," she said with pride at her accomplishment.

"I could use someone with your talents on my staff," the Speaker replied, taking another sip of her drink.

She still thinks that she is part of the solution, that there is going to be a role for her in what is coming. Becky wanted to laugh, but held back the urge. "You did very well reading it. I don't think we are going to need a second take; do you?" she turned to the cameraman who gave her a thumbs up.

"I should talk to the Pentagon," the Speaker said in a low tone of voice. "They need to be made aware of the situation."

"That won't be necessary, Madam Speaker," Becky said.

"But I should talk to them," she pressed.

"Perhaps later," she assured her falsely. *I'm not sure if it is sad or pathetic…she has no idea what is really happening here.* "For now, we need to get you to a place of safety. We have been moving the members of Congress down to the tunnels under the Capitol."

"Yes," she said, looking up. "If anything were to happen to me, all this would fall on the Secretary of State…and we don't want that happening."

"You're right," she said with an assuring tone. Becky moved around the desk and helped her to her feet. "I'm the most essential person in the government now."

"Of course you are," she assured her with a lie that the old woman needed to hear. "We need to get you to safety with the others."

"I have some ideas on this Ruling Council …" she said as she moved slowly through the office, with Becky at her side.

"I'm sure you do," she said. *Not that your thoughts matter.*

CHAPTER 13

"The hate of one reflects the hate of all."

Knoxville, Tennessee

Julius surveyed the Grumman LLV truck in the auto salvage yard with a skeptical eye. It was old, but still the same model that the post office used to deliver mail. It had been painted over with house paint that was peeling in many spots, a dull gray coat with the words, "GS Powerwashing" appearing on the side. The interior needed cleaning, but it was structurally sound from what he could tell. On top of the old delivery truck, the previous owners had attached a ladder rack. It had been in an accident at one point, and the rear bumper was dented. Two of the panels near the rear tires showed rust bleeding through from the back of the metal. The wheel hubs were rusted as well.

The search for a former postal truck had taken him to several such establishments. The other two that he had seen were in far worse condition. One had been made into an ice cream truck with a big window cut in the side—too much work to rebuild. The other, apparently made into some sort of camper near the end of its life, was so horribly rusted that he doubted that he would ever get it back in shape.

To anyone else, the old postal truck he was looking at was a junker, but to Bernstein it had all of the elements he needed. The owners of Pete's Salvage waddled over next to him, his hands stuffed into the pockets of his filthy, faded blue coveralls. "She may not look like much, but she still has some miles left in her."

"Does it run?"

Pete pulled himself up into the vehicle and overflowed the seat. He turned it over and the truck hesitated, and then it kicked over. A billow of black and gray smoke rolled out from what was left of the exhaust system, stinging Julius's nostrils for a second. Pete gunned the engine and it actually started to sound smoother. "She's fine—she needs a little care," he called out from the driver's seat. After a few more moments of running, he shut the vehicle off and climbed down. "I know she runs on gas, but these things are beasts. Hell, the postal service still uses them today. They've been phasing them out for the new NGDVs, but it is taking forever. You know how the FedGov is."

"Yes, I have some idea," he said, feigning ignorance.

"What are you going to use it for?"

"Transporting freight," Julius responded.

"I have other vehicles that might serve you better than this little fella," Pete said. "This is pretty limited in what you can pack into it."

"I had my heart set on an old postal truck," he replied.

Pete shrugged. "Well, then, it sounds like your mind is made up."

"How much can it carry weight-wise?" Julius asked.

"About 1000 pounds," Pete said. "You could pack on more, but she's going to ride like a beast."

If I strip out some of the parts I don't need, I could add to the weight. In his mind, he tried to remember how much explosives Timothy McVeigh used in the Oklahoma City bombing. *I'll have to check the NSFCloud for that info.* "That should do fine then. How much are you asking for it?"

"I was thinking around $2000, given that she runs and all."

It was tempting to hand him the cash, but Julius knew that to do so might attract attention. Bartering was part of such sales. "I was thinking more along the lines of $1500, given how much I will have to put into her."

"I could meet you in the middle; let's say $1750," Pete said, rubbing the stubble of his beard.

Julius paused. "OK then. Is cash OK?"

Pete nodded, "Sure. Let's go over to the office and I will get you the title and a receipt," he said. "You've bought a good one there, mister. She's got a lot of miles still in her," he said as he waddled toward the faded, yellow, cargo container that had been converted to his office.

Julius didn't reply. It doesn't need a lot of miles. *It has the few trips she will have to make.*

The District

Rebecca Clarke stood with Jamison outside of the conference room, leaning in close so that her voice would not carry. The room was deep in the bowels of the TRC headquarters, far from windows or prying eyes. Still, given the sensitivity, she didn't want anyone overhearing what she had to say.

"Are you sure it is her?" she asked above a whisper.

"Jane Pistós, he replied. "Story Reprocessor Second Class. We hired her in about six months ago. We found the data on a flash drive in her apartment," Jamison said. "When we suspected her, I went with one of our internal security people, and we tossed her place. We don't know how she got the poll results, but chances are she lifted it from someone at the political desk. We haven't been able to figure out how she got through the security on the file though."

"How did she get it to the reporter?"

Jamison shrugged. "No idea."

Rebecca paused. This was new territory for her. It was one thing to kick off an investigation to look into who had leaked data from the TRC to the media; it was another to deal with the consequences of that. Memories of the night of the Liberation and those early days of the formation of Newmerica came rushing back to her.

She opened the door to the conference room and saw the young woman zip-tied to the chair at the end of a small table. Standing beside her were two security people, with no ties to the NSF. The woman glanced up at her with her one working eye—the other was swollen almost completely shut. Her lower lip was cut and a caked drizzle of blood clung to her chin. Her dark, olive-skinned cheek was purple from having been hit—hard. She wore a plain white exercise shirt, marked with blood splatter and scuff marks. *She put up a fight, or my people were only giving her what she deserves.*

Rebecca took the seat opposite of her and tried to ignore the beating that the young woman had taken. She wanted to have pity for her, but this woman had betrayed not just her and the TRC, but Newmerica as a nation. Her initial instinct was to turn her over to the NSF, but she knew that the Secretary would flip this against her in a heartbeat. *No, this is my problem to deal with.*

"Well, Ms. Pistós," she began, crossing her arms. "You are in a lot of trouble." She caught a hint of sweat from the woman.

"I want a lawyer," she said with a growling voice.

Rebecca couldn't help but chuckle at that. "Seriously? You think you have any rights after what you have done."

"I haven't done anything."

"Really? You stole sensitive polling data and passed it to a reporter for publication. What you shared was confidential and classified. At best, you are a traitor."

"You would know," she said with a twisted grin.

Defiance. Normally that was a trait Rebecca admired, but not in this person. "I am a patriot," she said, adjusting herself in the seat. "You have chosen to turn your back on the people that put food on your table and a roof over your head."

"You don't know me at all," the woman said proudly. "I owe you nothing."

"Who put you up to this?" Rebecca asked.

Jane Pistós dipped her head slightly and shook it. "Go fuck yourself." One of the security people grabbed a handful of her curly, black hair and pulled her head back, taking a tuff of hair with him as he let go.

"How did you access the material?"

The woman said nothing.

"How did you get the material to the reporter? You know, we can pull all of your emails and phone records."

"The fact that the NSF isn't here tells me you aren't able to do that," Pistós replied. "Your goons tried to beat it out of me already. If I didn't talk to their beating me, why would I tell you?"

"Because I am between you and death," Rebecca said solemnly.

For a moment, Pistós said nothing, simply looking at Rebecca with her dark pupils. "I'm dead already."

"Not necessarily," she offered in the form of a lie. "If you cooperate, we might be able to find a solution where you walk out of here."

Pistós grinned, and Rebecca saw where a tooth was missing. "The best part of working here and getting to watch you is that I can tell when you are lying."

I'm not that obvious. "If I were you, I wouldn't be so cocky. I'd be trying to cut some sort of deal and live."

Pistós stared at her deeply for several awkward seconds. "It dawns on me, sitting here, that you don't know how bad things are for you, Madam Director."

"What do you mean?"

"There's a lot more of us than there are of you," she said confidently.

"More of who?"

"You think I'm the only person in your precious TRC that hates what you've done to our country? You can try and convince yourself there are not a lot of my people in the FedGov if you want to." The woman managed a single, pain-filled chuckle. "We are everywhere. We know all of your dirty little secrets."

Rebecca stared at her, wrestling with the next actions. *How many traitors are there? Is this the tip of the iceberg?* She had security people, but they were not trained in finding spies. *When the election is over, I can reach out to Alex and get her people in here and identify the others, if they exist.*

That left her with the decision concerning what to do about Jane Pistós. It was a shame she had wasted her life this way. Rebecca rose to her feet and looked at the two guards standing behind the young woman. "Finish it. Make sure no one finds the body." It wasn't the first time she had been forced to make that call, though she wondered if it was the last.

"Ma'am?" the man asked.

"You heard me," she replied. "Get her out of here discreetly; finish what you've started, and dispose of the body."

The guard nodded. Rebecca walked to the door; then she glanced back at the woman tied to the chair. Such a waste. *If only her dedication had been with us ...*

Arnold Air Force Base, Tullahoma, Tennessee

Raul enjoyed the clean sheets and bedding. The base housing they were set up in was more spacious and modern than the house he had been raised it, but from what Caylee had told him, they were not great homes. She had gone out and purchased groceries, and they had even arranged to order pizza their first night in. To him, it felt as if life might return to normal.

There were rules; she had been clear about them. Raul was to limit his time outside and there was no way that he could leave the base. They did drive to the base gym every morning, and there she gave him instruction in fighting techniques. Each time she made sure that the gym was empty so no one might recognize him.

The time in the gym was what he looked forward to most. Caylee was a good instructor, and there were times he was beyond frustrated, but he eventually mastered each step, swing, and kick. She pushed him hard, but always just enough so that he had to better himself. The physical contact of their sparring felt strangely satisfying to him. She enjoyed it too, even though she never said so.

Caylee had purchased thick, foam padding for their spare bedroom, which she had converted into a workout room. The trips to the base gym dwindled after that. Raul liked being out, but followed her orders. *She knows more about security than I ever will.*

They had a television, but Raul hated watching it after he saw a broadcast about himself that called him a terrorist. He watched game shows mostly after that, a few sitcoms, distractions really. It was hard to laugh at things on television after what he had experienced in real life. There was a time when he used to watch TV and laugh with his mother. It felt like it was a different lifetime, as if he were a different person. He left the volume on low most of the day so he didn't have to cope with silence in the house. Even the hum of forced laugh tracks was better than nothing at all.

Memories of his talk with Caylee when they arrived resonated with Raul still, even days later. She had been right about many things. He had embraced Newmerica before the events in Detroit. When the government turned on him, he had finally seen them for what they were. *They trample people's lives, spread lies, ruin whatever they touch. All I ever did was fire on those men attacking us. Now I am seen as the most wanted criminal in the nation.*

Caylee would leave for hours at a time, coming back with papers and a laptop on one trip. She spread them out on the circular, faux oak dining room table and studied them with an intensity that told Raul it would be unwise to disturb her. He saw blueprints in the paper, and she stabbed notes into her iPad, sometimes for minutes on end.

At dinner of their fourth day—a salad and spaghetti that Raul had prepared—he finally mustered the courage to ask her. "What is it you are working on?"

He expected her not to answer him, but Caylee surprised him. "My next assignment."

"What is it?"

"With the election coming, the President believes it would be in the best interest of the country to have the Truth Reconciliation Committee shut down. They are bound to be spreading a lot of disinformation prior to the voting. I can't fault him for his logic…but the ask is a tough one."

"They've been lying about me," Raul said firmly. "I would like to see them shut down as well."

She nodded quickly in understanding. "It isn't an easy op."

"How so?"

"First, the TRC is in The District. Since the whole swearing-in thing, they have done a remarkable job of turning it into an armed camp. You need proper credentials to get in close. I can get those, but it would not be easy; nor would it be convenient."

"Can you take the entire TRC down?"

She nodded, sucking one noodle up through her pursed lips before responding. "Oh yeah," she said as she finished swallowing. "Thousands of employees are working there. Normally, I would consider bombing the building they work in. The challenge is that the TRC is not only in The District. They have a lot of staff in LA, and a few in New York. Getting a bomb big enough to take the entire building down would be nearly impossible given their heightened sense of security. I could use some sort of poison, but after the attacks on Quantico and other NSF locations, they have measures in place to prevent that."

Her casualness in talking about killing so many people was not lost on Raul, but to a certain extent, it was no shock to him. Caylee had told him that she was a former operative. He had heard the rumors about operatives since he was a young boy. If half of the things he had heard were true, operatives were a combination of super-spies and covert secret agents. From what he knew of his companion, she was more than able and willing to kill when she had to—without hesitation. *She will do what she has to do…it is who she is.* "So how will you do it?"

"I have a few thoughts," she replied with a wry grin. "No system is perfect. The nature of their work means that the TRC has vulnerabilities, things I might be able to exploit. When you are working on something like this, you don't immediately go for the violent solution first. They built a system that is very dependent on human beings performing tasks. To do those tasks, they need data. Five stories under their HQ is their data hub, and it's a big one."

"Wouldn't that be hard to get to?"

She nodded, taking a bite of a piece of Pepperidge Farm garlic bread and chewing thoroughly before responding. "It is, but that doesn't make it impossible. The hard part is that they are bound to have backups and no one seems to know where their backup data is. So, even if I got there and somehow managed to take down their server farm, they probably have another location in The District that could spin up and continue their work."

"It sounds difficult. I would like to help you."

His offer surprised her a little. "Sure. You never know. Sometimes a fresh set of eyes can help. Personally, I like problems like this," she admitted. "It forces me to get creative. In some respects the kind of work that I do is…artistic. It's not your normal kind of art, but there are elements of art in the work if you are doing it right."

Raul said nothing for a moment. He was about to respond when he heard the name, 'Lopez,' come from the television. Both of them snapped their gaze to the set, Raul rising to his feet and moving into the family room area.

"Authorities apprehended the fugitive Raul Lopez's family being hidden with a terrorist cell of the SOL in Kansas," the announcer said. The image in the background showed his mother and sister, flanked by body-armored NSF police, being led into a building, their hands bound behind them with zip ties. His jaw hung open and he suddenly felt hot. "They are being held in protective custody in the Los Angeles Century Regional Correctional facility."

"Lopez is on the NSF's most wanted list," the announcer said as four images of Raul appeared on the screen in the corner. "Lopez is known to be armed and dangerous. Most recently he murdered several NSF security people in southern Ohio. He is believed to be in Kentucky or Tennessee, no doubt taking refuge with forces loyal to the Pretender President. There is a

$1 million reward for information that leads to the apprehension of this domestic terrorist." The images disappeared and the announcer went on to another story about wildfires in Oregon.

Raul moved to the couch and dropped into it, his mouth still hanging open. Caylee shut off the television and moved next to him. *My madre!* His sister looked terrified in the short video clip, and that tore at him. "Why would they do that to them? She didn't have anything to do with what I did!" A mix of anger and dread washed over him. It felt as if he were struggling for breath for a moment. His heart pounded in his ears, and it felt like the room was getting smaller.

Then he felt Caylee's hand on his shoulder, almost awkwardly. "It is standard NSF procedure," she said. "They want to send you a message. 'Surrender and save your mother.' Intimidation and manipulation are like drugs to them. They want to squeeze you into doing something stupid."

"We have to save them," he said after several rapid breaths of air.

Caylee shook her head. "Raul, that's exactly what they want you to do. They are prepared for that kind of reaction. Your mother and sisters—they are bait. The NSF is trying to force you to overreact or to turn yourself over to them."

"I have to help my mother and my sister," he pleaded.

Raul looked at her and she could see what he needed was a hug, but for the moment, she couldn't bring herself to do it. "We can't—not now at least."

"What kind of people would do something like this? Arrest innocent people…use them for blackmail?" he said, holding back the sobs that wanted to come out.

"This is what Newmerica is. You know that. This is what they do. To provide for the many; they suppress and punish the few and call it 'freedom.' When COVID hit, many people were willing to surrender their freedom for security. The people running Newmerica learned from that. It's a bad lesson for corrupt people to master."

He slowly broke their embrace. "We have to help my mother. She is innocent."

"They won't do anything to your family, Raul. Trust me, I know. If anything happens to them, they lose their leverage on you. They will be treated well. Those images on TV were for you, to try and break your will. No harm will come to her because if they do hurt her, you won't turn yourself in."

"Are you sure?"

"I am," she assured him. The sincerity of her words helped him regain his composure. "So what do we do?"

"Right now, nothing," she said. "You'll need to stay in the house going forward. A million dollars might get one of these airmen who are working security to think about ratting you out. It is best if you stay out of sight."

He hated that thought, but nodded in agreement. "So I am a prisoner?"

"No. This is for your own good, Raul."

He said nothing for a few moments. "Isn't that what they tell the people that are sent to Social Quarantine?"

Rarely did Caylee Leatrom wince, but it was evident with his last question. "Touché Raul, touché. You are not a prisoner. If you want to leave, I won't stop you. If you do that, I can't protect you though—plain and simple. I'm not ordering you to stay here. I'm a friend that is making a strong suggestion because she cares about you."

"OK," he replied, nodding begrudgingly.

"I will put out feelers," she said. "It will take time. I will get the full layout of where she is being held. I'll come up with a plan to get them out. California is hostile ground, but I have contacts that might be able to help."

"You will do this for me?" Raul asked.

Caylee smiled. "We spilled blood together. In my book, that makes us friends. After this TRC op, we will figure out a way to recover your family."

He drew a long, deep breath and felt his emotions slowly come under control. "Thank you Caylee."

"Alright then," she said, nodding off in the direction of the table where she had been working. "Let's get focused. Help me figure out how to hurt these bastards."

Michigan City, Indiana

The Three Sheets to the Wind Bar and Grille was not the traditional place for Colonel Reager to frequent. He didn't particularly like bars. For food, he usually had something delivered and he ate in the BOQ on base. Since his divorce and the loss of his former life, going out and socializing was something he struggled with. He did attend the obligatory parties, retirements, promotions, but beyond that Trip Reager kept to himself. Besides, he knew that Newmerica would be spying on the Indiana National Guard Armory in Michigan City, where his troops were quartered. Bringing guests in for a planning session was bound to hand the thugs in The District what they wanted, intelligence. They were far less likely to track someone leaving the base in civilian garb, merely out for a drink.

To be safe, he sent ahead Lieutenant Greenwood, his battalion intel officer. Larry sat at a table alone, with a half-consumed bourbon, refusing to make eye contact with Trip. No doubt he had jamming gear in his canvas briefcase; it would ensure that no one was able to monitor the pending conversation.

As he nursed his sweaty beer in the darkness of the Three Sheets, Trip surveyed the crowd. It was a working person's bar, not the kind that middle class professionals came to. There was a table of women, probably coworkers, who were loudly laughing at the other end of the establishment. The five guys at the bar had cornered the market on Walmart flannel shirts. A biker sat alone at a table, his body slowly merging into his tight, black leather vest and oil-stained T-shirt. Despite the no smoking sign, Trip could catch a whiff of cigarettes every time his older waitress passed him. *Unfiltered Camels*...the same kind his mother used to smoke. It struck him as strange that he could tell that aroma over any other cigarette.

When the trio entered the bar, he barely noticed them. One, the only female, wore a dull gray hoodie with a torn front pocket; another wore a light blue windbreaker with his name 'Ed' stitched over his heart, and the last one wore a sweater that was frayed around the cuffs. Trip made eye contact with the hoodie-wearing one and got a nod, and then the three of them came up to the table.

"Mind if join you stranger?" the woman asked. He caught a glimpse of her short, red hair at the edge of the hoodie covering her head.

"It's a free country," Trip said, giving them the appropriate countersign they had arranged. *Yeah, these are the people I was looking for.*

"I'm Rita, Southside Irregulars," the woman said, extending her hand. He noticed the paracord bracelet she wore and combined with a firm handshake, they told him that she was former military. The sweater wearer shook his hand next. "I'm Don with Windy City Overdrive, and this is Craig of The El Brigade." Trip gripped their hands tightly and they took their seats. The cell names for the Sons of Liberty always amused him and strangely made him feel proud. They came together out of their neighborhoods and had carved identities for themselves. He had studied enough military history to remember patriots like Francis Marion, the Swamp Fox, Nathaniel Greene, and Daniel Morgan's Riflemen. *The Sons of Liberty have deep roots in this country, and the imposition of Newmerica's policies have been like fertilizer to those roots, bringing more people into the resistance.*

"Hell of a place for a meeting like this," Trip said.

"We're the Sons of Liberty," Rita said proudly. "Historically, we've done our best planning in bars and taverns." The comment brought grins from her two compadres.

Trip didn't even try to suppress his smile. "I'm glad to have your people on board. We can use all the help we can get."

"The pleasure's all ours, Colonel," Don said. "After what you did in San Antonio, it's a damned honor to meet you."

Trip tried to ignore the reference to San Antonio, but couldn't. He preferred to simply change the subject as quickly as possible. "Thanks. For the op we have coming up. We can use all of the help we can get."

"We're ready and willing, sir," Craig said. The waitress came by, bringing her stink of cigarettes with her and took their orders.

Trip waited until she was back at the bar before continuing. "I've found that the local support is critical for eyes and ears. We will need every boot on the ground to pull this off."

"What is the plan?" Don asked.

"I can't give you all of the details, for security reasons. We are going to be securing several sites to allow free voting and make sure there is no fraud. These are the only locations in the city where the votes will be tallied. I have no doubt that the Newmerica crowd is going to attempt to shut those down, intimidate the voters, or otherwise cause a riot to make voting impossible."

"Where do we fit in?" Rita asked.

"I doubt their tactics are going to change much. They will bus in people from everywhere, and try to use mass to their advantage. The bulk of forces under my command will secure the voting locations themselves and the corridors where we will allow people in. I will have a mobile response unit that can be brought in along the perimeter when they make their move. I need the Sons to act as blockers. I want it to look like counter protesters—but we will make sure you are armed and protected as best we can."

"You want us to bring the hammer down on them?" Don probed. Trip didn't respond as the waitress approached the table and left the beers.

"I don't think you'll have to start anything. Those SEs are going to want violence; that's why they are coming in the first place. Once they start it, I need you to engage…tie them up long enough for my mobile response to arrive and take the pressure off. Given the geography and distance between the three voting locations, we can position you to adjust wherever the SEs decide to concentrate."

"What about the use of force?" Rita asked.

Trip knew that the question was destined to come up. "We need to be careful, but not stupid. Things are bound to escalate from non-lethal responses. I anticipate that they will be armed, and someone on their side is bound to pull the trigger first. I won't have your or my people get shot at and killed. If they open up, we will respond with gunfire of our own. It is important, however, that no one open up without my expressed orders. I don't want anyone taking the blame for killing other than me. Once I authorize the use of deadly force, your people will be free to do what they need to, but only *after* I give the order. That has to be clear."

"Crystal clear, Colonel," Craig said. The other two SOL leaders nodded.

"They have weaknesses," Trip said. "They operate as a mob. SEs almost always coordinate during riots with cell phones. We will be taking the cell towers out of commission at the start of problems. You, on the other hand, will be given secured military radios to coordinate. I'm going to arrange for our people to train you on how to use the gear and how to request support, confirm orders, the basics."

"A lot of my people, me included, are vets, sir. We know the drill and have the experience," Rita said firmly.

"Good," Trip said. "These people are going to press us and press us hard. They want images of bloodshed. Your people need to understand that it isn't our goal to rack up a body count, but to control the situation. That means targeting their leaders and taking them out fast. We have already seen that they have raided the armories and have technical that they are bound to bring into play. Those are high priority targets too."

"Technicals?" Don said in shock. "They might be able to mow us down quick with a few of those."

"I understand completely. We are going to get your people some good body armor. On top of that we are going to task some Humvees to each of your groups to counter them if they make an appearance. We have a few machine guns we can provide as well if you have talent that can mount them on trucks of your own."

"One of my members owns a body shop," Craig said. "I'm sure he can set us up with Technicals."

"Good," Trip said, pausing for a moment to take a sip of his beer. "Your people should do more than just be down on the streets. We have had years of watching these asshats riot. We know how they operate and can use that against them. Use the buildings and rooftops; establish good fields of fire. Get your snipers positioned as much as you can in advance. If you bunch up too much, you're tempting as a target. Keep your people spread out and using cover."

"Colonel," Rita said, taking a gulp of her own Bud Light before speaking. "I don't see this going down without blood being spilled. They want to hold onto their power, and you are putting us in the middle of Chicago, a city seeped in violence. This is going to do nothing more than incite them to come at us with everything they have. It leaves them little choice."

Reager sighed slightly, looking down for a moment at the scuffed and marred tabletop in search of solace, but only finding blank wood staring back at him. "The word I have from the White House is simple; these people are Americans. We have to remember that. They will capture video of everything we do and post it on social media to make us look like monsters. They did that with me before." He paused, unable to say the words, 'at San Antonio.'

"As tempting as it might be to kill a lot of them when this is over, and one day it will be, we need to be able to bring these people back into the fold. No massacres…but by the same token, we are not going to let them prevail because they have the numbers on us. I won't sit back and let them take shots at us without response."

"Whatever it takes then?" Rita asked.

Trip raised his glass of beer and tipped it toward her, clinking with her own. "Whatever it takes."

CHAPTER 14

"Fear is a virtue."

Denver, Colorado

The campaign event was packed and seemed to hang on every word of her speech. The Secretary of the NSF and the Vice Presidential candidate remembered the large rallies that the Traitor President held before his death. Those crowds seemed filled with conviction and enthusiasm. She found herself longing for supporters that loved her the way the Traitor had people throng to him. *It isn't fair. We have given the people far more than he ever did, but the people that show up for me have read a prompt on the monitor saying to cheer.* Even then, their applause and chants felt less than enthusiastic. Worse yet, they had been forced to bus many of the supporters into Coors Stadium where the event had been held.

She understood some of it. The Ruling Council had given the people prosperity and she was proud of that. Reparation points equated to dollars and many people had used that system to buy the material goods that made life better. Free education had allowed a college education for people who never had the opportunity to attend. The Youth Corps was out rebuilding the crumbling infrastructure and built new solar farms. Rent wavers meant that many could take the money they might pay for rent and spend it on other things. Yes, there was Green rationing, which was not popular; nor were the new taxes that had been imposed. These were offset with new paid federal holidays and raises to the minimum wage. Those companies that cut jobs because of the cost increases were forced to supplement the income of those employees who were impacted. Some creative trimming of the Defense Department budget had allowed for funding a great deal of the new programs. The nationalization of farms had removed several middlemen from food growth and distribution. Yes, there were occasional shortages, but few people complained.

As she saw it, the problem was that when you gave the people something, no matter how good it was, they always wanted more. *Many are ungrateful for what we have done. They don't understand the costs for some of what they want.* The first few years of the Great Reformation had been a smorgasbord of positive social changes. The bill was coming due. Inflation was a reality, and many traitorous companies had pulled up roots and moved their headquarters and operations out of Newmerica rather than pay their fair share. The good news was that many Newmericans enjoyed the resulting unemployment. *Paying people to stay at home and not work is the best way for us to get their votes. This Pretender President will take all that away from them and they know it.*

As she made her way to the backstage, the press waited, huddled like the sheep that they were. The campaign had filtered who could and couldn't be in the press pool. It was not a matter of fairness, but it made for a better projection of the story. She tolerated them, even though most of their questions were cleared in advance. In her mind, speaking to the press was a waste of her precious time. The mainstream media was the epitome of what Newmerica was all about. Most of them believed they were impartial. The majority were convinced their biases did not factor into their coverage. They believed their role in society was supreme and that the press was free. *We have conditioned them so well they don't understand that their true function is to tell the stories we need them to cover.*

Judy Caesar, the TRC representative who was coordinating the event, led the way, gesturing to the stage where the press was assembled. She passed her two NSF security staff; both gave her a nod that she knew was pure respect on their parts. The swirl of mixed thoughts made her smile as she took her place behind the podium.

"I'll be happy to take a few questions," she said, lying smoothly as she had done thousands of times before. Confidence rang in her voice despite the shiver she felt as a cold breeze danced off of her face.

A reporter from MSNBC spoke up and she knew he was on the cleared list. "Madam Secretary, what do you personally make of the massacre that took place at the Illinois border a few days ago."

"We have all come to know that the war criminal, Colonel Reager, was behind the vicious assault that left some thirty-six dead and wounded. Bloodbath Reager's reputation is well earned from the footage that I have seen…slaughtering innocent people. The fact that he was sent there by the Pretender President tells you all you need to know about how this man would lead our nation if he won." Becky's people had prepared the statement, and she had rehearsed it well, knowing that the question would be offered by MSNBC. It was almost perfect. It slandered the Pretender and sowed fear in anyone watching the broadcast.

"Is the Ruling Council preparing to use military force to protect the Voting Sanctuary Zones?" came a rapid-fire question from the AP representative.

"The last thing we want to do is to have to use force. Everyone knows that Newmerica is a nation of peace. You've seen the response of the Pretender in Whiting, Indiana. Violence. Carnage. We don't want to be forced to send in defense forces to protect our citizens, but this man, like his traitor-predecessor, seems bent on threating the very people he wants to govern. We are merely responding to his heinous acts."

"But will you use force?" the reporter pressed.

"Let me be clear; we will protect our people using every resource at our disposal." The words sounded much more convincing than the reality. Since the swearing in of the Pretender, the military had been paralyzed. A large number of personnel—no doubt racist seditionists hiding in the ranks for years—had abandoned their posts to report to the Pretender. When the Ruling Council attempted to press the Chairman of the Joint Chiefs into taking firm action to support the elections, he wavered, claiming that using the military for a purely civilian activity might be unconstitutional. *They are afraid of making a commitment in case they end up on the losing side.* That thinking had kept them on the sidelines during the Liberation. Now they were playing the same card against the Ruling Council. *Once we are elected, we will replace the head of the Joint Chiefs with someone who understands their primary role is to protect the government in power.* It was not an idle threat.

Names were already being drawn up.

Another reporter, a lanky female-looking person in a bright red blazer stood up, "We are getting reports of clashes along the Ohio and Kentucky border after the incident in Ripley the other day. Given that Ohio is on the fence in terms of support of the Newmerican government, would you care to comment on these reports?"

That question was not one she had anticipated and it instantly angered her. *Becky needs to rein these people in.* "I have heard several reports of clashes of NSF and defecting NSF forces along the border. These are minor. What I would like to react to is your comment that Ohio is on the fence in some way regarding its support of Newmerica. The Governor has been in close contact with the Ruling Council, and we have a strong and long-lasting working relationship with that state."

The reporter did not take her seat. "We are getting reports that at least a dozen counties are preparing to pledge their support to the President. There were reports on the web that our own polls show you lagging in some key states."

For a moment she said nothing but narrowed her gaze at the reporter. "What outlet are you with?"

"NeoFox," she replied.

"That figures," the Secretary muttered. She had heard of them, a pop-up news outlet, another ploy of the Pretender's administration. "I would caution you and other members of the press not to spread rumors of defections or imply that county leaders are in some way turning traitor to the legitimate government. I assure you, the good people of the State of Ohio know who is ensuring that they get their government stipends—their reparations, their social security, their rent abatement, and other support. It isn't coming from Tennessee where the Pretender is hiding. It comes from The District, the Ruling Council, and the ideals of Newmerica." The woman from Fox lowered herself slowly to her seat.

Another reporter shot to their feet. "Do you have updates on the Raul Lopez investigation, Madam Secretary?"

This was a prepared question that she welcomed after the NeoFox reporter. "I'm not at liberty to go into the details of the investigation. The NSF has a lot of resources working this case. We are closing in on this terrorist, and I am confident that at some point soon, we will have him in our custody." Most of that was the truth. Several teams were moving into Kentucky and other states. Leads were pouring in and each had to be classified, qualified, and investigated. Sooner or later Lopez would be brought to justice for his crimes against the state. That was something she looked forward to.

Another reporter's voice, a male, barked out from the rear ranks. "What can you tell us about the upcoming investigation by Senator Lewis?" he said loud enough that it could not be ignored. She held her scowl back since this was another failure on the part of Becky's people to filter the questions being thrown at her. "A lot of accusations have been made on the Internet about a so-called operative program. We have all seen those documents that were posted. If true, it seems that you have had a role in a number of illegal activities. What do you say to those charges?"

It was hard to conceal her rage, but somehow she managed, through gritted teeth. Questions about the operatives were not to be discussed—she had that agreement with the TRC on the matter. "I cannot comment on Senator Lewis's apparent crusade against the NSF other than to say it is based on reports someone posted on the Internet…which tells you a great deal about their validity. I look forward to having the opportunity to provide clarity to the good Senator on these matters so we can move forward." Every sentence she spoke was a lie, but they flowed with utter calm and control.

Judy Caesar stepped forward, clearly sensing the loss of control. "Ladies and gentlemen, thank you all. Now the Secretary has to go to a fundraiser at the convention center." She followed Judy off the stage and behind the curtains that concealed them.

"What in the hell was that?" she demanded of the young TRC staffer.

"My apologies, Madame Secretary. They were instructed to stick to their scripts. I was very clear about that."

"Not clear enough," she growled, dusting off her lapels with furious little thrusts. "Those questions were totally unacceptable. They weren't on the script."

"I'm sorry," she said, almost pleading. "Some of the reporters apparently felt emboldened. We will block those questions and answers before they go out—you have my word on that."

"You had better," she said in a low tone. Judy took off and the Secretary turned to her two NSF detail staff. "Those reporters…the two that asked those questions. I need them brought in and interrogated for their possible links to the Pretender. When you're done with that, have them sent to one of our Social Quarantine camps. Perhaps a few weeks there will give them clarity as to their role."

"Yes, Madame Secretary," one of them said.

"And when little Miss Judy gets done with her efforts to block their questions, have her sent off to the same camp." *Perhaps a few weeks in quarantine will teach her to do a better job at handling the media.*

She relished the reaction that this would have with Becky. *She will be indignant…she may raise it in the Council session to attempt to force my hand. Her anger will only lend credence to the role I intend her to play in upcoming events. Any bitterness that she exposes will only provide validity to her role in the plot I have crafted.*

The Southern White House
Nashville, Tennessee

Jack entered the conference room and saw Caylee, with her back to him, staring out the window with crossed arms. She didn't turn around as he closed the door behind him; instead she stared out for a full minute of dead silence. "Good to see you, Mr. Desmond," she said, pivoting slowly. At times like this she creeped him out. *It is hard to forget that she was an operative, someone who had worked against us.* "How did you know it was me?"

"Your cologne," she replied. "You, like most men, wear the same brand every day—never changing. Ralph Lauren, right?"

Her observation was correct, but it only solidified a bit of the ookiness factor that she projected. "Yeah, it's Ralph Lauren," he conceded. "How do you know this kind of stuff?"

"You were trained in observation when in the Secret Service," she replied. "Trained to watch for gestures, actions, and the like which might indicate a threat. My training was similar with the agency and as an operative, but we always assume everyone is a threat of some kind. That forces you to use all of your senses." She moved in front of her laptop at the end of the table and slid into her seat.

They programmed her like a machine, to soak in everything around her. Somewhere inside that tough exterior is the real Caylee. I wonder if we are ever going to see her? In that moment, Jack understood why he was always a little suspicious of her. *She knows us all, but we really don't know her...we know the operative.*

"I take it your house guest is doing OK?"

"Raul is doing well," she responded. *She called him Raul, not Mr. Lopez...that means she is on friendly terms with him.* "He hates being cooped up. I cannot blame him for that. He wants to return to a normal life. I've tried to get him to understand that is never going to be possible, not entirely. This thing with them arresting his family has shaken him up."

"That's understandable. It's necessary, at least for the time being. The Newmerica government is keeping everyone on the lookout for him—public enemy number one. We caught an SE team in northern Tennessee that was clearly on the hunt for him. I have to believe there are more."

"I'd like to see that intel," she stated.

Jack nodded. "I can send it to you."

"Is there a reason that the President hasn't pardoned him? Wouldn't that take away the TRC's narrative about him being a domestic terrorist?"

Jack nodded slightly as he took his seat. *That's odd. She seems to have some sort of attachment to Lopez. Now she's advocating his cause.* "It might help, but this is not a simple decision. Politics plays a part in this. If the President pardons him prior to the election—when people are doubting his validity in the office in the first place—well, it makes it look like he sponsored Raul's actions. Once we win the election, the matter is less of an issue."

"Mr. Desmond," she said slowly. "Newmerica will never acknowledge the President's winning, regardless of how legitimate it is. You are a smart man; you know that."

Only Charli talks back to me that way, with such candor. "I know," he said an octave lower. "But after an election the lines will be drawn. We will know exactly where our support is. Then we can move to reunify the country."

"Civil war," she stated coldly.

"As a last resort," Jack replied. "Some of the geographies that support Newmerica will fold when we show up. As much as they like the system, loyalties are cheap in the enemy camp. The rest, well, we will use force to get them to comply."

"It will get messy."

"That's why I count on you," Jack said, flashing her a rare smile to hide how he really felt. The war was already on. It had started before the President had been sworn in. Jack had already been orchestrating the conflict for America for a long time. Everyone expects to see armies in the field fighting, but this is a different kind of civil war. *We are fighting precise digital attacks against targets. Neither side is willing to call it a war yet, but that time is almost upon us. The time for armies battling it out may come...Colonel Reager has already taken enemy fire and returned the favor. For now, it is a shadowy war.* He bore the burden for igniting the conflict alone. It weighed heavily on him. *After what they did to my family, I owe these bastards the blood I've spilled.*

"I'm not a warrior," she said flatly. "I'm an agent of chaos...a fly in the ointment...a person that causes trouble while solving trouble."

"I know," Jack returned. "I also know that Newmerica betrayed you, from the highest level. They played you like a pawn. I'm not going to do that."

"Everyone says that. Trust me. I won't betray you," she countered. "Politicians can't resist betrayal. It's in their genes. It is their go-to drug of choice. They love stabbing people in the back."

Jack leaned back in the chair and forced a grin. "I'm not a politician."

"You're the President's Chief of Staff. By your very nature that makes you political."

"Oh, I'm political—you have to be in my job. I spend a lot of time trying to hold together this fragile little alliance we have. I know what you mean about politicians; more than one has tried to turn on me. But that doesn't make me a politician. I'm in this for restoration of the country—nothing more, nothing less. I have no political ambitions. I didn't ask for this job; the President told me to take it. You didn't ask for your job either—that's something we share. When all of this is over, I will walk away. If you want it, I hope you do too."

Caylee seemed to study him for a long moment, staring into his face. He could feel her eyes penetrating him more than any CAT scan or MRI.

I hope he's right. I hope I survive and can walk away when this is over. "Alright then. Let's hope when the dust settles that both of us can walk away. In the meantime, I have been working on the little assignment you gave me—taking down the TRC."

We got too personal for a moment...so she's returning to business. "I take it you have come up with a way to pull it off?"

She cocked her left eyebrow for a moment. "I have a strategy, but it is complicated."

"Enlighten me," Jack said almost playfully.

She stabbed at her PC and the projector on the far wall flickered on, showing a single PowerPoint slide. Caylee's slide was plain, black-on-white text. Jack was struck by that because most presentations made to him were more decorative than filled with substance. It was titled, "How the TRC Operates." His eyes scanned the words, but he turned to her for the true meaning behind them.

"The TRC is a people-heavy operation. Big Tech has algorithms that look through social media and email for key words and phrases. Those get blocked and are routed to the TRC in The District. They have a massive data center buried stories under their HQ. The individual posts, videos, emails—whatever—are all filtered and sent to specialists who recraft them, flag the ones that need to go to the NSF or SEs for their action, and the staff rewrites or restructures the posts to fit the TRC's narrative."

"This seems labor intensive. If your slide is right, they have thousands of people sitting there, manually recrafting what goes out. Why don't they use artificial intelligence to do that work?"

"I dug into that. They tried it, but it didn't work. AI can craft text, but it requires a human touch to make it feel as if it were written by the originator. People could easily spot the text that the computers generated. So, in typical government fashion, they threw bodies at the problem—thousands of them."

"It seems like the data center is a single point of failure then," Jack said, nodding at the slide. "Take that out and the TRC is shut down."

"True. Unfortunately, the DHS people in the NSF figured that out as well. There's no easy way to take it down and no hope of getting out of there alive. I've gone over what info we have on the data center and it is secured better than some NSA sites. We could send in a team with explosives, but to get in and out would be a bloodbath—low chance of success."

"Bio attack on the building?"

"After the attacks a few months ago, DHS has done a good job of tightening up those loose ends."

Jack remembered the attacks he had directed against the NSF. "Car bomb?"

She shook her head. "Since the President was sworn in, The District is on an elevated level of security—code orange. I'm not sure we could get a vehicle with a large enough explosive charge in close enough to the building to take it down and kill the staff."

Caylee spoke about killing thousands of people in a casual manner that he appreciated. Jack had been the same way with the attacks he had planned. *She can't afford to think of the moral implications of her actions, not in her line of work.* "I take it you have found a flaw or two that we can exploit."

She nodded once. "Everything comes into the data center via the Internet from the West Coast. Rather than take out the data center, we can deprive it of the data the TRC needs."

"How do we do that?"

"We take down the Internet for The District."

Jack paused for a moment, and then leaned forward on the table, resting his arms on the polished wood surface. "Is that even possible?"

Caylee cracked a thin smile, a hint of pride. "It requires multiple ops, but it *is* possible. Almost all of the Internet traffic for The District comes through a series of exchanges—big buildings with servers, fiber optic lines, and manned by an army of geeks. These private companies have been outsourced with managing the traffic, bandwidth, and distribution." She paused long enough to change slides. "Three centers in Virginia handle around 90 percent of the traffic for The District. CoreSite in Reston, EvoSwitch in Manassas, DuPont Fabros in Ashburn and Equinix, also in Ashburn." Her slide showed aerial photographs of the massive buildings. Jack looked at them. *Hell, I've probably driven by at least one of these and never realized their importance.*

"What I am proposing is that we take these facilities out—in unison if possible. If we do this, the TRC will be cut off. Their people will not get the feeds to edit. They won't be able to send material to their other locations."

Jack's eyes opened wider at her words. "It will take down the entire Internet for The District, won't it?"

Caylee nodded. "I talked to cyber-specialists. It will, including all access via the phone networks. If you take down one site, the load can be shifted to another—but it slows Internet traffic in the process. Take down two, and you start an overload situation on those that remain. Take down all four, and The District will be totally cut off, along with most of Northern Virginia. The experts say it may cause a ripple effect all along the East Coast—massive slowdowns, system outages, you name it."

Jack turned from the images to Caylee. "How can it be that our infrastructure is so vulnerable? You would have thought that our foreign enemies would have taken advantage of this long ago."

"We have always given lip service to cybersecurity in this country. For years, our strategy has been to react to attacks and threats. These centers are guarded, not by a big force, but they have physical and organic security. While they are in Northern Virginia, they are spread out. It isn't an easy task. Most terrorists go for the easy, soft targets."

His mind raced with a storm of thoughts. *I hadn't planned to take down the entire Internet—just the TRC.* He tried to contemplate what the downsides of this change in scope might be, but none came to mind. *People will panic—they will be mad. Without the TRC directing their rage, it might fall on the FedGov and Newmerica.*

"How long will they be in the dark?"

She paused for a moment. "Depending on the breakage and damage, at least two weeks, if not longer. I will try to keep the body count to a minimum, but there's no way to avoid taking some lives as part of this. The more effective our attacks, the more people get killed."

I have a lot of blood on my hands already. It was a sobering thought. These attacks, like the ones he had orchestrated against the NSF, took out noncombatants. It weighed heavy on him each time he ordered such a mission. The only thing that steadied him was that Newmerica had inflicted damage on millions of people during its rise and grasp on power. *They killed Barbara and the kids, and they were innocent.* While he hated the idea of stooping to the level of his enemy, sometimes there were no alternatives. *There may be a reckoning someday for what we have to do to win, but for now, we need to be all-in.*

"This seems manpower intensive," Jack said, turning his focus away from the dead to the plan itself.

"Regretfully, it is. I will need multiple teams," she said, disconnecting her laptop. The projection screen on the wall between them immediately went black. Jack was impressed with her request. *Caylee isn't the kind of person to ask for help. It's not in her nature. She has always conveyed to me that she was a solo operator, not a team person.*

"There is an unanticipated side effect of this kind of attack," she continued.

"Which is?"

"If we struck at the TRC directly, the NSF would know that was our target. Since we are talking about taking down the Internet, it impacts the TRC, but also every other FedGov agency. They will be confused as to why we attacked in this manner. NSF is already stretched thin with the work you and Kara did prior to the swearing in. Now we will add a new layer of confusion in their ranks. Resources will be devoted to try to learn our real intent."

Jack's grin grew measurably. "I like that. I like to think that the confusion you mentioned is an ally."

"Sun Tzu?" she asked.

"No. Jack Desmond," he replied, referring to himself in the third person. *This may work.* A new admiration rose in him when it came to Caylee. She thought outside the box on this one. "I have some people that can help—former Navy Seals, specialists in this kind of operation. I will put them in contact with you."

"Excellent. I need demolition experts, comms people who understand this tech stuff. I have blueprints for two of these facilities, but I need geeks that can help me find further flaws with the facilities."

"I can make that happen," Jack replied.

University of Virginia
Charlottesville, Virginia

Maddie's parents slowed as they drove through the parking lot of her dormitory, coming to a stop where she was standing, waiting for them. The autumn breeze penetrated her jacket as she slid into the warm car. All around campus the leaves had fallen, except for a hickory tree that stubbornly clung to its brown, dead foliage. Seeing her parents in the front seat made her smile.

She had looked forward to her parents' visit. She had given thought to her meeting with Brad and Tina. She didn't want to tell them the details, but to feel them out about resistance groups on campus. If anyone would know about them, it would be her father. She knew his advice would be to stay away from them, but she hoped he might know something about them that would help her make the right decisions about engaging with the pair that had reached out and offered her protection.

"You didn't have to do a drive by, Dad," she said. "You could have come up."

"We know, but we thought it best," her mother replied as her father accelerated away from campus.

"I'm glad you're visiting. I graduate in a few weeks, and I will be home soon for Thanksgiving. Is there a reason for this trip?"

Her father's deep voice came from the driver's seat. "There is," he said, stopping at a red light. "We've had a little complication." There was something about the way he said the word, 'complication' that made her nervous.

"What's wrong?"

"Your father and I were at dinner in Midlothian and, well, we were seen by an old friend," her mother said. Her voice had become more serious.

Her family had changed their names; adopted new identities after the Fall. He had been a representative in the House of Delegates, a staunch Republican politician and well-known lawyer. When it was clear that they were on a list and destined to be rounded up like so many of his colleagues, they had gone underground. Being seen was bad—that had been drilled into her for years. "When you say you were seen, are you *sure* they saw you?"

"It was Doris Mosley," her mother said. "She even came to the table and said hello. We couldn't get away from her."

"What does this mean?" she asked as her father drove through the intersection, putting more distance between them and the campus.

"She doesn't know what name we are living under, but Doris has to know that Social Enforcement is looking for us. No doubt she will tell the authorities she saw us, if nothing else, merely to cash in on the reparation points for the tip," he said. "They will start combing the area looking for us—bringing in NSF assets. If we stay put, it is only a matter of time before they find us."

Maddie heard something in her father's voice she had not heard in a long time—fear. He had worked hard to keep his family out of the Social Quarantine camps. A lot of his close friends and colleagues had simply disappeared in the night. Social Enforcers looted their homes. Some moved in and claimed the property. The people that were taken away never seemed to come back. The thought of that happening with her parents suddenly swept her with anxiety.

"So what are we going to do?" she asked nervously, leaning between the driver and passenger seats.

"*We* aren't going to do anything yet," her father said firmly. "Your mom, David and I are going to move again. I hate doing it…we'll lose the equity we built up in the house, but there's no other way. We may need to get new identities," he said with a dejected voice.

Her younger brother David was going to hate that decision. Maddie had learned to adapt to the moves easily because she was off in college. David was moved from school to school, never getting friends for more than a year at a time.

"What about me?" she asked.

Her mother turned, reached back, took her hand, and squeezed it. "You are close to graduating," she said. "We want you to finish. We will relocate, but you will remain here."

Maddie's mind was a blur of emotions. She was angry at what had happened to her family; furious at Newmerica who would do this to people; afraid for her family; worried that she might be discovered; concerned about graduating. Slumping back in her seat, she said nothing for a long minute as her father continued to drive.

"Where will you go?" she finally said.

"Virginia is too risky. We are thinking of going to Tennessee or West Virginia," her father said. "They are safer than being here…less risk of being seen."

How long do we have to live on the run, hiding who we are? "This isn't fair," Maddie said as if she were a petulant child. "We haven't done anything wrong."

"We don't like it either, honey," her mother replied as the car turned a sharp corner. "If they find us, it will be trouble with the SEs."

"We're a threat," her father added, his voice slightly crisper, angrier. "We represent opposition, and that is one thing that the government can't tolerate. They can't have dissenting voices. They intimidate…use fear and threats to silence anyone that might speak out against them. They know that the only real danger to them remaining in power is people who believe they can and should be removed. Ideals the opposite of their ideas can topple them. So they crush and suppress everyone that might dare to speak out." There was fire in his voice, and Maddie had heard it many times before. It was her father the politician, the lawyer, the man who had represented his constituents. *They haven't crushed him, not entirely.* She wanted to smile, but the burden of the news seemed to prevent it.

The car angled into a small diner several miles outside of town. "We don't talk about this inside," her father said. "We're going to sit down and have a meal as a family."

Maddie nodded as the sedan came to a stop. *I can't bring up Brad and Tina…not now. They already have too much on their minds. With my family at risk, I need all of the allies that I can muster. I have to rely on my instincts.*

CHAPTER 15

"The loudest voices are the ones that are right."

Livingston, Tennessee

Deja had never traveled to a foreign country. When she was younger, her mother could not afford such luxuries and even with the Great Reformation, she did not make enough to afford such a trip. Her mother talked about driving with her grandparents across the country, but that was a daunting task now. Electric cars had limited ranges and long recharge times, and gasoline-powered cars required Green ration cards. Some friends had gone to Canada by train when she was younger, but they hadn't spoken highly of the trip. As Detective Gallagher drove through Livingston, Tennessee, she wondered if Tennessee was different than a foreign country.

Being in the south was bad enough. Her grandparents on her mother's side were born in Alabama and had filled her with stories of the redneck and prejudiced people that lived there. While the last shots of the Civil War had been fired over a century and a half earlier, there was a feeling that the war was not over. No matter how much progress came to the south, to Deja, it felt as if the red clay soil was hostile ground…a land of white supremacists looking for a reason to lynch innocent victims. It was only confirmed when they drove through Livingston.

The American flag had been banned since the Liberation. Anyone possessing one faced social justice and criminal charges. Bounties had been offered to turn your flag in for cash, or in exchange for a new Newmerica flag. Yet in Livingston, the stars and stripes was displayed everywhere. The post office on Main Street had a flag fluttering in the autumn breeze in defiance of mandates from the Ruling Council. Several houses had flags hanging from their porches. She was angry to the point where she couldn't articulate it. *That flag is racist! These people are racists for flying it. They are broadcasting that they are corrupt.* As the car turned into the parking lot of the Overton Motel, she saw a seemingly happy black family walking down the street, and even that irritated her. *How can they betray the rest of us, living in a community filled with such hate? What is wrong with these people?*

The Ruling Council had replaced the tainted red, white, and blue banner several times since coming to power. It was the only way to ensure that every disparate group was represented—give each faction some aspect of a flag. A single flag could never do that. The old flag was for a nation that had been built on slavery, on corruption, and on genocide. It represented a history that was horrific in every way. Yet here, in Tennessee, people were now breaking the law, flying symbols of oppression. *I am in a foreign country...one filled with traitors.*

Deja remembered what the country was like before the Liberation. The government never seemed to care about people. The Ruling Council had changed all of that. Reparation payments had helped a lot of people buy things they never could afford. You could augment them by simply turning in violators, which was easy. As a Social Enforcer, she had taken things from those that defied the Ruling Council. In the early days the pickings were far better; when families were shipped off to Social Quarantine, their goods were often divvied up by the SEs. *It was only fair...those people were traitors.*

Under it all was the feeling that the old American nation was built on a foundation of evil. All one had to do was look at the treatment of the Native Americans or the slaves brought from Africa. In old America they tried to ignore those scars in favor of looking at the positive things. Newmerica had changed all of that. The ugliness that was the rot in the heart of the old nation was laid bare. For Deja, that was part of the healing—making people admit their flaws and their roles in the oppression of others. *Our forcing people to acknowledge their inherent flaws was a growing experience for them.*

She, like others, had heard that Tennessee had betrayed Newmerica—

but until she had crossed the border and had seen the place, she did not realize how different it was. They have turned their back on everything that we built over the last five years. As she glanced around, she saw a nearby convenience store with a digital slogan board of the Truth Reconciliation Committee. It was still running with the words, "Equity is within reach if you believe it is," followed by the TRC logo. *They have not entirely crushed Newmerica here.* It was one of the few things that made her smile.

It had not been easy to get across the border from Kentucky into Tennessee. Their rental car had been checked, though the police had not spotted the hidden cache of weapons in their luggage. Their IDs, which Gallagher provided, had been for auditors on a business trip to visit a client. She had even changed clothes to quasi-business attire so that she fit the part. The Tennessee Highway Patrol that had stopped them had scrutinized their story and paperwork, scanned the Federal IDs and logged them, and done a cursory check. The IDs passed muster since they were legitimate identification cards—among the few advantages of working within the NSF infrastructure as far as Deja could see.

The others of their party were waiting in Gallagher's hotel room. The thick drapes were pulled, plunging the room into darkness until the lights flicked on. They had not spent much time together since their rendezvous in Kentucky, driving in two separate vehicles. Now that she saw the party sitting on the twin beds checking their weapons, she felt more normal. Two of the group were males, or she assumed they identified as such. Their arms were massive, thick muscles covered by tattoos, one with the screaming eagle logo of a military unit, if she remembered correctly. The two nonmales were very different. One, Gloria, was small, short, almost perfectly filling the false role of an auditor. *She is not much of a threat.* The other was a thick-around-the-waist person adorned with a number of piercings along her eyebrows and in her nose. She identified as a female, or so she claimed, but there was little feminine about her. Her hair was short, looking as if she had cut it herself using a mirror. Her round, plastic rimmed glasses seemed too small for the pudgy cheeks. Her name was Donna, an SE from Lexington, Kentucky, though Deja wondered how much help she would be if trouble reared its ugly head. Gallagher had insisted on blending their team with SEs and NSF staff.

Deja pulled the chair from a small writing desk and sat down as Detective Gallagher spoke. "Well, we made it this far," he began. "Now it's a matter of waiting until someone spots this Raul Lopez. Once they do, we are poised to bring him in."

"How is the progress on that?" asked the male with the eagle tattoo. His name was Chad.

"The last message I got a few hours ago said that the NSF has fielded over 90,000 leads."

"Shit!" the other male, named French, snapped, shaking his head. "They'll never get through all of those."

"A million dollar reward is going to have everyone turning in everyone else," Gloria said.

"It's going to take them a while to filter through all of that," the detective said. "The attacks on the NSF have crippled our analytical capabilities. We've tapped DHS to help on this one, but it is going to take time to narrow down to the credible ones. Those are the ones we will get our eyes on."

"So what do we do in the meantime?" Donna asked.

"We wait."

"Are we safe here?" Deja asked. "We are in hostile territory."

"It's not hostile," Gallagher said. "They have flipped and are going back to America."

"They're traitors," she spat back. Donna nodded in agreement, which made Deja unsure whether she was happy about that fact. "Newmerica gave these people everything, and they turned their back on them for a false President."

Gallagher shook his head and crossed his arms. "You're overreacting a bit, Deja. Don't let the flags fool you. Plenty of people down here support Newmerica. Right now, they won't show their colors. There's too much of that extremist patriotism going on. They are laying low. This entire state is not behind that asshole in Nashville. We have more support than you might think. This isn't hostile. It's different—more like the old days."

"This isn't nostalgia for them," Chad said. "People saw that stuff with the Social Quarantine camps being 'liberated' and began to question things. They never had good reason to do it before. With the Pretender suddenly popping up, they actually think things can return to the way they used to be."

"A lot of them never accepted the new normal," French said. "We should have been harder on people…pounded it into them what freedom was all about."

"It's those damned churches," Donna said. "You can't have people out there—people not governed by the state—teaching other people what is right and wrong. It confuses people…gives them the wrong ideas. Consistency is the key to keeping people in line. Churches are more of a problem than a solution."

Deja found herself nodding. Her grandmother insisted on going to church until it was forced to close due to the new tax laws the Ruling Council had passed. The loss of the church had not hurt her grandmother one bit from what she had seen. "That's all part of the problem, but it's not the root cause. Our issue is that we have been too soft on people. When a kid like Raul Lopez can turn traitor, it simply means someone didn't do their job of looking for problem children. We should have done a better job of finding dissidents. Sending them to camps wasn't good enough." *We should have killed them...and their families. Trying to reeducate people is a waste of time. Examples need to be made, ones that will be remembered.*

"I'm not so sure about that," French said. "We have done some pretty dark shit to get where we are today."

"We did it for their own good," Gloria said; her high-pitched voice seemed almost in contrast to the harsh words she spoke. "Some people are so stubborn. You have to beat it into them. I'm not so sure that Deja is too far off. If we had been a little harder, Raul Lopez might not have happened in the first place."

"God knows they have held us down for generations, beaten us back," Deja said. *No amount of pain we inflict is ever going to make things right.*

"I've looked at Lopez's file in detail. There was no indication anywhere in his background that he was a radical. I mean, shit, the kid joined the Youth Corps. The kids who do that are pretty committed."

"Are they?" Donna asked. "Maybe he joined to take advantage of the program."

"I saw his file," Gallagher countered. "Whatever changed him happened in Detroit. Up until then, he was like any other kid."

"I saw the same file," Chad said. "The kid had religion in him—Catholicism. No doubt that messed with his head."

"Or," Gallagher offered, "Maybe the local SEs leaned on them too hard. There were reports of their violence against the Youth Corps group."

"We don't have to know what triggered him," Chad returned. "It doesn't matter. The fact that he could think that it was OK to stand against Newmerica is the problem. Deja is right; we have been too soft on the individuals that have stood against the will of the people. If we had cracked a few more heads, put a lot more of them in the grave, this Raul kid never would have even thought to pull a trigger and start a riot."

"Fear is necessary, but it's not a necessary evil," Deja replied. "If you use fear for the right reasons, for the right outcomes, it is the best tool we have. We can't afford to have more kids turn on the country like this Raul did." The words flowed from her mouth as if they were part of a poem or a song. They described what she felt in her heart.

There was a silent pause in the motel room as each of them reflected on the words that were spoken. *We are all feeling a bit of tension that didn't exist a few months ago...challenges to the Ruling Council are rare.* That emotion, the tenseness, hung in the stagnant air of the dark room. "Well, all our superiors think this Lopez is either here or in Texas. We have teams operating there. We should consider ourselves lucky. Texas is a tougher nut to crack than Tennessee." Deja understood that comment far too well. While Texas had technically been part of Newmerica, it had been the epicenter of resistance until the last few months when Tennessee had stolen that spotlight.

Deja didn't feel lucky to be in Tennessee. It wasn't at all how she imagined a southern state—it was far worse. People were willing to demonstrate their disloyalty here without fear—the fear they all should have. No matter how much they tried to sugar coat it or compare it with other places like Texas, it did not feel right, or safe. We are surrounded by people who don't think the way we do, and that makes them threats. Her hand drifted down to the gun in the holster on her hip. Touching the handle gave her a sense of security.

We can't find this douchebag Lopez fast enough ...

The Western White House
Nashville, Tennessee

Charli greeted Caylee with a warm smile as she entered the room. For weeks at a time Caylee had disappeared. While Charli and Jack suspected that it had something to do with the deaths of the NSF Secretary's mother and brother, neither bothered to ask. She presumed that Jack didn't want to know if Caylee had been involved—such knowledge might taint his impression of her. Charli didn't ask out of professional courtesy. *I have spilled a lot of blood for this cause myself; who am I to judge her?*

Charli didn't talk about the restless nights to anyone other than Andy. They usually came when storms rumbled nearby. For Charli, that triggered nightmares about the Falls Church bombing, and she was jolted awake. Andy understood and did what he could to calm her. She tried to console herself that they were the enemy—NSF investigators that would have taken down Jack's restoration of the Presidency. Saying it, and coping with the thought that she was responsible for the deaths of hundreds, if not more, ate away at her in the quiet of the night.

"Thanks for coming in," Charli said as she closed the door behind them. "Can I get you anything?"

"Thank you, Charli," Caylee responded. The fact that she used her last name registered with Charli. *Caylee doesn't usually do that. It's a sign of trust, or respect, or both.*

"Look, I'll get right to the point," she said, opening her laptop. "We've had a few incidents recently. Nothing major—simple fender bender car accidents. Each one has forced us to divert the motorcade. Another one happened two days ago."

"Go on."

"Statistically, it's more accidents around this building than we have had in over a year. It stands out to me and my people."

For a long moment, Caylee said nothing in response. "You think someone is probing your security."

Charli nodded. "It's possible that I'm being overly cautious. But I'd like your take."

"Given the circumstances and who you are protecting, I'd be disappointed if you weren't being overly cautious."

It was a compliment of sorts, the kind that only Caylee could deliver.

"I had my people pull video footage of the surrounding area to see if we could spot anyone that might be doing observation. We did find this man," she said, turning her laptop toward Caylee. Two images were blurry. He had dark hair, barely visible under two different ball caps. Both images showed someone that seemed to be dressed casually, one time in a red T-shirt, another in a blue golfing shirt—none with identifying marks.

Caylee walked over to the laptop and stared intently at the images, zooming in on them with the mouse pad.

"With the new incident a few days ago, we were a little more ready. We spotted this man, who I think may be the same person." She reached down and pulled up a third image. This one was crisper, clearer. His Ray-Bans did a good job of hiding his eyes, but his cheek structure looked strikingly like the others. Caylee leaned in on the new image, squinting as she looked at it.

"Can you show me where these alleged accidents took place?"

Charli nodded and led her out. It was an unusually warm day. Indian Summer was what the weatherman had called it. The pair of them walked like two professional women out for a stroll as she ushered her through the locations. At each one the former operative stopped, drinking in the scenes, silently soaking up the ground. It took the better part of an hour for them to hit all of the sites. At the last one, where the accident had recently occurred, Caylee finally stopped.

"What do you want to know?"

"Is my hunch right—are our procedures being tested?"

"That looks to be the same person," she said. "Given what you have shown me, I would say you are up against a professional. Amateurs sometimes stalk their targets, but those types are just that—stalkers. They are more prone to take advantage of situations. Like the creep going after some famous movie star will make their move on them when they are in town for a premiere or a press junket. If this is an assassin, he's measuring what you do to find a way to manipulate the environment."

"Is it an operative?"

"Unknown," Caylee replied. "The United States has enemies beyond Newmerica's usual suspects. Whoever this guy is, he's willing to operate close to the White House here. I wouldn't rule it out."

"Some of his bad drivers are SEs. It *feels* like a Newmerica thing,"

Charli pressed. "We have one of the drivers under surveillance now."

"If I were doing it, I would use pawns to throw you off the scent. Then again, he's operating here, basically outside of Newmerica. It might be the best that he can do, using loyalists to do his dirty work."

"Do you know this guy?" Charli asked.

Caylee shook her head. "If he's an operative, he's not one I know. It's not like we had annual meetings or anything. Our very nature is secrecy. I met one or two because of missions, but that was the extent of it. No, I don't know who he is."

It was a shot in the dark and Charli knew that when she asked. *Damn, it would have been perfect if she recognized him.* A man brushed past them on the street, and she eyed him carefully as he went down the sidewalk, aware that they were talking in public. No one was within earshot of their conversation as the man turned the corner onto Rosa Park Boulevard. "We checked cell tower traffic, but it is hard to sort out in a meaningful way. Thousands of people work down here."

"He's going to use multiple phones anyway, probably some burners," she countered. "He's not going to live in the area; he'll be commuting in, probably on public transportation. If he is an operative, he will be mapping your cameras, so moving them or adding more will throw his game off a bit. He will make his trail hard to catch."

It's like trying to catch a ghost. "Caylee, this is your world. My universe is around keeping the President alive. If this guy is an assassin, that's something you understand better than me…I'm willing to admit it. What is his play? How would you be approaching it if it were your assignment? Any insights you have are going to be helpful in nailing this bastard before he strikes."

Caylee surveyed the street in a long moment of deep thought. "This isn't far off from some stuff Jack has me working. Chances are he's learned that the target building and immediate perimeter are solid, solid enough for him not to risk trying to penetrate it. It's not enough to get in; you have to have a reasonable chance of getting out. Being an operative means you're good, but not suicidal.

"The motorcade is a hard target too, but it is exposed," she said, sweeping the street again with her eyes. "You can't use a rifle, not a traditional one. Even if you had an M 107, you know, the 50 cal sniper rifle, you can't see inside the vehicle to hit your target anyway. If he's using accidents to change traffic flows and your route, he's either trying to stop the target so that it is easier to hit, or guide it to where he can spring his trap."

"No rifle," Charli repeated. "So…a bomb?"

Caylee gave her a slight shrug. "That limo is a tank if I recall properly. The only way to get at someone inside it is to use appropriate force. In this case, I'd bet on explosives—a lot of them. Chances are he is already assembling whatever his device is. You may want to try tracking unusual fertilizer purchases, that kind of thing, but if he's smart—and I think he is—he's likely doing small purchases to avoid detection."

Shit. Charli had suspected as much, but hearing it from Caylee was strangely relieving. "We've tack-welded all of the manhole covers. It would take a lot to pry open the limo. How would you get the bomb to the target?"

"I wouldn't," she said flatly. "I would get you to bring the limo to me. This will be a sizable bomb we are talking about…it has to be sizable to take out the limo."

"That's why he is playing with us then…he's trying to guide the motorcade to a killing zone."

"That would be my approach. It allows him to do the job and get away." Caylee cupped her hand to shield her eyes as she turned to look in another direction.

"Anything else?" Charli asked with trepidation.

"I trained at the Farm in Virginia. There are some basics about assassination attempts. Unless you are a crazed fanatic willing to die for your cause, you have to have the means to get away. Otherwise, you're a liability if you are apprehended. He will also need the means to detonate the device. That can be done with a cell phone and experience. We learned in Iraq that it also means he has to be close enough to make sure he sets it off at the right time."

Charli processed the information carefully. "We can arrange for jamming of cell service around the motorcade. It will be a bit of an inconvenience to everyone in the area, but it isn't for long."

"I'd also recommend doing sweeps of license plates. Build a database of the ones that should be here, and the ones that don't belong."

"I'm way ahead of you on that front," Charli replied. "We've been doing that for two weeks already."

"That's a good start. This person is going to have a fallback mechanism of some sort. You don't have a plan without a backup plan, and that backup plan has a backup plan or three. That's the way of operatives. People think it's all about the investigative work or the actions we undertake. In reality, the world I live in is about planning."

How do I counter someone like this? Changes to perimeter security were a start. *I can start inspecting vehicles for explosives, deploy more detection dogs...but the scope of this is big.* She glanced up the street and saw a group of newspaper boxes. *Things like that, which could hide a bomb—they have to go.* "Do you have any other advice for me?"

She paused, lowering her hand from her brow, then taking a step closer toward her, closing in on her personal space. Charli didn't flinch, but a part of her understood the person in front of her. *Caylee is a killer, dedicated, and professional. She is skilled, almost artistic in her work.* There was also acknowledgement that she was like the woman she faced. It was, in that moment on a Nashville street, a chilling realization. *She's a mirror of me.*

"This person will disguise himself. He will disguise his bomb too. It will be big; it has to be to take out the limo. Take nothing for granted. Constantly change your approach; alter your patterns. He will take refuge in things you do over and over the same way. Don't give him that. The more things alter, the harder it is for him to execute an effective plan."

I have limited staff, and some with not much experience. Damn it all! "Anything else?"

"He's confident, maybe to the point of being overconfident," she said. "In these pictures you showed me—he isn't trying to conceal himself. He's standing there, drinking his coffee in two of them. If it were me, I would not be out in the open. That kind of observation can be done from anywhere—but he has chosen to do it in public."

"Maybe he's only playing a game with us."

The former operative shook her head. "No—though I wouldn't rule out arrogance on his part. He thinks you are incapable of stopping him. That's how strongly he feels that his plan will work at this stage."

"Overconfidence ..." Charli said. "That's not a lot to work with."

"It is the flaw of Newmerica. They think themselves smarter than anyone else. Their cockiness emboldens them. It makes them think they are beyond reach. Five years of having utter control and power does that to people. Remember this though; it is a flaw."

"Thanks Caylee," she said with a hint of resignation in her voice. "You've given me a lot to think about."

"Catch him," she replied coldly. "If you don't, everything that has been done up to this point is wasted effort."

CHAPTER 16

"Do you like the weather today? Thank your government and the New Green Deal!"

Indiana National Guard Armory, Michigan City, Indiana

Trip was about to leave his quarters to head over to his office when his iPhone rang. He expected to see the word, "Spam" but instead saw his wife's name. For a moment he didn't respond. Since their divorce he had only spoken with her once, when their pet dog Murry had to be put down. There was a lot of bad blood between them near the end of their relationship and talking only seemed to make things worse. Heated words were like missiles—once fired, they couldn't be recalled. By the time of the divorce, Trip had simply given her everything she asked for and more. He had a lot of fight in him, but couldn't bear to unload it on her.

He touched the green connect button and held the phone to his ear. "Hello Nancy," he managed.

"Trip."

Then came a few moments of silence. His ex-wife continued the conversation. "Are you OK?"

Am I? Trip liked to think he was fine, but stationed near the Illinois border, facing what he thought was an inevitable confrontation, he was not sure how to respond. "I'm fine," he managed.

"I saw you on the news," Nancy said. "What are you doing up there? You know that is going to lead to trouble." Her south-Texas drawl was still as seductive as ever.

It had never dawned on Trip that the incident with the tank might be on the news. *No doubt the TRC has spun it up that we started it all.* "I'm here because the President wants me here."

"You could have gotten yourself killed a few years ago," she scolded. "Hell, you still might. You don't need to be there."

It was odd that Nancy was concerned about him. He hadn't expected that. Usually the words between them were so short, angry, and curt. "I have my duty."

"You could have said *no*. They owe you that much after…well…you know …"

San Antonio. She had a hard time saying it even after these years. *I probably could have said no, but it would have caused drama that was unnecessary.* Fighting for what was right, fighting for America or its values—that was who Trip Reager was. It defined his existence. Saying no would have been contrary to that. "I'm an officer in the Guard. We have a President now and he's my Commander in Chief. That means I do what I'm told. You know the drill." He almost called her 'honey' at the end, but those days were long gone.

"When I saw you on TV, I—I didn't know what to think. I got worried. It was like you were being deployed overseas all over again. That anxiety I had when you took another tour of duty, it all came back."

Trip felt the urge to quell her fears, as he had done when he'd gone off to Iraq. Despite the bitterness between them, something was still there. He heard it in her voice and felt it in his soul. "You know me, Nancy; I'll keep my head down." It wasn't a lie. Trip also wasn't telling the whole truth. He had always believed that you couldn't lead your troops from the rear. If and when the shooting started, he intended to be close to it.

"You haven't asked about Jessie," she prodded.

"No," he said slowly. "I haven't."

"She's our daughter, Trip." It wasn't a statement—it was a plea.

"She turned on our family, you included," Trip flatly said. That was bitterness that Trip couldn't shake. Ultimately it was the wedge that tore their family apart. Nancy had done all she could to connect with Jessie, but she had been rebuffed over and over again. Nancy blamed Trip, especially after the events in San Antonio. Trip could forgive many things, but not a child that turned against her own parents. He wished he could; there was even a bit of regret from time to time, but in the end he always found himself in the same place…Jessie's betrayal.

"I spoke with her a few days ago. She lives in Hartford, Connecticut. She's working in a college library up there."

Trip wasn't sure how to respond and struggled because he knew he had to say something. "OK."

"You should try to patch things up with her," Nancy pressed. "I think she's in a good place now. She's very active on campus still. She took my call though, and that's a good start."

Active on campus—*she's still fighting for Newmerica…fighting against me.* "I don't have anything to say to her," Trip replied slowly.

"You need to do it while there's still time."

She thinks I'm going to die. Does she know something I don't? "There will be time when this is all over," he finally said with a breathy tone. "Jessie has my number. She can reach out to me at any time. She doesn't need you fighting her battles for her. If she wants to talk, she knows my number."

Nancy's voice wavered slightly. "She's like you, damned stubborn."

"You used to like that about me."

"It used to be something I admired," she conceded. "Now it makes me angry and sad."

She's disappointed in me, still. "I can't change who I am, Nancy."

"She's your daughter. You're her father. You can't shut that off. You have an obligation."

I shut her out of my life a long time ago…you know that. "I have an obligation here," he said firmly. "This is where I need to be. If Jessie wants to bury the hatchet, she can find me when all of this is over. Until then, my responsibility is with my country and my President."

"You haven't changed, Trip," she said with a faint sob.

A part of him wanted to say, "I'm sorry," but he couldn't. The only sorrow he felt was for the pain he was causing her still. *I thought getting divorced would allow her to move on—but she can't. She still is thinking of me and of what we had before all of this bullshit happened. Newmerica cost me everything—my wife, my family, my life. God damn. They will pay for that.* "I'm glad you called, Nancy. I appreciate it. I really do."

"Watch yourself, Trip," she warned with another muffled sob. "The other side—they know you. They'd like nothing more than to have your head."

"Don't you worry," he assured her. "I have every intention of coming through this alive." Nancy hung up and Trip slid the phone into his fatigue pants pocket. *Newmerica does this; it stomps on our values; it tears families apart; it trades our freedoms as payment for a false sense of security. It does it and tells us it is for our own good.*

They took from me everything I cared about and twisted it into something I don't even recognize. They have painted me as a war criminal, made me into a monster. By God, I will make these people pay!

Hartsville, Tennessee

Wyatt's Auto Repair and Body Shop was almost as filthy outside as it was inside. It had begun life as a full service gas station decades ago. The pumps and underground tanks had been pulled during one of the many recessions. The convenience store closed shortly thereafter, unable to even compete with 7-Eleven, which wasn't saying much. The cinderblock structure had been turned into a three-bay repair shop. The former parking lot was filled with cars, some customer drop-offs, some abandoned vehicles, and a few for sale by the owners.

The one thing that Wyatt's had going for it was that the owner, Wyatt Dawson, was a committed supporter of Newmerica. Julius Bernstein had gotten his name from an NSF approved list of contacts in Tennessee that were still loyal to the Ruling Council. Julius had gone beyond the list, doing some digging into Dawson's background. During the four waves of COVID, he had taken full advantage of the monies offered by the government. His business had never been a big moneymaker, but the influx of free cash from the government had been a boon for him. His loyalty had been bought and paid for over the last few years. He made more money with his doors closed than he ever made running the shop. To Julius, that meant he could be trusted. *He'll do what he's told out of fear that the gravy train will come to an end.* It was the kind of pressure that the operative liked to use—*money equals self-interest which equals compliance.*

Brown paper covered the windows on the closed bay doors and his work; only one of Dawson's people worked with the owner on refurbishing the old postal truck. Julius stopped by, unannounced in the evenings to make sure they were progressing on the project. The garage stung of oil, grease, and a hint of ozone when the welder was running. The old truck was up on a hoist, looking far worse from the bottom than the top.

Dawson spotted him and walked over, his blue coveralls barely visible under the filth and sweat stains. "She's not much to look at," he said to Julius, jabbing his thumb over his shoulder at the truck. "Damn thing is rusted out. The frame's bent too."

"I need it repaired and painted."

"Well, you see," Dawson said. "That's the thing. It's going to cost more. I had to track down a loaner vehicle in a scrapyard for parts. There's not a lot of these around once the post office is done with them."

Julius stared at the unshaven man whose girth was twice that of his own. He was tempted to say, "Money is no object," but he knew that a man like Dawson would simply take advantage of that. He was a little perturbed that he had gone out to another vendor to get parts. *He's creating loose ends that might come back to bite me at some point.* Julius drew a long, slow breath. Loose ends could be resolved; they merely took time. "How much more are we talking about?"

"At least a thousand, maybe two," he said, grinning.

"That seems a little steep," Julius countered. "How much did you bring back from that dump?"

"It's not only the materials; it's the time."

Julius did not respond immediately. "I'm good with a thousand more," he said. Dawson nodded. "We are going to have to bang together a new set of quarter panels. Most of what is there is rust."

"This isn't a museum level restoration," Julius said. "Get them patched up."

"If we do that, they won't hold together for more than a year or so."

"That's OK. A cosmetic repair is fine. What is more important is that it be able to handle a heavy load, like we had talked about and that she is properly painted."

His words made the taller, bulkier man frown. "I've beefed up the frame—nothing pretty, but it will hold a lot. We used replacement parts for the suspension. These fuckers don't have a lot of smoothness to them.

It'll hold what you asked for, maybe more. The ride might be shit though. I can improve it, but it will require extra *dinero*, if you catch my drift."

"I think we understand each other fine. Don't worry about how it handles. It needs to look like what it is, a postal truck."

Wyatt Dawson shook his head slightly with those words. "No offense, but this is one of the weirdest jobs we've done. You have us rebuilding a postal truck, painting it up like new and all, and you don't care about the body work. What are you going to use this for?"

Julius took a step closer to Dawson, enough so that the big man's lack of deodorant punctured his nostrils with a full assault. "We had an agreement up front, if you recall. No questions. It should be enough for you to know that I work with the NSF and you are being paid well for your services. Understood?"

Dawson eyed him suspiciously. "Yeah, I understand. It seems strange, that's all."

"The NSF appreciates your discretion, Mr. Dawson." There was no threat, merely an implication of a threat—hence the mentioning of the NSF.

The big man turned and lumbered back under the vehicle. Sparks flew from a Tig welder being used by his assistant; the brilliant blue-white light flickered throughout the garage, casting strange shadows. Julius held his hand up to block the blinding light for a minute; then he turned and left the garage.

As he stood outside in the blackness of the night, he heard a rumble of thunder off in the distance. Pulling out his phone, he checked the footage from one of the cameras he had placed near the so-called Southern White House. It was an expensive little system, one he had secreted under a small café table at a deli a half-block up from the Estes Kefauver Federal Building. Every day he went to the table and discreetly pulled the memory chip.

Julius was watching for several things. First was any change to the terrain around the building. One thing had happened; the row of newspaper boxes outside of a small stationary store were removed. Chances were pretty good that the Secret Service was behind that and to his trained eyes, it meant that they were taking additional precautions—things they had not done before. Removing the boxes meant they couldn't be used to conceal explosives.

The second thing he was watching for were the faces of known members of the Presidential detail. The app that he was running was good at identifying facial profiles that he had set up from his observations. One came up as he flicked through the video, flagged with a flashing red circle.

The female was short with crisp, blondish hair. She was with another woman, a little taller, more muscular. They stood on the street corner and seemed to be looking up and down. He paused the image, zooming in on her face.

This is my enemy. Staring intently at her face, he followed the features. He had picked her up before in images. The earpiece she usually wore was not in place, but it was her; Julius was sure of it. He had seen her before, handing out orders to the other detail members. That meant she was in a command role, if not the detail leader herself.

Zooming back out he looked at the other female, tagging the new person's face as one that he wanted to track. *Who is it? A new member of the detail?* The way they seemed to be looking up and down the street—it was not a casual observation taking place. They are doing their own surveillance, studying the ground where I operate. He wished he could hear what they were talking about.

For Julius, it was a warning and one that he took seriously. They suspect something is amiss. His last staged accident had occurred two days earlier. At the time he knew he was pushing the envelope, running the risk of detection. *Is this video evidence of that?*

A number of things ran through his mind. The first was whether it was worth killing the Secret Service leader he saw in the video. It was tempting. She would never expect anyone to go after her...only the Pretender. There were issues with such an assassination though, namely that it would tip off the Secret Service that he was potentially planning something. *Even a staged accidental death might elevate their security.* That was a risk he was not willing to take.

Their presence also made him realize that he could no longer afford to test security the way he had. It was OK; he had gotten the information he desired. The use of a mobile bomb would allow him to position the explosive almost anywhere along the route. *A postal vehicle is almost invisible in the city. No one pays attention to them.* He wouldn't have to alter the motorcade route unless it was diverted to a street opposite of him.

He was still thinking through how to trigger the bomb. Of equal importance, he was attempting to figure out how he was going to get out of the city. Once the President was killed, there would be a lockdown, probably on the level of what happened in Boston after the marathon bombing or in The District after the Liberation. Mass transit and the major roads would be sealed off; searches would be done. If he did everything right, he would be invisible; they wouldn't know to be looking for him. *If they have figured out the accidents were staged, they may have picked up an image of me. That could certainly complicate matters.* It meant that he had to be a greater distance from the assassination scene than originally planned, which meant a more sophisticated trigger.

Another distant, almost strained slow rumble of thunder shook the night air. This time it was louder, warning of the pending storm. Julius shut down his phone and moved the zipper of his jacket up slightly. Everything was going as planned. When he got the word, he would assassinate the President of the so-called United States of America. *Their dream of rebooting America will die with him, in fire and death.*

Arnold Air Force Base, Tullahoma, Tennessee

Raul settled on the couch and began to change channels on the TV, mindlessly flicking past shows that seemed dull. Caylee brought in fresh popcorn and settled on the sofa next to him as he surfed.

Suddenly he saw his mother on the screen and froze. The show was 20/20 and the banner at the bottom said, "Anatomy of a Terrorist." His mother was weeping, talking quickly, her words stabbing out from the television and into his soul. "I keep telling them that he is a good boy. He never would be involved with these people. He loves Newmerica. This has all been some horrible misunderstanding." The camera managed to catch the two guards that stood behind her as she sobbed, wiping the streaks of tears from her puffed cheeks.

The narrator, whose voice was deep and polished, spoke up. "Sadly, in such cases, close family members are often the last to realize how their loved ones are radicalized."

Caylee reached over for the remote control, but Raul moved it away.

"You don't want to watch this," she warned. He ignored her. *I have to see this.* The clip of his mother crying, because of him, seemed to draw the air out of his lungs for a moment.

Next came a psychiatrist, a woman, or so he assumed. He ignored her name in the banner and the California university where she taught. He stared instead at her as if she were in the room with him. "We've seen this before with domestic terrorists. They want to take advantage of everything that the FedGov offers, but at the same time, they develop hatred of the government. They often have influencers, people in positions of authority, who they trust, and they convince them that the very foundation of their beliefs is wrong. These people, these authority figures, find ways to weaken their resolve to the point where they are rebuilt into weapons of terror. If you have a terrorist, you always have this kind of person in their life."

The narrator spoke again. "So who was the person that turned a young, naive kid from Alvarado, Texas, a Youth Corps worker, into Newmerica's most wanted criminal? When we return from break, we'll talk about that."

The image went to a car commercial for the new Chevy Strider, touting its extended battery life. To Raul it was all background noise. He slumped into the sofa, letting the remote drop next to him, opposite of Caylee. Slowly he turned to her.

"You shouldn't watch this, Raul," she said.

"Why are they doing this?" He knew Caylee would answer him honestly—that was her nature.

"As I said before, they want to flush you out. That's why they grabbed your mother. They want to apply pressure."

"Why am I so important to them?" he pleaded. "All I did was help free some people they were mistreating."

"You did more than that, Raul. You broke the cardinal rule of standing up to those SEs in Dearborn, and that led to riots. Yes, they were the ones that led those riots, but the government can't have any one standing up against the system. And it encourages others to keep people from standing up against the system."

"I don't think you understand the kind of symbol you are," she said. "You were their supporter, and you turned against them. If that can happen with you, it can happen with others. It's not enough to bring you to justice, Raul. They have to make an example of you. Every day that you remain free is an act of defiance to them. It tells others that they can be defiant."

"I don't want to be a symbol of anything."

Caylee shrugged. "I have to imagine that a lot of people in history have said the same thing. Unfortunately, you don't get a say in it. Both America and Newmerica see you as representing something to them… one simply is more benevolent than the other. It isn't about you as a person; it's about public relations at this point. Both sides want the hearts and minds of their followers. The difference is that Newmerica has to have compliance from the people. To get it, they will intimidate, lie, and even kill." The last word drifted off with Caylee. *That is what she has had to do for them. She was their tool. She murdered for them.*

"What can I do?"

"Don't give in," she said slowly. The ominous musical sounds of 20/20 came back, flashing the red letters of "Anatomy of a Terrorist." This time, the narrator, was on the screen. "We talked in our last segment with experts who understand terrorists like Raul Lopez. They say that they are almost always corrupted by someone in authority and they turn traitor. So who was that person that misled Lopez and took him down his path of betrayal?

"To get this answer, we need to talk to one of his closest friends, Paco Morales. Paco was Raul's confidant and served with him in the Youth Corp. When the rioting broke out as a result of Lopez's actions, he was held hostage by a cell of the Sons of Liberty until he was rescued a week ago. He can offer all of us a glimpse into the mind of Newmerica's most wanted criminal."

Paco! The last time he'd seen him was in Monroe, Michigan. Seeing Paco's face was both pleasing and disturbing. Makeup had been applied to the bruises on his face, but not well enough to fully hide the swelling. *They didn't rescue him; they captured him.*

The narrator seemed so warm, so friendly, and at the same time, so evil to Raul. "I'm glad you are willing to talk to us," he said. Raul knew that Paco had no choice in the matter, but the commentator was making it look voluntary. You were Raul's closest friend, weren't you?"

“Yes,” she said carefully, Paco’s eyes darting past the camera. *There is someone else there, in the room with him. Paco’s afraid. I can see it in his eyes.* “We worked together in the Youth Corps. We were assigned to clearing an old, abandoned factory outside of Detroit. We were very close.”

“The Youth Corps does a lot of great work, especially in the inner cities removing blight,” the narrator said smoothly. “You knew Raul well?”

“We were best friends,” Paco said. That answer wasn’t forced—Raul could tell. His memories of his friend came back and it seemed they were from a lifetime ago.

“Did he look up anyone that might have misled him, taken him down the wrong path in life?”

“You have to know this. Raul is a bit of a loner. He kept to himself. I do know he thought a lot of a priest at our church,” Paco offered. “Father Ryan. He spent a lot of time with Raul.” Raul cringed at the words. *They are making him say these things…I was never a loner.*

The interview stopped, but the narrator continued as a black and white image of Father Ryan plastered the screen. “The man that Paco referred to was Father David Francis Ryan, a Catholic priest. What no one knew at the time was that Ryan had been moved from two parishes; both had priests who were implicated in child sexual assaults. While he was never formally charged, Ryan also had ties to a terrorist organization, the Sons of Liberty. This was the man that guided and corrupted Raul Lopez. He—“

Raul shut the television off. “He was not a child molester! He didn’t corrupt me. He saved me!”

Caylee reached over and put her hand on his shoulder, squeezing gently. “This is how they operate, Raul. They never said he was a molester; they simply planted the seeds in the minds of the viewers. I doubt that a man of the cloth was some cold-blooded terrorist, but they need to implicate him in those activities.”

“It’s all a lie.”

She nodded. “It is. A well-crafted one at that. The media is not an independent entity. They are now a tool of the state. The TRC logo was in the corner during the entire broadcast—you probably didn’t even notice it. They approve these kinds of programs. Given your status, I would be surprised if they didn't have someone on their team write the entire script.

"They are packaging you like a product being sold to the consuming public," she continued. "Doubt, suspicion, fear—these are all things they want in the minds of the viewers. It makes it harder for you to be safe. This was all about getting your name and face out there, on some true crime show. The media has already tried and convicted you. They had to; the government would not allow it any other way."

"And now they have Paco."

"Yes."

"All to get me."

"Yes. It won't end there. If they get you Raul, they will parade you out, do a show trial for everyone to see. They will execute you as a lesson to anyone else that might stand up against them. They will package your death the same way that they did your life. As long as you remain out of their grasp, you are a danger. They have to bring you in or kill you trying because if they don't, it will give others hope."

This was wrong; he knew it in every joint of his body. It had never been quite so clear to Raul as it was sitting in front of the black television screen. *They will stop at nothing. They have declared war on me, my family, my friends.* "I will not let them make me a symbol that they can use. I am not something to be sold to people. I am a person. I am not a terrorist; I saved those people in that camp. I did what I did because it was right. They had no right to capture my mother, Paco…or speak lies about Father Ryan."

Caylee looked at him and offered only a thin smile for a few seconds before finally speaking. "You've looked at your enemy tonight, Raul. It isn't a person; it's an entire system that is working against you. You aren't caving in, which is what they want. That program was designed to break your will.

"I liked you before…but now I respect you," she said.

CHAPTER 17

"Individual needs corrupt the needs of the whole."

Arlington National Cemetery, Virginia

The Secretary of the NSF moved through the graveyard as her security detail skirted the perimeter. A thunderstorm had passed, and she had sat in her limo for nearly an hour waiting for the rain to abate. Each step on the ground felt like she was walking on a sponge. *This is going to destroy my shoes.* Thankfully, she knew her aide would have a backup pair tucked away in her luggage. It was yet another inconvenience that she was forced to endure.

She had tied the visit to a campaign stop in Northern Virginia. The night before she had been in Florida, which she had hated. Florida, as it had been for more than a decade, was a battleground state for politics. With the rise of the Pretender, it was more of a battlefield than ever before. It held onto a large number of Electoral Votes and while she despised the antiquated system, those votes would be needed for her and her running mate to claim legitimacy in the upcoming election. *Once we are in, the Electoral College can be discarded. We will have a new Constitutional Convention, one that will return the votes to the people rather than some vain attempt to balance urban and rural states' power.* Northern Virginia felt like ground where the administration would easily win.

The plan had been to have the convention, but then the Pretender President had emerged from whatever rock he had been hiding under. For the first time in a long time, she and her fellow members of the

Ruling Council found themselves forced to play defense—responding to the actions of real opposition. *If we had only pressed harder, put more people into quarantine, cracked a few more skulls, there wouldn't be any opposition. Once we are in legitimate power, voted in, we will finish the job we started.*

She trudged across the wet grass, looking for the gravesite. She was last here for the funeral, a few weeks earlier. Caylee Leatrom had killed her mother and brother in cold blood. The rogue operative had assassinated them. *They were innocent. My mother had never hurt another person. Ever.*

She stopped before the grave marker that had been erected for her mother and brother. It was tall, nearly seven feet in height—a carved marble angel holding a trumpet, pointing skyward. It loomed over the dead soldiers' small markers...*as it should.* Both her mother and Gabe were buried here; their names were still wet from the rain. She stood and looked at the monument for a long minute, trying to remember the last time she had spoken with either of them, but she couldn't summon the memories.

The Army had balked at her putting up the monument, but had eventually caved to her demands. *My mother and brother were victims of war as much as any of these dead soldiers were.* The military treated the ground there as if it were sacred soil. She knew the reality; it was Robert E. Lee's former home. This dirt was not sacred to her; it was the ground of oppression—of slavery. *Now it is the final resting place of my family...national heroes. The military can fuck off.*

Her mind went to Leatrom and brought forth an anger she did little to suppress. *We trained her, gave her the best of our assignments—and this is how she repays us? Murdering my innocent family members, posting her mission reports and memos about the operative program on the Internet!* Caylee's actions went far beyond defiance and insolence. She was a traitor, a criminal, a professional killer. *When we catch her, I will see her tortured, slowly—painfully. I will be there too, so that she knows who is giving the orders, so she can see the justice in my actions.*

Looking at the massive marble monument, she stood mute—nursing her thoughts of vengeance and anger at those who had done her wrong. Despite a few setbacks, things were still going her way. Senator Lewis would be moving forward with his hearings into the NSF and her operatives, but measures were in play already to make sure those hearings never happened. No matter what evidence he gathered, it would never be made public. *I will not be roasted by some Senator for my actions. Everything I have done was for the good of the nation and our people.*

Fixing the election was far more complex than it was to fix a mere Senator. The plan she had formulated, however, would generate a great deal of sympathy for her and her running mate. *Daniel is such a child at times; he is simple to manipulate.* She had ample blackmail material on the Chairman of the Ruling Council and had already shown her hand in absorbing the Social Enforcers. Once her new plan unfolded, Daniel would fall in line quickly. He has little choice. If he becomes too big a problem, well, he has a lot of enemies out there, enemies that are more than willing to kill a sitting President. *If I can't find such people, I can handle matters myself.*

Staring at the monument, she reflected on her career. Loud and boisterous when she had been elected to Congress, her peers often disregarded her. It didn't matter. She had learned the lessons of the Traitor President. It wasn't necessary for the press to respond positively to you, only that they mention you at every opportunity. She said things that were inflammatory, nasty, and—at times—unrealistic. Each time she did, the press covered her.

She had been a key instigator in the Liberation. She and her people had prepared lists of conservatives and supporters of the Traitor. Because of her covert efforts, the liberators that had seized the Capitol and the White House had rounded up many of those that might prove troublesome. The opposition disappeared overnight. Those that were not on one of her lists went into hiding. Those that thought her to be a fool were taught a harsh lesson about her brilliance. Memories of the tunnels under the Capitol the night of the Liberation didn't haunt her; they gave her great satisfaction. *The looks on some of their faces when they realized who had taken them down...me...I will savor those forever.*

There had been worries in those first few days of the Great Reformation she had engineered. No one knew what had happened to the Traitor President. She knew if he was alive, he would be communicating, rallying his supporters to take Washington back. When he didn't emerge, the assumption was that he had died. It was Becky who had come up with the idea of staging his arrest and him dying in custody. It wasn't as good as the public trial she had desired, but it served a purpose. *His death was meaningless. He didn't go out fighting; we made it look like his death was a footnote to his life.*

Staring at the monument, she knew her mother would be happy with it. She was deeply religious, something that had never stuck with Alex or her brother. The angel was for her, like having the priest at the memorial service. Studying the marble statue, she was pleased at the one she had chosen.

The memorial service for her mother and brother had been private, for family and close friends. Becky had wanted to cover it, to make her appear more sympathetic in the eyes of the public. Becky never seemed to understand Alex, despite all of the work she had done to try to foster some sort of relationship with the head of the TRC. *I don't need sympathy. I need loyalty.* Alex had turned it down, blocking news coverage of the event.

Her phone chirped and instantly she became angered at the interruption. Pulling it out of her jacket coat, she glanced down at the text message. "Sabretooth." That abated her anger almost instantly. The code word meant that the material from her covert project was complete. It wasn't enough to force a smile, but she felt a surge of accomplishment…a ray of hope. *This will change everything. It will solve many of my problems, and the problems our nation is facing.*

She spoke to the grave marker softly. "Momma. I am going to be elected the Vice President of the country soon. You'd be so proud. It's all because of you. You worked hard to get me through college and you dealt with of the press hounding you in those earlier years. If it weren't for you, I'd never have gotten this far." Her voice wavered slightly, and she felt her eyes start to water.

Being Vice President was an undesirable job. It had very little authority. She could only name a few of them from history, and most were seen as jokes. *I have no desire to be the person to fly around to state funerals or visit natural disasters.* Presiding over the Senate—all that meant to her was that she would be filmed in the background of CSPAN, sitting there, attempting to not look bored. Its only real advantage was being next in line to become President.

Being such a figurehead was not her destiny. Daniel was nice and had an edge to him, but he was not the kind of person to lead the nation as President. To her, he was the means to an end. *There will be conflict, even if we win the election. Whoever is President will have to deal with that and it will be complicated and messy. The Pretender is not going to sit back and accept the results of the election if he loses. He will fight.*

Daniel would be useful for a while. *People need someone to be angry with, and it might as well be him.* In due time, his ineptitude would reveal itself. It is one thing to organize ANTIFA, another to run a nation. *Then, when the time is right, Daniel will be replaced...by me.* Turning, she saw a camera crew in the distance, filming her. No doubt it was some news team that was hoping to capture a moment on film. A part of her was angry; this was a private moment. *Did Becky have them trailing me, hoping to capture something on film?* She didn't doubt it. It was tempting to order them off, or have her detail seize their equipment. *Then again, this is an image that might help me, make me look more human to my detractors.* Pretending to ignore them, she stepped forward and touched the angel, and then wiped a tear from the corner of her eyes.

Momma—you will be so proud of what your little girl has become... and what she will eventually be,

The District

"I apologize for this call," said the voice on the other end of the phone as Rebecca Clarke sat in her office. "I assure you, this is purely routine."

Rebecca had half-hoped it was in response to her inquiries about Judy Caesar. After the campaign event in Colorado, Judy had seemingly disappeared. All that Rebecca had learned was that Judy had last been seen being approached by a Social Enforcement team outside of the Denver Airport. Her inquiries as to what had happened to her staffer had resulted in stonewalling, denials, and outright lies. She had left a message with the Secretary of the NSF—polite, almost apologetic—but so far Alex had not returned her call. *She is doing it to spite me—an act of defiance. Judy is a proxy for what she would like to do with me if the chance presents itself.*

This call was not about Judy's fate, and her mind was slowly wrapping around that fact. Her admin had told her that it was a call from The District NSF office, and blowing off a call from the NSF was not something that Rebecca was up to. "No problem at all Supervisor Simpson. What can I do for you?"

"We found a body in the Anacostia three days ago," he said. "We just got it identified. I regret to inform you that it is one of your staff."

She felt her stomach clench. "Oh my God," she feigned. "Who is it?" A part of her already knew the answer to the question before he responded.

"Jane Alexi Pistós," the deep voice of the supervisor said.

"What happened to her?"

"Due to decomposition on the body, it's a little tricky for us to pin down. It is clear that she was beaten…she had a few broken bones."

This was the moment that she had been dreading. It had haunted her, the order she had given to kill and dispose of Pistós over a week earlier. It had taken years to get past the nightmares of the events that took place at the Capitol. Ordering the death of the spy in her department had been easy to do, but hard to live with. Almost every night she woke up to the dark eyes of the woman silently staring at her. No words, no movement—just a disturbing stare.

As much as she had hoped her security people would be able to hide her body, there was this ever-present fear that it would surface. It had been like a nagging toothache that occasionally throbbed. Now it had… and she was going to have to deal with it. "That is horrible," she said. "Is there anything I can do to help?" A bit of paranoia crept into the dark recesses of her mind. *The NSF is bound to be monitoring this call, checking for voice stress levels. Are they going to sense my hesitation or deception?*

"It seems clear to us and the medical examiner that foul play was involved here. Given the condition of the victim, this doesn't seem like a robbery or sexual assault. That tends to point to someone that had a grudge with the victim—someone that knew her."

"That's awful."

"Yes, it is ma'am," the NSF supervisor replied. "It would be very helpful for us to get access to her emails at work, conduct interviews with coworkers, and see if we can identify anyone that might have had a personal grudge against her."

"I want to cooperate with you in any way possible. I hate to think that someone would do something like that to one of my people. I will assign someone on my team to help you, if that is alright?"

She got his contact information and after a few more pleasantries, slowly replaced the receiver on the phone cradle. For several minutes she did nothing but sit in her office, mentally playing out everything that the NSF might ask for. She had already asked her people to destroy the security camera footage from the night that Pistós had been killed, along with several other days' worth so that it would look like some sort of equipment failure. She couldn't think of any risk or harm in coworkers being interviewed—chances are none of them knew that Jane was a traitor. If they did, they would only implicate themselves.

Rebecca came to the conclusion that she had very little to worry about, but that didn't shake the fear. She wasn't worried about the investigation as much as the nightmares. This was not going to do away with those dark eyes shattering her sleep. No, it was going to get worse.

I need sleeping medicine...something to get me through the night. Yes, that would do it. A prescription for Ambien or something like it and the nightmares would not keep her up any more.

Let them come and ask their questions, run their little investigation. In the end, it is just another dead government worker. *Once they find no trail to follow, the whole thing will get swept under the rug.* It was that way when the city police had been the Washington Metropolitan Police Department. *It will be the same with the NSF.*

Then we can focus on what is important—winning this election.

The Southern White House
Nashville, Tennessee

Jack sat across the desk from the President as his Commander in Chief and momentarily remembered his time in the Secret Service. The image he saw before him was wrong and he finally understood it. It was the desk. The Resolute Desk of the Oval Office was not what the President was sitting behind. He was seated behind nothing wrapped in history. It was a plain desk, a government-issued, dull wooden desk from some GS-15 that had been appropriated for use. For Jack, it was a reminder of things that were lost in the Fall.

"Mr. President, I agree. This is a sign that the campaign stops are working," Jack said, nodding to the printout of the story from NeoFox. "The TRC took it down, but they had at least a million hits before they did."

"So their own polls show us gaining ground," he said with a hint of satisfaction that was rare. "It's a start."

"What's more important is that this got out in the first place," Jack said. "The TRC doesn't make mistakes, not like this."

"Are you saying it was deliberate?"

"No, sir," Jack said. "I think we have someone in the TRC, someone that is loyal to us. This has all the hallmarks of an unauthorized leak."

For a moment the President said nothing, but he was clearly thinking. "There are people out there that are behind us, Jack. I've felt that all along. Remember that policeman in New Jersey after I was sworn in? Millions of people out there remember America. They are willing to take risks to see it restored. If I knew who this person was, I'd give them a medal."

Jack didn't tell the President the reality of the risk that the person had taken. *The NSF will go on a mole hunt. They will go all out to find this person. If I knew who they were, I might be able to help them. Right now their anonymity is their only defense.* "Yes, sir," was all he could muster.

"How goes our plans for providing secure voting on the contested states?"

"We are more prepared each day. Our pre-deployment activities are going well. We are starting to see some activity on the part of Newmerica. The Maryland and Pennsylvania National Guard have been mobilized. Across the country, the Social Enforcers are mobilizing. The SEs in California and Oregon are renting buses, so they are planning to go somewhere—no doubt where our people are going to try to secure voting. My people are getting reports of the NSF upgrading their gear as well."

"They're plundering the armories?"

"Yes, sir."

"We expected this," he said with a resolved tone. "They can't allow us to have a fair vote. They can't risk it."

He knows this is going to lead to bloodshed. It bothered him. The wrinkles on his face when inevitable conflict came up told the story of his anguish. That garnered respect from Jack. *He knows people are going to die, but he isn't wavering from his conviction.* No man should contemplate such actions and not have it bother them. "The SEs are a considerable force. They have at least 200,000 in their ranks. While they have structure, each group still tends to operate independently. There's coordination, but it is damn thin."

"That should be good for us."

Jack nodded slightly. "I hope so. It also means that the individual teams will not react in concert with any plans. Some are bound to be more violent than others."

"They created an army out of a bunch of angry kids," the President said, leaning back in his chair. "They don't trust authority; it is part of who they are. Now they are five years older, and that distrust is still a part of them. Taking orders from a central authority will rub some of them wrong. They will have a hard time working with each other—despite the fact that they have had some degree of structure in place."

"Those are my thoughts as well," Jack said. "They have the numbers, but they don't have the control."

"Good, we need some advantages. I'm a little worried about the timing for us to deploy though," the President said.

"Sir, we have pre-deployed National Guard and supporting forces in friendly territory. If we move too soon before the election, those troops are going to find themselves under siege. We want voting to happen, but they will turn the major cities into battlefields to prevent it. Our plan calls for us to move the day before the election, blitz our message to the people as to where legal voting can take place, and secure the election."

"About that," the President said. "It seems fairly low-tech."

"By design, sir," Jack replied. "The last thing we want is for their allies in Big Tech to try to hack us. I assure you; they are going to try. Dumbing down the technology frustrates the hell out of our enemies. They want us to use tech because they have an advantage when it comes to penetrating that tech.

"We are using paper ballots with hidden watermarks on them, making them impossible to duplicate. Voters will have their thumbs dipped in indelible ink to prevent anyone trying to vote more than once. The ink has an ultraviolet dye that we can check. The dye is going to stay on their skin, even if they somehow get the ink off. We validate each ballot so we avoid hanging chad situations, and tallying happens as we go with people we have certified as not being part of the Newmerica government. No flash drives like the last election, no mail-in ballots, no bogus voter rolls. IDs will be triple checked. We won't have a replay of the events in the last election."

"You've convinced me, Jack," the President said. "It feels like we have planned for everything."

Jack shook his head. "Sir, these people are desperate. They are not showing it, but I know them. We have plans in place, but they are going to throw curve balls at us, try and throw us off our game. Where we are playing honorably, they are not burdened with that aspect. We have self-imposed limits based on our morals and values. Our enemies shed their morals a long time ago, and their values are subject to change depending on what they desire. People with shallow values are the most dangerous."

There was a rapid knock at the door, and the President's secretary entered. "I'm sorry, sir, but there's something you need to see on TV." She moved over to the remote in front of the flat screen and turned it on. The banner at the bottom read, "Breaking Story: Bombing at the US Capitol." Jack was stunned to see the image of the Senate Chambers side of the building. Black smoke billowed skyward. The front façade of the building had collapsed in a cascade of rubble and debris.

"For those of you tuning in, it appears an assassination attempt was made at a meeting of the Ruling Council. We do not have reports of injuries or deaths yet, but as you can see, the Senate Chambers have been attacked and bombed. Military units are being deployed in The District as we speak …"

The President looked at Jack. "Please tell me we had nothing to do with this, Jack."

"No, sir, not that I'm aware of." He found himself torn. A part of him hoped that the Ruling Council was dead…it would make matters easier.

If the attempt failed, it could backfire on us...generate sympathy for the enemy.

"Damn it!" Jack added as he glared at the image. "We are going to need to get out in front of this. No matter what, they are going to lay the blame at our doorstep."

University of Virginia
Charlottesville, Virginia

Maddie had limited the amount of time she spent watching the bombing on television. Pris was furious about it. "It was that fucking Pretender. He did this! All conservatives are terrorists, like we've been told!" When word finally came that only a handful of staffers had been killed in the explosion, that the Ruling Council was still alive, Pris finally conceded to turning the TV off. "We need to finish what's been started," she growled. "Quarantine is not good enough. These people have to be eliminated."

Her only response was to nod. This was her roommate who had no idea that Maddie was a conservative—talking about waging genocide. Pris was not just raging; she meant the things that she was saying. Worse yet, most of the campus felt the same way. *No doubt there will be protests in favor of the Ruling Council. It's too big a thing for them not to protest.*

In her mind things had gone from bad to worse. She wanted to keep her head down and maintain a low profile, but she remembered what Brad and Tina had told her—she was being observed. *If there are protests, I will need to be there, if only to blend in.*

The next day she started her daily trudge across campus. Banners were already crudely hung on the outside of buildings with the words, "Vengeance!" and "Bring the Bombers to Justice!" painted on them. One even misspelled the word, "Vengeance" which made her smile, if ever so slightly.

Her plans for the day were to do what she always did—go to class, go to the library, have dinner in her room, and keep to herself. Her pottery class was cancelled so that participants could attend the protests. As she crossed the campus, the presence of Brad surprised her. Maddie saw him next to her but did not stop and talk because of his warning that she was being observed. She didn't want to risk exposing him. She felt his hand, for a moment, in hers, passing a note into her palm. Then, as quickly as he appeared at her side, he was gone, turning and walking off in a different direction. She caught only a fleeting glimpse of him, walking under the now barren oak trees of the campus.

She didn't open the note; instead she stuffed it in the front pocket of her jeans. She didn't take it out and read it until she was back in her dorm room. Pris left their room for dinner, and once she was sure she would not be interrupted or seen, she pulled out the note.

"Same place, 9 p.m. tonight. GBA."

As she stared at the note, she felt her heart beat faster. The fact that Brad and Tina were reaching out to her was not likely good news. With her parents having been exposed days earlier, she wondered if the same people had discovered who *she* was. It was a sinking feeling, one tinged with desperation and stark fear. Her parents and brother were hastily making plans to change identities again. Maddie had hoped to simply make it through graduation before having to cope with her family change. Was this note a prelude to her identity being doxed?

Mentally she convinced herself for a moment not to go to the meeting. If she didn't go, the problem didn't exist. The budding lawyer in her devoured that logic, wadding it up more than the note she had just read. *I can't ignore this. That doesn't make it go away. They want to tell me something, and I need to hear it.* She mustered courage and prepared to go. Once more her pistol was slid into her backpack. While she felt somewhat secure, facing Brad and Tina came with a bit of trepidation.

She arrived at the abandoned Rotunda, thankful to be out of the stiff, cold, autumn wind that was blowing across the UVA campus. Her footfalls were soft as she made her way to the North Oval Room, where a lone light was on. As she cautiously peeked around the half opened door, she saw that it was not only Brad and Tina; three others were in the room, talking in low tones.

When she entered, the room went quiet. Brad flashed her a smile. "Ah good. I'm glad you came." Gesturing to the others, he said, "Everyone, this is Madison."

The three strangers turned toward her. The first was a person she assumed identified as a female. She was slender, dressed in black jeans and a long-sleeved, gray, T-shirt with a zippered hoodie bearing the new

UVA logo. It had originally been the crossed swords of the cavaliers, but most people recognized that the name had come from the Civil War cavalry. The school had changed the mascot to, 'The Stalwarts' and had replaced the crossed sabers with two crossed up-thrust fists. "I'm Francine," she said. Maddie shook her hand gently.

Across the table a younger male with a slight paunch rose to his feet. "I'm Lee," he said. The other male, slightly older, gave her a wave from his seat. He was muscular, clearly someone that worked out…was, perhaps, on the football team. "I'm Lonnie."

Giving them a courtesy nod, she put her backpack on the table and took the open chair closest to her. "I didn't know there'd be others here," she said.

Tina spoke up from the far end of the table. "I hope you didn't think you were the only one," she said. "We thought it was worth getting everyone together, especially after the events yesterday. With this assassination attempt on the Ruling Council, we fear it will embolden the Social Enforcers on campus and elsewhere. You've probably seen the banners on campus…these people want blood."

Brad weighed in. "We have a source in the Chainbreakers, one of the campus SE groups. Word is they suspect that there are a few free thinkers like us on campus. They have plans in place to start doing a little surveillance of their own—trying to identify the conservatives. I don't have to tell you after this attack, what will happen if they find us."

"Do they know about any of us?" Francine asked nervously. Maddie had the same question.

"I haven't gotten the list yet," Brad said. "I thought it might be easiest to reach out to all of you at once and give you the heads-up. You need to remain more observant than usual. Watch out when using your phones or sending anything electronically that might imply you have conservative tendencies."

Maddie could feel the tension in the room. Lonnie spoke up. "Do you really think they are monitoring our devices?"

Brad nodded. "We've heard about that from other campuses that have groups like ours. You have to understand. These SEs are now part of the NSF. They are a bunch of thugs, but they have access to a bigger set of tools as a result. That makes them dangerous."

Tina spoke up, sitting backwards on the chair at the far end of the table. "Look, we know that others like us are out there. We need to be able to warn them too. If your friends have similar political preferences, it would be good to pass the word on to them. If you are comfortable, share their names with Brad or me. We need to bring them into the loop and let them know they are at risk." Maddie drank in those words. *How many students like me are out there?* Despite the danger that Brad and Tina were laying out, there was something comforting in the knowledge that she was not alone.

"What else can we do?" Lee asked.

"Try to blend in," Brad continued. "That's how we have had to operate since the Fall, hiding in plain sight. Don't do anything that might make you stand out. Go to the protests—I know it sucks, but do it. They want revenge for the attack, and it doesn't matter who they deliver it against. Acting like them is one of the best ways to throw them off."

Tina weighed in again. "We all have to be quieter than normal. They may be tracking us for all we know. Brad's contact has given us solid information in the past, so we have every reason to believe that he is being truthful now. If we get word that the SEs are going to make a move on us, we will get word to you. We will rendezvous here, and we will work to get you off campus before anyone else can get their hands on you."

Maddie understood the implied message…*be ready to move.* There was a sense of admiration for what Brad and Tina were doing. *For a long time I was alone and afraid. Knowing that others on campus think the same way I do is reassuring. They are taking a big risk by helping us. With the election coming up soon, maybe things are going to turn our way for a change. The campus SEs are trying to find us…and I am afraid of what they will do if they catch us.*

CHAPTER 18

"The only virtues that matter are those that are sanctioned."

Livingston, Tennessee

The only thing that dampened Deja Jordan's anger at the news reports was the frustration regarding her assignment. The news footage of the bombing at the Capitol had been played almost 24/7. CNN had already composed a musical tone for the disaster, and every time she heard it on the television, it made her fists clench and her body grew tense. It was clearly the act of the Pretender and the terrorists he surrounded himself with. *They need to kill him now...get it over with. This farce of an election can't be allowed to happen, not after this.*

A tip had come in two days before, one of thousands that had been filtered to her and their team in the motel. An Airman from Arnold Air Force Base had said that he saw Raul Lopez in the gym several weeks ago. He had even gone so far as to identify where Lopez and another person, a woman, were living. The allure of a million dollar payoff was something that couldn't be overlooked easily. Others on the team had written it off, but to Deja it made sense. Having Lopez on a military base would ensure security. She had persuaded the others to take a closer look.

The Air Force base presented a myriad of problems in terms of getting in. Deja solved it by getting a job as a delivery person at the Domino's that delivered to the base. The first time she had gone in, she was nervous, but the security team there only gave her a cursory inspection. Pizzas were delivered there all of the time. They checked her

ID, did a brief look at her car using mirrors to make sure there were no explosives, and let her in.

Base housing was easy to navigate. Deja delivered her pizzas, carefully driving by the target house each time she was on base. The curtains were drawn, but she could tell that lights were on inside. She never saw the occupants of the house, but she did see an old model Kia Seltos in front most of the time. Whoever was in the house was keeping to themselves.

After her fourth penetration of the base, she sat down with Detective Gallagher and the others in the dimly lit motel room. "I never got eyes on the target, but it makes sense that he's hiding there," she said.

Gallagher was skeptical. "We wouldn't be able to get in with a whole team. Not to mention that if someone raises an alarm, you'd be trapped in the middle of a military base filled with armed personnel. The risks seem too damn high."

"Too high for the NSF," she countered. "I'm a Social Enforcer. You seem like a good enough guy Dale, but you have been conditioned to think like a cop. Think of it from their perspective. If it is Lopez in that house, they think he's safe. No one would dare go after him there, for all the reasons you point out. SEs do this kind of stuff all the time; we bust in and toss the place quick. It's one of our best approaches, being willing to take the risks."

"What if it isn't him?" Gloria asked.

"If not, we get out fast," Deja said quickly. "Everything is built on us moving and acting quick."

"What about the woman that was with him in Kentucky?" Chad asked. "From what you've told us, she's special forces or something along those lines. If she is with him, a small team is not going to cut it."

Deja nodded. "I've been thinking about that. Lopez can't get out much; he can't afford the risk of being seen. So if he has protection in the house, it's whoever is driving that car. It sure as hell isn't him going out for drives around base. We only move if the car isn't there."

"How do you see it going down?" French asked from the bed where he had plopped himself.

"Pizza delivery is the key to getting in. We do it with a team of three. I'll tell the guards I'm training a new driver that puts two of us in the front of the car. We have one in the trunk. So far they haven't checked the back of the car. We go in with a legitimate delivery—do a drive by and see if he's alone, drop off the pizza, drive back and hit the house. If we move fast enough, we nab Lopez, tie the little shit up, toss him in the trunk. If we do this right, we are in and out in five minutes."

Detective Gallagher still wasn't on board; she could tell by the way he ran his hand through the gray-cropped hair of his head, over the wrinkles on his forehead. "Your target is likely armed Deja. You go in, there is likely gonna be some gunplay."

"Two of us will be dressed like pizza delivery people that happen to be at the wrong address. Our third can circle to the back, and come in when we do. If it is Lopez, he won't know what hit him."

"And if it's not?" Gloria asked.

"We zip-tie 'em, gag 'em, and get out."

There was a lot of resistance in the room; she could feel it. Deja went over to the stack of printout tips they had received. "We've been poring over these tips, and this is the best that we've had. You saw them. None of us think that Lopez was seen at a laundromat in Knoxville, or at an ATM in Nashville. You saw that one about him buying a slice of pizza at a Royal Farms gas station—do you think that's him? He's high priority for us, which means that the opposition is going to keep him hidden. What better place than a military base?

"Their arrogance is their weakness. They think that parking him on base makes him safe all by itself. I say we go in and check. It sure as hell beats spending time here, wading through a bunch of bullshit tips by people who are trying to make quick cash. This makes sense; you know it. I say we go for it."

Donna, another SE in the group, spoke up. "The girl is right. You can't do this the way the NSF does, all formal and safe. I say we go in and see if that prick is there. If he is, we bag him."

Gallagher eventually nodded. "Alright, we try it your way."

Deja couldn't help but smile.

The District

The Secretary of the NSF had her arm in a gray sling and she rubbed it slightly as if it ached. It was all for show; she had a bruise from the explosion that had taken down the façade of the Capitol. To her, it was important that the media see her as injured. She didn't want their sympathy; she wanted them to see her as *human*, more relatable. Being the survivor of an assassination attempt did that.

The blast had been more frightening than she had expected. Her ears had popped and the concussion had knocked her off her feet. The wave of dust had ruined one of her favorite suits—a small price to pay for the photo opportunity it offered when she had been taken out of the building. Her hairdresser had struggled to get all of the debris out of her straight black hair. Her ribs and back ached, either from the fall or from the massive invisible wave that had rippled out from the explosion.

Timing the explosion was easy; she knew the arrival times of the other members of the Ruling Council. Some, like Becky, were predictable. She always liked showing up at the last minute before the meetings started, no doubt to generate the illusion of how busy she was. In this case it would play well for the later stages of the plan, making it look as if she had timed the explosion so she wouldn't be hurt when it went off.

Their usual meeting room in the Senate side of the Capitol was not usable, so they had commandeered the Ways and Means Committee chamber of the House. With most of Congress gone since the Liberation, no one complained when Daniel had pressed to take the room for their meetings.

From her perspective, Sabretooth was unfolding as planned. The bombing was never meant to kill anyone on the Ruling Council, but to scare them—shake them to their core. It would incite every one of them into wanting action and retribution. Outrage would cloud their logic, allowing her to unfold the rest of the plan with no one questioning her motives or reasoning. *Most of them are so simple; they never would suspect my involvement in the first place.*

"Where are we on the investigation?" Daniel pressed. She noted the small bandage on his forehead where he had been injured by a bit of marble that had nicked him. She remembered the hallway outside of their meeting room—immediately following the explosion—how Daniel was trembling, the blood running down his hairline.

She slightly shifted in her seat. "We are gathering intel still, as you can imagine. Whoever planted the explosive somehow got through the security around the Capitol. We have no indications of this being a suicide attack, so we are reviewing all transmissions in and around the Capitol. It's a lot of data, but my people suspect that this was an insider—someone who used their position to circumvent security." *There, the seeds are planted.*

"What about the media?" Daniel demanded.

"We are labeling this as a domestic terror attack—with heavy hints that this is the work of the political opposition," Rebecca said. It was a prudent move on her part, laying the blame for an assassination at the feet of your political opponents. The media was more than willing to do so, even if the evidence pointed elsewhere. Regardless, everything was happening exactly as she had hoped it would.

"Of course it was!" Treasury Secretary Barbara Collingsworth said. She was easily the oldest member of the Ruling Council, despite her attempts to dye the gray out of her hair. Her anger was pointless; she was implicated in the fake evidence that the NSF Secretary had at her disposal. *Your pointing of fingers will only backfire on you before I'm done.*

The NSF Secretary spoke up, "While that makes sense, I'd prefer to go where the evidence takes us. We are checking emails, security feeds, etc. I don't see any harm in pointing the finger at the Pretender at this point, but you never know where the evidence will take you." In this case she did, because the evidence had been carefully crafted.

"We need to accelerate the process, Alex," Daniel said, glaring at her. "The election is almost on top of us. The people need to know for sure that the people in Nashville were behind all of this. We need something solid, something tangible."

She gave him a nod, not as much out of respect, but for playing into her hand. "I will put more people on it—but these things take time." *I want them to think that I am being thorough...that there is no rush to judgment.*

"Whatever it takes," he said, pounding his fist on the table. It was rare that she saw this rage in Daniel. There was a bit of satisfaction in it. It meant that the bombing had gotten to him, rattled his cage. *His ego is such that he is treating this as if it were directed solely at him.* From what she knew of him, when he was emotional, he was easy to manipulate.

"This election is complicated enough as it is."

Once more, she shifted in her seat. "If we do find out that the Pretender was involved, how would you envision us proceeding?" It was a loaded question, deliberate on her part. *Let him make the call, so if anything backfires, all of the blame is his to bear.*

"If he ordered us killed, we should pay them back in kind," Daniel said through gritted teeth.

"Our allies are not going to react well to that," the Secretary of State said. "It makes Newmerica look like some third world country where assassinations are tolerated."

"I don't give a shit what our allies think," Daniel fired back with another pound on the conference table. "Britain and France whine and moan, and Germany pontificates every time we do anything around the globe. It is easy for them to criticize what we do. No one tried to kill them. Do you really think that the English Prime Minister wouldn't retaliate if some Irish asshole took a potshot at her? I will tell our allies to mind their own business. This is an internal security matter."

Daniel paused for a moment, clearly attempting to reel in his rage. "If they had succeeded in this, everything we fought for would have been lost. I know none of the people in this room are willing to lose all of that. We finally have this country on the right track. I won't hand it back to these fascists ever again. I don't care what the world stage thinks about it. If the opposition did that, we will hit them back. No one tries to blow me up."

"I will set things in motion," she said, holding back her smile. "Strictly precautionary."

Arnold Air Force Base, Tennessee

Caylee sat in the chair with her legs draped on the table and watching the press conference from The District. Across the table, seated in the same manner, was former Navy SEAL Travis Cullen. Travis had brought in a bag of Kettle corn, and the two of them were on a break, watching television coverage of the bombing aftermath.

Travis had been tasked by Jack to assist Caylee, and she appreciated his talents. He was a meticulous planner; then again she expected that from a SEAL. Their plans for taking down the key infrastructure to blind the TRC were progressing well, thanks to his contribution. Travis had a few comrades in arms who were loyal to his cause as well, which gave her additional people on the ground.

She eyed the coverage, tossing a popped Kettle corn kernel into her mouth. "Look at her," she said, pointing to the screen.

"Who?"

"My former cunt of a boss," she said. "The NSF Secretary. That sling is bogus. See, she's wiggling her fingers, fidgeting. I've had a sprained arm. You don't want to make any movement that is going to cause pain. That sling is fake."

Travis nodded. "Yup. That's all for the cameras," he confirmed. "And have you looked at the damage?"

She returned the nod. "Mostly external. The bomb had the right amount of force to do the job, but it looks like it was planted to do only structural damage rather than kill. When you look at the shot, you don't see them picking up nails out on the Capitol lawn. They are flagging a few things—bomb fragments. If I were doing it, this thing would have been wrapped in things to kill people. They have only three dead, all staffers. Whoever this was didn't make a bomb to kill a lot of people… intentionally."

"All boom, nothing anti-personnel," Travis confirmed. "You know what this makes it, don't you?"

"Either a complete novice who panicked and pulled the trigger early, or a false flag attack," she said, taking a few more kernels from the paper plate where she had poured them.

"That's what I told Jack," Travis said. "This whole thing smells of a false flag, a justification for them to do something shitty back to us. Did you catch the President's response?"

She nodded. "It seemed sincere enough. The TRC will edit it, remove anything that might make it appear compassionate. They want this to happen." She thought for a moment about her conversations with Charli regarding an assassination attempt. *If gives them plausible reason to attempt their own assassination attempt.* As tempted as she was to pick up the phone and call Charli, she knew that the head of the Secret Service had already pieced that together for herself. *Charli's smart and fast; she will see this for what it is.*

Caylee swung her feet to the floor and leaned over the table where the blueprints and maps were spread out. Travis followed suit, grabbing the last handful of Kettle corn and stuffing it into his mouth. They had been going over the plans for crippling the TRC for several days, to the point of exhaustion.

The two facilities in Ashburn, Virginia were ones that Travis assumed responsibility for taking out. She admired the creativity in his work. So many professionals in her field were all about brute force, but Travis was someone that studied a problem and came up with a unique solution to resolve it. In the case of the Farbros facility, he saw that the water main that came into the building was higher in elevation than half of the building in terms of data warehouse equipment. "It's as simple as opening the main down the block, planting explosives in the pipe and blowing it." Half of the warehouse would be submerged in a matter of minutes, and there was no quick way to repair the pipe after the blast. "This isn't about some guy coming in and welding it." Just to make sure, he would spot weld the shut-offs in the open position for the entire block. While it only destroyed half of the hardware, the building couldn't possibly reopen without extensive repair and cleanup. "No water," he said with a wicked grin when he presented his plan to her, "No toilets. Even the geeks have to shit now and then." The best part of his plan was that he could set the explosives the day before, so that freed him up for other operations.

The Equinix facility was more of a challenge for the former SEAL. His solution involved infiltrating the building and planting explosives around the backup generators and cooling towers. The server farm required a lot of cooling, and he seemed to know a great deal about those systems. "Take out the cooling system, and all of the hardware is worthless. Travis planned to disable the warning system as well, ensuring that the server room temperatures would rise quickly to the point where hard drives and other hardware would fail before anyone could start taking them down safely.

"Where did you learn about cooling systems for data warehouses?" she asked.

"Bumblehive," he said. Caylee understood the reference instantly—Jack Desmond had orchestrated the destruction of that facility's equipment. *No doubt Mr. Cullen had a role in that operation.*

Travis shifted the blueprints, pulling out the EvoSwitch site in Manassas. “Have you come up with an approach for that beast?” he asked, gesturing to the seven-story, obelisk like structure. “They have a lot more feet on the ground than the other sites.” He pulled out several photographs of the well-armed assault weapons.

She knew the problem all too well; they had discussed it several times. “I looked at the building, and I think it will be difficult to circumvent their security,” she conceded. “I could get in, but not with enough gear to do the job and do it right.”

“OK,” Cullen said, leaning back. “You want to use a plane? Manassas Airport is only two miles away. You could fake engine problems, bail, send the plane right into it. If we load enough explosives, it will do considerable carnage.”

She shook her head. “Nice thought. We’d have to purchase a plane, outfit it, and the minute I bail, there’s a chance of it going off course. While I want to take the building down, I’d prefer to walk away from this alive.”

“I take it you have another idea?”

She took out her phone, pulled up a photo, and showed it to him. His mouth slowly fell open. “Are you thinking what I am?”

“Their security barriers are around the entrances. The rest of the perimeter is standard security fence, midgrade stuff.”

“Lowest bidder bites you in the ass every time. The fence has camera monitoring, but that is easily circumvented.”

“The fence might stop you.”

“So I cripple the cameras, go in and cut the uprights of the fence at the base, right at the ground. I don’t have to cut all of them, just enough to drive through.”

“Yeah. It’s a low tech solution, but I think it has a high probability of working.”

He nodded, which from a former SEAL was an encouraging signal. “And for CoreSite in Reston?”

“I’m still refining the plan. They have a contract with a local company for fire alarms, fire retardant systems, and response systems. If I pose as one of their inspectors, I should be able to get free run of the facilities. I bring in my ‘inspection equipment,’ which is a series of bombs; I can plant them everywhere. I found the specs last night on the equipment they have—so I need time with an electrician, but I think I should be able to disable the systems."

"It's going to take time," he said.

"Two days to do the work," she replied. "I will kill the fire alarms, make them look like they are working fine. When we start the op, I can remote detonate the explosives. The fire department will not get the alert; their suppression system won't come on. Easy peasy," she said.

"Manassas makes me nervous still," he said bluntly. "I think you need to heist a cab and work through how you are going to pull it off. You know, make some practice runs."

"I'm just as worried about Fabros," she countered. "We're only hitting half of the facility with a flood; that leaves a lot of hardware they might be able to use to get back up."

"I say we game this stuff out, simulate the attacks, come up with contingency plans," Travis said. "There's a number of places where this shit can go south, and we need to be prepared."

"Agreed," she said. "We also need a good inventory list and ID where we can source the stuff we need. I'd prefer to buy local so that we are not trying to transport explosives and incriminating stuff across state lines."

He nodded in response and pulled out a yellow legal pad. Caylee shot a glance back at the perpetual coverage of the bombing at the Capitol. She saw the image of the Secretary of the NSF at the press briefing for what seemed like the tenth time. *What are you up to? This feels like an op, all planned out. What is your game?*

For a long moment, she regretted killing the Secretary's mother and brother. *I should have killed the NSF Secretary when I had the chance.* At the time, she wanted to hurt her former leader, and killing her wouldn't have hurt her as much as losing loved ones. *I won't make that mistake again.*

Nashville, Tennessee

The police station still bore evidence of the NSF. The sign out front and a vinyl banner proclaiming it as the Metro Police Headquarters was tied down over the NSF sign. The officers had removed their patches from the NSF and had replaced them with the Metro Police of Nashville sunburst logo, which they had worn before the Fall. Charli stood in the interrogation room, waiting.

Jacob Markowski of Spring Hill, Tennessee was led in. At her behest, police had picked him up at the Motel 6 that he had been calling home. He was a good old boy; she could see that in his taste of Walmart flannel and Wrangler jeans. The reddish beard that he sported showed a smile with slightly discolored teeth—a hint that he used chewing tobacco. The two arresting officers forced him into a seat, attaching his handcuffs to a link on the floor-mounted table.

Charli considered Social Enforcers to be the lowest form of life in Newmerica. They operated without rules, beyond the law. They picked their own targets, like bullies, inflicting justice as they saw fit. During her years of hiding, she had seen the results of their actions—dead bodies, beaten savagely, SEs taking victim's houses and personal goods as their own booty. They had ruined careers and killed without fear.

She had seen the professional profiler's take on SEs. Many were individuals that worked low-end jobs. To them, being an enforcer was a sanction to intimidate others without repercussions. Others were college graduates, usually with degrees in philosophy, gender studies, diversity and inclusiveness, or other non-money-earning degrees. For these individuals, being an enforcer gave them a purpose, a sense of being in society—justification for spending their parent's money in school. Some were self-proclaimed 'Internet warriors' who bullied others from the comfort of their parent's home. To Charli, the profiles did not tell stories of people to be looked up to or people who had redeeming qualities. They are losers, bound together to lord power over others. ANTIFA and now the SEs gave a group of loud voices a sense of authority at the expense of the lives and reputations of others. Looking at Jacob Markowski, she didn't see a man; she saw an opportunist thug.

Markowski had put up a fight, so resisting arrest had been easy to level at him. He had also been caught with a copious amount of marijuana, enough to get him on distribution. She didn't care about those charges; she wanted to know about the car accident that he was involved in near the Southern White House.

The President had gone on the air, denying the charges coming from the media and the Ruling Council that he had ordered their assassination.

The denial was good, well written, perfectly delivered—but she knew it wouldn't change anyone's mind. It had forced her hand; she had to bring Markowski in for an interrogation.

Charli waited for the door to close as she sat in front of him. "Who are you supposed to be?" he asked snidely. "I've already talked to these guys. I got busted for weed. Big damn deal."

She flashed her badge. "Secret Service."

The smirk on his face faded. "Why would the Secret Service want to talk to me?"

Reaching down, she pulled out a photo of him next to his car at the scene of the accident. "You tell me."

Markowski glared at the image for a moment. "Yeah, I had an accident. So what?"

"Who paid you?"

"What do you mean?"

"Cut the bullshit," she commanded. "You don't live here. We ran your bank and credit records; there's no way you could have afforded all of the pot you were arrested with, let alone pay the bill at the Motel 6. You were paid to stage that accident. I want to know who did it."

He looked both confused and frustrated at her accusations. "I don't know what you're talking about."

"Does he look familiar?" she asked, pulling out a blurry image of the man she suspected of being behind the accidents.

"Never saw him before," he said, shifting in his seat uncomfortably.

"You know," she said slowly. "Being involved in a Presidential assassination can get you the death sentence. Conspiracy is a nasty business. With the Lincoln assassination, Mrs. Surratt hung just for letting the assassins plan the operation at her house. What do you think they'll do to you Jacob? Don't answer that. I already know. A chubby guy like you…even if they don't execute you, you'll probably end up as someone's bottom bunk bitch in prison. I might be able to get you into a Supermax prison once we take one back. No daylight, but the risk of rape drops dramatically. You can rot there, forever, being a failed assassin accomplice"

"I—I—look I don't know anything about no assassination attempt," he stammered, suddenly shedding his arrogant demeanor for stark fear.

"Who is he?" she demanded.

"I don't know."

"Where did you meet him?"

"He showed up at my house. He knew I was an enforcer. Said I could make some easy money. All I had to do was get into an accident."

"How'd he pay you?"

"Cash—a big wad of Obamas and Clintons," he said. "All I had to do was a fender bender. Hell, the insurance company is even paying to get it fixed. That's why I stayed here; it was cheaper than having it towed home."

Add insurance fraud to the list of charges. Charli watched him squirm in his seat like a trapped animal and realized that he probably wouldn't have much useful information. "You met with this man, correct?"

"Twice. Half up front, half after. I thought it was easy money, that's all."

"Do you have a phone number for him? Any photos?"

"No. Like I said, he just showed up. Said he was NSF, even had a badge."

That's helpful. It confirmed that the mystery man was tied to Newmerica. *He's seen my target, clearly.* "Here's the deal," she said coolly, resting her elbows on the table between them. "As it stands, you are implicated in a conspiracy. No matter what, you are going to be held, if for nothing more, than for your own safety. You see, if I tell the media we have you, and plaster your face on the local and national news, this guy is going to see you as a loose end. He doesn't strike me as the kind of guy that likes loose ends, if you catch my drift."

The color slowly drained from his puffy, pink cheeks. Charli drove home her want from the man. "If you cooperate, that will likely work in your favor. Of course, as I see it, the alternatives for you both involve a short and painful life."

"Wha—wha—what do you want?"

"I need you to sit with a sketch artist," she said. It was old school, but combined with the photos she had, it was bound to be better than the blurry photo alone.

"OK—a—anything," Markowski stammered.

It was a start, but a part of Charli felt like she was already behind the eight ball. *So far I am reacting to this unknown figure. She liked life the other way, where the bad guys reacted to her. With the assassination attempt of the Ruling Council, it would be only a matter of time before they wanted to meet out their pseudo-justice.*

CHAPTER 19

"Those who deny systemic racism are the worst kind of racists."

Arnold Air Force Base, Tennessee

Caylee squatted low and reached for Raul, only to have him grab her left arm and roll, throwing her onto the foam matting they had put down in the spare bedroom.

She twisted during the roll, coming up on her knees and her left hand; she grabbed his right wrist with her free hand and twisted it. Raul flinched in pain, but turned hard away from her, breaking her grasp.

She rose as he turned about and faced her—smiling, fists at the ready. *He's getting much better.* It was hard not to feel pride in his progress. Relaxing, she held her hand out. "I need to get ready to go."

Raul relaxed as well, taking a moment to wipe his brow with the sleeve of his sweaty T-shirt. "I wish you didn't have to go."

"I've stocked the kitchen—so you are set until I get back," she said.

"That's not what I'm talking about," Raul said. "This plan of yours is dangerous."

"Which is why I have to go," she countered. "I have been doing this kind of work for years. Trust me, I won't take any risks that I don't have to."

"I don't have a lot of friends left," Raul said.

She walked up to him and rested her hand on his shoulder. "Trust me. I'll be back, Raul." Her words were sincere. Living with Raul in the house didn't feel like part of a mission. They had become good friends.

She could have walked away after getting Raul settled. Jack

Desmond had not asked her to stay with him—that choice had been hers. At first it had been a decision of convenience. Once she had gotten him back to Tennessee, her obligation was over. She had stayed because she didn't have anywhere else to go. The more time she spent with Raul, the better friends they had become. It wasn't romantic, not on her part at least. She did care about him, however. It was a strange emotion for her. Rather than flee from it, she embraced it. *Maybe I can afford to have friends now.* She was friendly with Jack, Andy and Charli, but Raul was different. She had opened up with him. On top of that, in some respects, their little house had become a pseudo-home to Caylee.

"You take too many risks," he said.

What defines too many? "It's not the number of risks; it's the severity of them. You counter that with planning. We have planned these out in detail," she said.

"You told me that no plan survives contact with the enemy," he said back.

"That's why we have contingencies," she said. "Don't worry Raul. Once the dust settles, I will be back here." *I like it here...for now at least.* "In the meantime, you know the rules."

"Stay indoors; be cautious of everything; and when in doubt, shoot first," he said repeating what she had said to him on numerous occasions.

Smiling, she gave him a nod. "You'll be fine." She started for the stairs intending to gather her gear. *I have a long road ahead of me and a tanker truck to steal.*

The District

"I don't believe it." The Chairman of the Ruling Council, Daniel Porter, stared at the laptop screen in utter shock. The Secretary of the NSF, who had shown him the mountain of evidence, savored the moment. *This was the man that helped bring down America by coordinating ANTIFA, and now he is stunned senseless. This is not a man that is worthy of being President.* She felt that her decisions around her project had been completely justified. *A smarter person would suspect the truth, that this evidence is fabricated.*

"I didn't want to believe it either," she said. "But you've seen it yourself. Senator Lewis, Rebecca Clarke, Barbara Collingsworth...they all conspired behind our backs with the Pretender to have us killed." She had rehearsed the line twice in front of the mirror earlier that morning.

"But Barbara was injured in the blast," he said, giving her a quick glance, and then turning back to the laptop screen.

"We still don't know who planted the bomb or how it was set off. Maybe it was a mistake, or maybe she intended to get injured so that we wouldn't suspect her."

"But Becky? I knew her back before the Liberation." His face reddened and she could see the panic sweat starting to form on his brow. "She has always been loyal—dedicated to the cause."

"I can't speak to that," she said carefully. "You can see the same evidence I have. My people pulled this right off of their hard drives and building security systems." She chose her words carefully. *I don't want to make it look like I am pushing him to a conclusion and merely serving him the information to arrive at the right conclusion.* "I would be remiss if I didn't state the obvious. They couldn't have done this alone. While we know who the key conspirators are, there are bound to be others that provided help. As the investigation continues, eventually dozens could be implicated." *Once we start rounding up dissidents, I can use this to get rid of anyone that ever spoke out against me or the Council, and no one will bat an eye. Their actual guilt is irrelevant. We can rid ourselves of those that are weak at heart, who lack faith in what we are making.*

Daniel dipped his head deep, resting his elbows on the desk top, visibly shaken by the revelation that she had presented to him. It was tempting to talk, but she had learned that silence often was far more effective in manipulating others. He didn't raise his head, but stared almost straight down as he broke the silence. "Who else has seen this information?"

"No one beyond the investigators," she replied. "I thought it was best to share it with you as Chairman first." She wanted her running mate to believe that she was the loyal supporter, further distancing herself from her targets.

He raised his head slowly; his eyes were starting to turn red. He had not been crying, but from the look on his face, he was close to it. For a half-minute, nothing was said as he stared intensely into her eyes. "This is coming at a horrible time. We are days from the election."

"There will never be a good time," she countered. "While you may be tempted to wait until after the election to take action, I remind you that these people tried to kill both of us in a plan to reinstall the Pretender. Their initial attempt failed, but they may get desperate and try something that could work to cover their trail."

"It will shake our people's confidence."

"We can manage that. The TRC is still in control of the media and Internet messaging. We can spin this any way we desire."

"Regardless," he said, sniffling slightly. "Arresting them means trials. It will erode the confidence of the masses in what we are doing."

"Daniel," she said in a soothing tone. "We do not have to hold formal trials. If you want, I can simply take care of matters."

"They have committed crimes against the state…against both of us personally."

"I know. Sometimes extreme measures are called for. I feel the same way you do. If I have the NSF arrest them, they will lawyer up. It will get ugly. Becky is smart. So is Barbara. They are likely to say things in open court that will hurt our administration, simply to save themselves. They will bring in experts who will claim the evidence is false. They will do whatever it takes to save their own skin. Having it in a traditional court of law will expose some of our investigative techniques."

"Just killing them—that makes us look lawless. I need a better alternative, Alex."

"We can use the SEs. They are not bound by the burdens of the legal system. They will still get a fair trial in a People's Tribunal, something we can use in the media to bolster our regime. Using the Social Enforcement approach will give the appearance of legal justice without all of the messiness and risks." In her mind she pictured the show trials blasted out on the Internet. It was even harder for her not to smile. *When the people see what we are willing to do, even to ourselves, thoughts of not supporting us will evaporate. Everyone will fall in line.*

"I am concerned about the TRC," she added. "Rebecca is well respected by a lot of her top people and with the election just days away, we need to carefully control the messaging around changes in the Ruling Council. We need a firm hand at the wheel over there—someone that can manage a large organization effectively. More importantly, it has to be someone that can be trusted."

Daniel nodded. "I know you have a lot going right now, integrating the SEs into the NSF. Do you think you could handle the TRC? Just until we get through the election."

"Good boy, Daniel. It will be a challenge," she said. "But I will do anything to protect what we have built."

You may win the title in the election, but with the TRC and the NSF reporting to me, I will hold the real power behind our administration. I have no intention of giving that up.

Hartsville, Tennessee

Julius Bernstein walked into the bay and saw the postal delivery vehicle; its new coat of white paint made the light coming through the dingy windows reflect around the garage of Wyatt's Auto Repair and Body Shop. While Newmerican postal vehicles were a flat black, the Americans had opted for a more traditional paint scheme. Outside he heard the Uber driver pulling away, ensuring he was alone at the garage with the two people that had worked on his project. Julius walked up to the vehicle and slid open the door, looking inside. Even among the stink of oil and antifreeze, he could smell the new car aroma in the cab as he looked around.

When he had received the call that the truck was done, he was thankful. Only an hour earlier he had received the go-code word from the Secretary of the NSF herself—*Peregrine*. It authorized him to execute his plan, and the van was the lynchpin of that operation.

"We had to work all night to finish it up for your deadline," Wyatt Dawson said. "With the changes you asked for, it should be able to hold about 2,000 pounds."

Julius worked his way to the back and rolled up the big door. The interior had been recently painted, and the fumes hit him as much as the pristine nature of it. "She's a beaut isn't she?"

Julius looked back and saw him and the other mechanic whom he had seen working on the postal truck. Both were smiling proudly. He understood what they were feeling. *People should feel gratified by the work that they do.*

"I am pleased," he said, jumping up slightly, grabbing the strap, and pulling the big door closed. As he turned, he saw Dawson handing him the keys. "She runs fine now too."

Julius took the keys and slid them into his pocket. "You did an outstanding piece of work, both of you," he complimented them.

"I know we went over your budget, but it was worth it, as you can see."

Julius nodded, glancing for a moment at the truck behind him, then turning back to Dawson. "You've done your country a great service. I thought you should know that."

"Well, thanks—" Dawson began. His eyes widened as he saw Julius pull the pistol out. Before he could make another sound, the gun went off, popping Julius's right ear with its crack-boom.

The shot hit Wyatt Dawson in the heart. Blood squirted into the air. He dropped to his knees, then fell to his left side on the filthy concrete floor. The other mechanic panicked. He turned and ran for the door at the rear of the garage. The jumble of tools, tires, and parts blocked a direct path to the exit, forcing him to take three extra steps to get aligned to hit the door.

Julius drew a breath and held it as he tracked his target with the gun patiently, coolly. He fired, hitting him in the shoulder. No doubt the bullet entered his chest as well. The man spun and cried out as he fired a second shot that hit him in the throat. It must have hit his spinal column based on the way his head flopped to the side as he dropped lifeless to the floor.

Julius silently looked at the two bodies. Dawson's made a gurgling noise—nothing new to Julius, who had heard similar sounds from dead bodies before. The other mechanic's left foot twitched for three or four seconds. While he watched and waited for it to stop, he pinched his nose and blew hard to re-pop his eardrum.

It took a few moments for him to find the controls for the big bay door. He backed the postal van out; then he went inside and closed the door, carefully wiping his prints with a handkerchief. As he walked to the front office of the station, he flipped the sign to the main entry door so that the 'Closed' portion showed to the public. He used the handkerchief to hide his prints. Julius searched for a few moments, finally finding a container full of gasoline. He splattered it around the garage, right up to a barrel filled with garbage and cardboard. Dropped a small, timed explosive device in the old metal barrel. In fifteen minutes the evidence of his actions would be ablaze.

Walking calmly out, Julius got into the driver's seat and started the engine. He was pleased to see that Dawson had taken the effort to fill the gas tank for him.

As he drove away, he found himself grinning slightly. *People should feel gratified by the work that they do.*

Georgetown, The District

Rebecca came out of her Georgetown brownstone as she had hundreds, if not thousands, of times, with her two security people walking both in front of and behind her. The house had belonged to a prominent conservative lawyer before the Liberation. When the SEs had forced him out of town, she had simply moved in, laying claim to it for herself. It was quaint, especially compared to some of the riverside mansions that other members of the Ruling Council had taken as their own. She didn't like that optic, so she had chosen a smaller place to live. *We need to at least appear that we are living the ideals we espouse.* Clearly most of her peers didn't feel that way.

The TRC ran over 200 pieces during the last five years about the duty of Newmericans to take public transportation. She was only a short walk from a Metro station, but found it to be filthy. While she compromised as to where she lived, though Georgetown was far from the project housing of the South East District, she didn't want to ride the trains or take a bus. Her bright Tesla Roadster was parked in the street and she angled toward it.

From the corner of her eye, she saw several people moving on the sidewalks, walking fast, seeming to close in on her. For a second, she panicked. The attack on the Capitol had frightened her, as it had many people. *Was this an attack?* She started to recoil, to turn and start back toward the safety of her home. Her security people drew their weapons, but the people only held up badges and shoved them in the faces of her two protectors. They lowered their weapons and let the people walk past.

"Rebecca Clarke?" a stocky, young, black female asked in a demanding tone. She held up her badge and Rebecca saw the Latin phrase,

"Tutor of Licentia," with a large "SE" under it. *Social Enforcement? What could they possibly want?*

"Yes," she said slowly. "What is all this about?"

"We're taking you into our custody," the woman said, putting the badge back into her breast pocket, and then reaching down and pulling out a white zip tie. "For your own safety."

"What the hell?" she managed, taking a half-step back. "Frank—Bob, do your job!"

Her security people didn't respond other than Frank, who shook his head. "You don't have the authority—"

The stocky woman grabbed Rebecca's shoulder and swung her around so violently that her purse fell off her other shoulder and to the ground. Before Rebecca could react, her hands were being thrust upward in the center of her back, hard, painfully. "I demand to know what this is about?" she said.

The SE turned her around and then Rebecca saw her...Alex. Rebecca's heart sank. *What is she doing here?* Her presence alone seemed to indicate that things were far more serious.

"These SEs are taking you in Becky," she said as she slowly walked up to her.

"For what?"

"Treason. Conspiracy. A botched assassination attempt. We're still early in the investigation. I'm sure other things will turn up."

Rebecca ignored the confident tone of the Secretary of the NSF. "This is all bullshit!" she fired back. "I had nothing to do with the Capitol!" She looked around at the SEs and saw that her own security people were also being zip-tied. Instantly she realized the gravity of what was unfolding. *I've been set up.*

"I've seen the evidence," Alex said as the stocky SE pulled her down the two steps toward the sidewalk. "As has Daniel."

"What evidence?"

The Secretary chuckled once, barely audible. "Don't play innocent with me. I've seen the videos and I have read the emails."

"I've been framed!" she said, hoping that the SEs might pause, give her a chance to explain.

"You should consider yourself fortunate," her former peer said as she led Rebecca to a nondescript white government van that was parked in front of the Tesla. "I suggested outright execution. Daniel felt that we needed to show the world that we were lawful though. So these SEs will take you before a People's Tribunal, review the evidence, and deal with you as they see fit."

A Tribunal! That gave her a sinking feeling. "I'm a member of the Ruling Council! I want a lawyer! I have rights!"

The SE leading her laughed out loud. "Look bitch, you tried to blow up the fucking Capitol. You'll get what's coming to you. Rights? Ha! Fuck your rights," she said as the van's side door opened.

Rebecca reeled her head around as if to make one more plea to Alex. When she saw her dark eyes, the look of grim resolve on her face, it summoned up memories from five years ago. "I didn't do this and you know it!"

"Wrong answer, Nightingale …" Alex said, turning and walking away.

Five Years Earlier
Washington DC

There were multiple sets of tunnels under the US Capitol. One set had a transportation system that shuttled Senators and members of Congress, via a subway, to and from their office buildings that flanked the Capitol itself. The other set of tunnels ran from the visitor center over to the Capitol. While far from secret, the private subway was rarely seen.

Rebecca led the Speaker of the House through the bustle of the ANTIFA mob that had seized the building, to an elevator, then down to the subway access. The white tiled walls and ceiling were illuminated by florescent lights.

Once they reached the small subway terminal, Rebecca saw the other members of Congress just past the open, blue, subway cars. Most stood on the tracks while others sat on the nonpowered rails. The system had been shut off. Along the sides of the rails, where they could have walked if they so chose, members of an ANTIFA squad, "The Red Devils," lined the track, armed with various assault weapons. The air was moving, but a bit humid. *They must have never planned on so many of them being down here at once.*

The Speaker paused at the edge of the drop-off to the rails, turning back to her. "You don't have to do this," she stammered slowly.

"Help her down," Rebecca said. One of the men in black bloc reached up, picked up the frail Speaker, and gently lowered her onto the train track. Rebecca climbed down on her own, along with several others who joined her.

Looking to her right, she saw Daniel, and beyond him was Alex. Unlike her fellow members of Congress, Alex wore a black, tactical vest and was with the people that had assaulted the Capitol. There was a look in her dark eyes, fiery and excited. Rebecca understood the wave of emotions. It had taken remarkably little time to secure the building and round up the delegation.

Alex shifted next to Daniel. "They somehow got out," she said angrily.

"Who?" Becky asked.

"The Texas delegates and Senators," he said with frustration. "They had a fundraiser out of town and all left early for the airport. We missed bagging them."

"We should rush the airport," Alex said defiantly.

Daniel shook his head. "We missed others too. We don't know for sure that we have the President yet either. It's nothing to worry about. How much trouble can they cause?"

"I wanted them too," Alex said. Where Daniel and Rebecca came from the campuses and ANTIFA, Alex was different. She had been in Congress, struggling against the corrupt system from the inside. *We wouldn't have been as successful without her help.* She had provided Daniel with the means to get into the Capitol quickly, to negate security, and she provided the plans for rounding up the Congress people and Senators. It was clear, with the aggression in her voice that she wanted the Texas representatives—and wanted them immediately.

"Let it go," Daniel said. "We've already won a great victory here. Besides, after tonight, they will never be able to go back to the way things were." Rebecca heard the passion in his voice and hung on every word.

He turned to her. "You have the statement?"

Reaching into her belt pack, she pulled it out, a single-sheet of folded white paper. She had worked hard to pick the right words, keeping the message short and to the point. Like the address she had coerced the Speaker into reading, it was meant to be heard by everyone in the nation. "I have it right here."

"Go ahead," Daniel said with a smile. "You wrote it. Read it to them."

This was an honor she had not expected. When she had written the statement, her assumption was that Daniel would be the one reading it. For him to trust her with such an honor made her blush momentarily.

She motioned for the news team that had followed her. "You film this, but only release it when I give you authorization. Understood?"

The CNN team nodded nervously, clearly aware they were surrounded by ANTIFA troops armed to the hilt. They positioned themselves as Daniel and Alex flanked her; their filming lights hit her square in the face.

Her fingers were trembling as she unfolded the paper. "People of our nation. The time of reckoning has come. The people you have crushed under the heels of your oppression have risen for the cause of freedom. Your children have unshackled themselves from their racist pasts to set right more than four centuries of tyranny."

She paused, steadying her grip on the paper to stop the trembling of her fingers. "Tonight we have secured the future. A new age is upon us. A rebirth of our nation will begin in a great reformation. But to take those steps, we must acknowledge and accept that there can be no turning back from this historic moment. There can be no reconciliation without shedding the broken system of government that has bound us and held us back."

Her eyes stabbed at the camera and she felt her jaw set. "This rebirth begins here in Washington DC, but it is unfolding everywhere. I encourage our great family of revolutionaries to rise up and seize what is rightfully yours. Take control of your state capitals; shake off the shackles of capitalism and oppression. Tomorrow begins a new age—a new America."

A roar of support came from the ANTIFA in the tunnel. Rebecca stopped, carefully folding the document and returning it to her belt pocket. *This is the speech I only dreamed of delivering...and now it is happening. We are in control!*

Alex was the first to move. While the camera was still filming, she produced a small pistol with a turquoise handle. In three quick, long strides, she walked up to the Speaker of the House, who was being held upright by an older Senator Rebecca couldn't quite identify. The Speaker saw Alex and summoned the energy to rise to her full, tiny stature.

Alex extended the weapon, aiming it at the Speaker's forehead only a yard away. The Speaker, to her credit, didn't waver in her gaze or stare at the weapon; she looked Alex in the eyes. "You don't have to do this," she said in a quivering voice.

"From the day I came to Congress, you treated me like shit. You stabbed me in the back a hundred times and grinned to the cameras when doing it. You broke every promise you ever made to me." Pure venom dripped from every syllable that she spoke. Rebecca could see the rage and could taste the hate in the moist air. Other members of Congress could too. They began to move away from the Speaker so as not to be caught in the gunfire they most certainly expected.

"No…no…you got it wrong. I saw the greatness in you. I was grooming you for my job. I was teaching you how this place worked… and you were a fantastic student. I was doing you a great favor. We are allies—we are the same."

Alex's eyes closed slowly as she clearly attempted to curb her rage. "I didn't need your help. I made myself. Look around you, Nancy," she gestured to the elevated gunmen on both sides of the subway track. "We have taken what is rightfully ours. Your era in history is over."

The Speaker's head shook back and forth, "No—no—no. You need me. You need people like me on this Council you're calling for. They will come for you at some point with everything they have. You won't kill me," she said with a hint of defiance. "You need my experience and connections."

"Wrong answer," Alex said and the gun barked in her hand.

The bullet hole in the forehead of the Speaker of the House was small, but behind her was a massive gush and spray of blood. She fell from the side of the older man who was holding her up, dropping limp to the floor. Screams came from several of the prisoners who moved even farther down the tracks, as if they might somehow get away.

"Pull the ones on our list," Alex said coldly as she turned around.

"We don't need her, but some of the other members might be useful." Daniel pulled out his iPhone and began scrolling through a short list of Congress and the Senate, pulling them off the tracks and ushering them to the rear of the platform. Rebecca watched as the process ended only a few minutes later.

The camera crew was still filming, focused on Daniel Porter as he finished the task. The other members of the nation's leadership kept back at least ten feet from where the body of the Speaker lay on the tracks.

Daniel paused, looking at Alex, who gave a nod of approval. He then surprised Rebecca by glancing at her. "Do it," she said softly, just enough for him to hear.

"Free the nation!" he roared. "Kill them all!" The gunfire in the tunnel and Rebecca's ears popped, muffling the screams and the sound of bodies falling on the tracks. It was over in a few seconds. There was a slight haze in the air, and a long procession of dead bodies. The image was seared in her mind.

The light from the CNN crew went off and left her alone there, in the darkness. She knew she should be feeling sad, but she didn't. *They deserved this. Such is the fate of tyrants.*

Georgetown, The District

Rebecca wasn't helped into the back of the white van; she was tossed. Alex's last words hung in her ears, along with the memories of that night five years earlier in the subway tunnel under the Capitol. When she had finally authorized CNN to release the footage, she had edited out the slaughter that had taken place and the shooting of the Speaker of the House.

As her arms ached from hitting the van floor, she realized the error she had made. *The Presidency means nothing to Alex…that's why I am here. She wants it all, and Daniel is being manipulated to play into her hands.*

I should have released the footage of her shooting the Speaker.

CHAPTER 20

"If you think you are possibly being oppressed—you are."

Manassas, Virginia

It had been a busy few days for Caylee Leatrom. She had infiltrated the CoreSite activity posing as a fire inspector—disabling their detection and suppression systems, and planting a half-dozen fire bombs. From what she could tell, no one suspected a thing. The timers on the explosives were set to go off in an hour, and she knew she'd be done with the work at EvoSwitch in Manassas, one way or another.

For two nights she had gone along the fence line, using a portable torch to cut the vertical rises on the security fence. She didn't have to sever them, only to damage them enough to substantially weaken them. *I would have been done in one night if my torch hadn't run low on gas.*

The most important phase of her plan was securing the right vehicle. She went to a gasoline transfer station in southern Virginia for that, hijacking a Sheetz delivery truck. It was almost comical, when she flagged over the driver, and then pulled the gun on him. "You stealing this to sell the gas?"

In a rare moment of humor, she had been blunt. "I was thinking of blowing it up," she told the driver.

He grinned broadly. "Makes no difference to me. Since they have been shoving those shit-fuck electric cars up everyone's ass, half my buddies have lost their jobs driving trucks. You want to blow up the company's truck, you've got my damn blessing! Hell, I won't even report it missing for a few hours."

"Thank you," she said as he climbed down.

"God Bless America," he said, giving her a light salute with two fingers off the bill of his cap. *Did he somehow know I was using this against Newmerica?* It seemed unlikely, but Caylee had given him a quick salute back.

Not everything was going quite as planned. The NSF had a major office less than a mile from the EvoSwitch building. It was an FBI field office before being absorbed into the NSF. Regardless of what it had been, its proximity was unnerving when she had spotted it. The Newmerica allies in Silicon Valley had not allowed the facility to show up on Google Maps or any other site, essentially making it invisible on the Internet. She had to admit that it was a brilliant move on their part. *Regardless, I'll be making the attack in the early morning hours, so they should be understaffed. When it does happen, they may think it is nothing more than a building fire.* While the odds of the NSF's best and brightest responding was limited, it was something she had not anticipated.

She had prepped the truck with two devices, in case one of them somehow failed—a suggestion from Travis Cullen. The phone numbers for the detonators were on her phone speed dial. As she sat in the cab, parked off a wooded side road in Prince William County, she mentally reviewed her checklists.

At 3 a.m. she drew a deep breath. "Show time," she muttered to herself.

While Caylee had practiced driving a nearly identical rig back in Tennessee, that one had been empty. The full gasoline tanker handled a lot differently—it was more sluggish. Turning was slow and required a lot more effort, despite power steering. Getting up to speed was going to be a challenge, given the turns in the road. *I'll have to bail out after the last turn, right after I get it into the top gears.* That was concerning because she knew it would be close to the fence itself. *There's no way around that; I may have to wing it.* While she was confident that the truck would do the job, there was always a chance things would go wrong.

The big truck turned off of State Route 234 and into the industrial park where EvoSwitch was located. Caylee worked up through the gears as she saw the facility in the distance. The trick was to be going as fast as possible, but still be able to make the last turn without rolling over.

In the darkness, the facility parking lot was well lit, illuminating the gray windowless structure. The gears ground as she struggled to keep upshifting.

Swinging wide on the road into the opposite lane, she struggled at craning the big tanker around the last curve. She could feel the vehicle side sliding slightly, but she did not even think of hitting the brakes. Her heart pounded in her ears as she lined up the side of the building in her sights, punching the gas pedal and moving up the gears.

The truck hit the autumn grass as it headed for the area of the fence that she had weakened. She jammed the shift into the last gear, and then grabbed the cut piece of two-by-four she had prepared. Jamming it down on the gas pedal, she wedged it up against the bottom of the seat as the tanker's engine roared. I'm as lined up as I can be.

Opening the door in the cold, early morning air, Caylee jumped out.

Her landing was far from graceful as she rolled on the cold, dew-covered grass. At the moment that she sat up, the truck hit the heavy metal security fence. The sound was a sickening metallic grinding as the fence buckled under the impact, but clung to the front of the vehicle. The battering ram of a tanker truck dragged it across the nearly empty parking lot, making sparks and a sickening metallic moan as it gave way.

The fence altered the angle of the truck enough to force Caylee to utter, "Shit!" Instead of hitting the building perpendicular, it was now roaring at an angle. *Would it even penetrate the structure?* A heartbeat later she saw it collide with the exterior of the structure, blowing through the outer wall and driving into the building's interior, stopping as half of the truck was in, and half was out.

Caylee pulled out her phone when she heard sounds of cracking and collapse. The weight of the vehicle, which was filled with gasoline, was too much for the interior floor. In a loud whooping sound, it collapsed, pulling the cab downward into the first basement level and sliding the truck a few yards inward.

She was about to send the call that would detonate the bombs she had placed on the vehicle when they went off on their own. Roughly 10,000 gallons of gasoline ignited in a ball of fire that was so massive she could feel the heat from where she lay outside the facility. Two cars in the parking lot exploded as well, adding to the conflagration that was roaring skyward in a billowing mushroom-cloud-like, rolling, orange ball of fire. A tire shot out—either from the blasted truck, or a car in the parking lot—bouncing some twenty yards into the darkness.

The fire was so intense that it instantly plunged a large section of the structure into flames. The gasoline from the tanker burned so hot, she got to her feet and started to jog back toward the road. Because the truck's cab and part of the tank itself were now down into the first sub-basement, she could only assume that the fire was burning deep in the substructure.

There was a rumble from deep inside the structure. The flames were so brilliant, she could not make out any piece of vehicle. Cullen's projection had shown the heat would be so high that it would melt concrete and easily devour the aluminum and steel of the building's interior. It didn't matter that they had working fire equipment—nothing would easily extinguish this blaze.

Satisfied that this facility was done, she started walking cross country towards Route 28 to the south. Finding a vehicle to steal would be easier there, and she wanted as much distance as possible from this site. In a short few minutes, the bombs she planted at CoreSite would be going off, engulfing that building in fire as well.

As she moved out into the darkness, framed by the roaring blaze behind her, she heard the distant wails of fire engines. Caylee allowed herself a smile. *You're too late.*

The District

Senator Lewis's upper lip was swollen and his left eye was surrounded by deep purple. His shirt collar had blood splatters. He was angry; she could see that through the two-way mirror where the Secretary of the NSF reveled in his plight. "I want to talk to him, alone, no monitoring or recording," she said.

"Of course, ma'am," the detective said, motioning for the other two officers to leave the room.

As soon as they left, she stepped down the two stairs and opened the door to the room. His brilliant blue eyes locked onto hers, and his anger intensified; the red in his cheeks went fiery crimson at the sight of her. "I should have known you'd be behind something like this, such a blatant abuse of power."

"I tried to reason with you…to get you to do what was right for the nation."

"Checks and balances *are* what was right for the nation."

"We could spend a lot of time debating that," she said coyly, savoring every moment. "But I don't take political advice from a traitor."

"I'm no traitor!" the Senator snapped.

She held out her iPhone and tapped the play icon. The video showed the Senator and the cabal her people had created, talking about bombing the Ruling Council. She let it play for only a minute…that was all it took.

The expression on the face of the Senator went from angry to shocked. "I—that isn't me! This is a fabrication—a lie!"

"The funny thing about a lie. It can become the truth if it is told to the people enough times. Sooner or later people believe in it…hell, they will fight to protect the lie. And in this case, Daniel and others who have seen it believe it."

"You created this to frame me!" the old man said bitterly.

"You can keep denying it," she said, pacing in front of the table that stood between them. "Or you can confess. Frankly, I don't care which. Either way, your hearings into the NSF are dead and buried. Oh, and my people found the bugs you planted at the NSF too." Memories of Burke Dorne showing her the listening devices still infuriated her.

"I have no idea what you are talking about," he said. His defiance was the same…no hint of guilt. *Maybe he didn't plant that bug.* "When I get in court, I will eviscerate you. I will prove that the video and these ridiculous charges are fake!"

There it is, the defiance and fire that spared his life that night in the Capitol subway tunnel. Her smile broadened as she spoke. "If there were going to be a traditional trial, you might be right. There won't be. You are going to be turned over to a People's Tribunal where you will get the justice that you deserve. Your interpretation of events will never be public." *Your opinions and views will die with you.*

Lewis's head shook. "I deserve—"

"—nothing!" she snapped, cutting him off. "Social justice is justice in our country; even you know that. When we are done with you, our SEs can do some digging into your family. They might not have done anything wrong, but being associated with a conspirator and traitor isn't going to work in their favor."

He lost his fury—his anger. As it flowed out of him, he realized what was unfolding. For half a minute he said nothing, looking down at the table. "I'll stop my hearings. I will tell everyone it was all a big mistake. You don't have to go through with this."

The Secretary smiled. "Another mistake on your part, Senator. I *do* have to do this." She turned and left the room as the old man broke down, sobbing uncontrollably. The sounds of his whimpers were something that she would relish for some time to come.

University of Virginia
Charlottesville, Virginia

Maddie Steele grabbed her gym bag and backpack. The note her roommate Pris had found under the door and handed to her simply said, "Go time." She had prepacked clothing, what few personal effects she had, and her textbooks. As she lifted the bag, she regretted packing the books, but in the back of her mind, she knew why they were there. She wanted to finish what she had started at the university. *I've gone this far; one day, I will complete my degree.* The bags had weighed so much that she had tucked her Smith and Wesson EZ9 into her pants waist, making sure her sweater and hoodie covered any hint that it was there.

Pris looked at her. "Where are you going?"

"Out."

"For the weekend?"

Maddie glanced down at the bag. "Something like that."

"Good for you," Pris said. "You never leave your room except to go to class." Her attention immediately shifted to her iPhone. "Hey, are you able to get on the Internet?"

Pausing at the door, she turned to her. "Not at all today," she replied. "No one has been able to." It had been an annoyance to her, but her mind was focused on one thing—leaving.

Walking across campus she saw a large group of angry students gathered off to one end of The Lawn. Their voices were louder than normal, tinted with a bit of rage that puzzled her. Some held their phones in the air, as if that were some sort of symbol, one that Maddie didn't understand. People seemed drawn to the group, and she saw a number of them were wearing their black bloc. *Something has happened to get them all riled up. They can't be this upset over the Internet not working.* She shook that last thought. *Of course they could! Social media is how they define their existence. If they can't get there to scream their opinions or attack others, they have nothing.* She held back any trace of a smile over their angst.

Maneuvering around the growing crowd, she made her way to the Rotunda, glancing around to make sure no one was following her. The sounds from the growing crowd were muffled in the large opening, bouncing off the abandoned ceilings and walls. She made her way to the North Oval Room.

Inside, she was surprised at the number of people. Brad and Tina stood on the long wall opposite of her. Easily a dozen students were crammed into the room, each with luggage. One girl had two big roller bags—as if she had packed everything she owned. The faces of the students were concerned; some were downright frightened.

"Ah, Maddie," Tina said. "I'm glad you came. Things are getting out of control quickly. We need to move soon."

"What has happened?"

"Haven't you tried to get on the net today?" Brad asked.

Shaking her head, she responded. "I couldn't. I assumed the campus net had gone down for some reason."

Brad now shook his head. "No. Someone attacked the Internet hub sites around The District last night. It has cut off most of the East Coast from the net. Even New York has been affected. From what I was told by a computer social science student, with everyone trying to connect, it's overloading the other hubs and they are collapsing…or whatever it is that servers do."

I was right; they are upset over losing their Internet access! There was an eloquence about it all; taking down the net threw the people that hated her into a frenzy. It would be funny if it weren't so dangerous. *They don't know what to do; they just know someone has to pay.* "So we have to leave because of this?"

"We got word that they have a list with many of our names on it. This attack will set the campus SEs off. They are going to want to look for someone to blame. I was hoping that we had another week or two, but this attack has changed that. We need to get all of you off campus," Brad said with a tone of assurance. "We've got three cars waiting. We'll get you to someplace safe."

Francine spoke up, clutching her soft-sided athletic bag tightly in her lap. "You're asking us to trust you. We barely know you."

"That's fair," Brad said smoothly. "Look, you have to start trusting someone Francine. These people are coming for you, for all of us. You're welcome to go back to your dorm room and wait for them to come—or you can come with us. We aren't going to force anyone to do anything they don't want to do." Tina nodded firmly in agreement.

"Where's someplace safe?" a young man asked. He was wearing a UVA lacrosse hoodie.

"Front Royal. There's an old 4-H camp up there on a mountainside. It's rough, but isolated," Tina said with a comforting grin. It's going to be winter soon. The thought of living in an old camp had little appeal, but then again neither did a beating by an angry mob. *I can make it work. It is no longer safe here, not if they have our names.* A ripple of sadness washed over her. *Will I ever get to return here?* She knew the answer to that question, and it tore at her soul. *For now, my college career is on hold.*

"We need to get you out of here," Tina continued. "Grab your stuff and follow us." Tina, Brad, and another young man she didn't know led the rest of them out of the room and to the back of the Rotunda. They pulled back a piece of plywood that had been nailed over an old doorway. There was barely enough room for each person to squeeze through with their luggage. They quickly made their way to University Avenue where a car and two vans were parked. The other students on the campus seemed to ignore them; they were heading to the gathering at The Lawn that she had passed. Someone had gotten a bullhorn, and she could hear the cries of "terrorist attack," coming from the growing protest.

She shuffled into the van and sat next to a girl she didn't know. "I'm Maddie," she said, extending her hand.

"Clarice," the younger girl said, shaking her hand.

"You frightened?" Maddie asked.

Clarice nodded. "I'm feeling better now…now that we are getting out of here."

"Me too," she said as the van's old gasoline engine turned over. As it jerked into motion, she wondered how she would get ahold of her parents. *They will worry about me.* She was tempted to call them, but the packed seats in the back of the van offered no privacy.

Each passing moment made her feel safer; each mile brought a bit more calm.

Arnold Air Force Base, Tennessee

Deja drove slowly down the street, which was lined with identical houses. She leaned forward and squinted in the darkness at the house where she suspected that Raul Lopez was hiding. The car was still not there and while the drapes were closed, she saw light from the inside creeping out between the two curtains on the front window. *Someone is home.*

She had come on the base to deliver a pizza earlier and had noticed the car not being there, which she took as a good sign. When she came back, she had Gallagher with her, wearing a red and blue Dominos ball cap, looking woefully too old for the role of a future pizza deliveryman. She had given the guards a free pizza the last time she came through, claiming that with the Internet down, they had made one too many. The guards were more than willing to wave her through the second time.

"That's it. The third one from the end of the street on the right," she said. Gallagher leaned forward and looked at it. "IT looks like someone is in there," he said as she slowed the car even more. In the trunk of the vehicle was Chad, curled up in a tight ball, no doubt hoping they would pull over soon.

"We use stun guns," Gallagher said, pulling his out and checking it. "If we start firing actual guns, it is going to attract a lot of attention, quick."

Deja didn't like it. The SE way was to use brute force, including guns. It was a point in their plan she had conceded though. It wouldn't do anyone any good to get caught with Lopez before they got off base. "Yeah, yeah," she said. "But if that fucker pulls a gun, this taser shit is history.'

She angled the car into the short driveway and turned off the engine. "Grab the delivery case," she said, hitting the button for the trunk release. By the time she stood up, Chad had unfolded from the trunk and was already making his way toward her.

"I'll do the talking, Gallagher. You hit him as soon as we get confirmation it's him."

"Right," he said. He held the red vinyl pizza carrier in front of him with the taser under it. Chad moved off to the side as they started to walk up to the small, cement porch. "Chad, go to the back door."

"On it," he whispered back, moving in the shadows around the small house.

As they reached the front door, she drew a long breath. This was where it all paid off…the hours of roadblocks, being shot at, wading through tips. Her instinct as a Digger told her that this was where Lopez was hiding out. *We're going to get you, you little fuckface. Then I will see you burn.* She reached down to the right side holster where she had strapped on the taser and wrapped her hands around the pistol grip.

Deja reached out and hit the doorbell. Inside the muffled ding-dong went off. She heard footsteps getting closer. The knob turned, and the door cracked open. For a moment, she saw half of his face staring out at her from behind the chained door.

"Pizza delivery," she said with a fake, happy tone of voice.

Arnold Air Force Base, Tennessee

Raul looked through the narrow crack of the security chained door and saw two pizza delivery people. One of them was old with crew cut hair. He looked nothing like someone delivering pizza. He was holding a red pizza carrying bag, but from what Raul could see, it was limp, as if it were empty. The other person was a muscular, black woman, who greeted him with, "Pizza delivery."

It looked and felt wrong—far beyond the fact that he had not ordered pizza.

Caylee's training with him kicked in, almost as if it were instinct. Action overrode hesitation. Raul moved to slam the door shut and succeeded. Right next to the door was a small table with a loaded Glock on it, which he grabbed. A thud on the door was followed by a cracking-kick that knocked it wide open, busting the chain in the process. The older male stepped forward, still holding the pizza carrier flat in front of him.

Raul brought his free hand down hard on the pizza carrying bag. He heard a 'zzzit' sound under it. A stun gun! He never felt the wires embed into him; the hit on the bag meant that they had struck the carrier, not him. The man was furious, filling the doorway, tossing the bag to the ground and fidgeting with his stun gun as Raul swung the Glock around on him.

He squeezed the trigger smoothly, exactly as he had been taught. The pistol had a nasty kick, but it roared. The shot hit the man in the upper body on the left side, sending him teetering backwards. Raul went low, rolling to the side, knowing that the female was going to come through the door. For a few moments it felt as if everything in the room were moving in slow motion. The older man fell, and the doorway was filled with a blurry image of the female.

In a haze of motion, Raul squeezed off another round; he thought he caught her right leg, but he couldn't be sure. She was fast, darting in, leveling her stun gun toward him. He leaned a little to the left, and then jerked hard to the right to throw off her shot as he tried to bring his own gun to bear on her again.

He never felt the stun gun barbs hit him, but he felt the shock instantly. Raul's entire body seemed to go rigid, and the pain made every body part roar in agony. A part of him knew he had to keep moving, but it was as if his body were refusing the command.

Somehow, he managed to raise his pistol again and aim at the woman at the other end of the wires. Caylee clenched the stun gun with both hands at this point. *I can do it—I can get off another shot.*

Then he felt it. Another lightning bolt of agony hit him from behind. His vision blurred for a moment; it was so painful, so violently jarring. He wanted to shoot; he wanted to turn and see who had attacked him from behind, but instead his body locked up. He went down face first on the carpet, the ripples of hot torturing agony searing at every attempt to move.

Another pain came, a knee jabbing into his lower back. The female in front of him moved forward, and he felt a hand grab the pistol and toss it toward the kitchen. The person on his back grabbed his arms as he struggled to break free; then his arms were zip-tied behind him.

As quickly as the electric charges came, they suddenly stopped.

"Who are you?" he demanded defiantly.

Hands tossed him over on his back. Looking up he saw the female on her knees in front of him. She reached down and held his face, eyeing him suspiciously. There was a moan from the doorway; the older man that he had shot was clearly still alive and in agony. *Who are these people?*

"Raul Lopez," the female said grimly. "You are a prisoner of the people," she said. "Gag him," she told the man standing next to him. "Toss him in the trunk."

"What about Gallagher?" he said, pulling out a large red and black kerchief.

The female went to the door and struggled to drag the man in. The moans stopped as he crossed the threshold. Raul craned his head around and saw that the color seemed to be draining from the man's face. "He's bleeding out," she declared, closing the door. "We need to leave him here."

"You can't do that," the other man said.

"The fuck I can't. We can't fit him in the truck with Lopez and if the guards see him bleeding, we are screwed," she said angrily. "He knew the score. Those shots are going to draw a lot of attention fast."

The man tied the gag over Raul's mouth, knotting it hard over his left ear. "You make a sound," he whispered close to Raul. "And I will gut you." To make his point, he held out a big buck hunting knife, waving it in front of Raul's eyes. *He wants to hurt me; I can see that.* In his mind, he pictured Caylee. *Don't give him a reason to do it, Raul. You need to wait until the time is right.*

The female rose over him to her full height. "Let's get him loaded. I don't know how much time we have." Hands grabbed onto his shirt and pants and he tried to shift his legs, only to find that they too had been zip-tied. The last image he had of the house that had been his temporary home was of the ceiling fixture over the entry near the front door. *Come on Caylee...show up and kill these assholes!*

As much as he wished it, she never appeared …

CHAPTER 21

"There are no crises—there are only opportunities to excel."

Nashville, Tennessee

Charli Kazinski sat in the 'Perch' inside of the command and control center for the secret service in the old Commerce Union Bank Building about a half block away from the Southern White House. The red brick structure had been slated for a major renovation when the Fall unfolded. After the overthrow of Washington DC, the rioting in downtown Nashville had left the owners with little incentive to complete the work. While the business of the Secret Service was done at the White House, the tactical operations were coordinated in the old bank building. Chari and her people moved in while it was still being rebuilt, and now, from her elevated central seat, she could survey the banks of video screens that almost completely surrounded her.

Since her talk with Caylee, she had undertaken additional measures for security. The President's motorcade was always escorted by a decoy. From time to time she had the President ride in what appeared to be a backup SUV simply to throw off a would-be assassin. Monitoring had been dramatically increased as was rooftop surveillance in the blocks around the hub of federal activity for America. Despite all of the additional measures, she felt like she was fighting an uphill battle. She remembered her training years ago. "The assassin always has the advantage—they get to choose when and where they will strike and with what means. Our job is to make that planning as difficult as possible."

"Chief," came a call from one of the observers. "I've got something out of place here."

Charli moved from her seat to stand behind the agent. "What have you got?"

"This post truck," she said, pointing to the image that the street camera picked up. "It's two hours early, and it is not parked where it usually is, by a block and a half."

One thing about the postal service; they are consistent. "Run the plates," she said.

"On it," the agent said, accessing the database. A few seconds passed before she responded, "It's not on our list of frequents."

It's possible that it is a replacement driver—driving a different truck. While that would account for the vehicle being parked in a different area, Charli stared at the truck and saw the sunlight shimmering off of it. The light reflection caught her attention. "Postal trucks are old, usually with a lot of signs of wear and tear. That one looks like it has a fresh paint job."

The agent sitting in front of the computer furiously punched at the keyboard. "The license plates don't match. They are federal, but not for a postal truck," she said more to herself than to her team. *Damn...this could be an attempt.*

"People, we have a probable explosive device," she said loud enough for everyone to hear, moving back toward the Perch. "Contact the detail and have them divert immediately," she commanded. "Have the decoy go into the loop." The loop was a holding pattern of streets outside of Nashville proper. "Contact the Nashville PD, and tell them we need the bomb squad where that vehicle is parked." She wanted to order the evacuation of the nearby buildings, but if she did, the bomber would know that his plot had been foiled and would likely get away. It was not an easy decision. A truck of that size could kill hundreds of people. Memories of the Oklahoma City bombing tugged at her. The decision gnawed at Charli, but she knew she was making the right call. *I need him in custody.* "Rewind that video. I want to see the driver and where they went."

The room seemed to tingle with excitement as agents did their work. "Got him," the agent called out, sending the image to the large, central flat screen that was suspended from the ceiling. "He's walking down

9th Avenue heading toward Broadway." The video on the big monitor, showed what appeared to be a postal delivery person. The traditional satchel was slung over the uniform shirt as the man casually closed the door to the truck and walked away. "Zoom in on the face and freeze," she said. "Everyone check the time stamp. I want him followed."

As her people went over the data, Charli glared at the face. It wasn't too far off from the police sketch Markowski had provided. His hair was different, cut shorter with a hint of gray to make him look older. *That's our man, the one that has been fucking with me for weeks.*

"Chief," I have a road obstruction, Demonbreun and 6th. Flat tire in the street. Local law enforcement is on the scene," an agent called out.

"That's his diversion," she said. "Have the locals take that driver into custody," she commanded.

"I have our target," Agent Truman called from her seat. "Christ Catholic Church at 9th and Broadway, four minutes later," she called. Truman didn't wait for her to give the order; she moved the short video stream up from her screen onto the large, main screen. Charli watched as the faux postal worker walked under the camera at the church. *He's not delivering mail—he's walking right by them.*

"I've got him," called another agent from the floor. "Frist Art Museum, two minutes later—in front of the Holiday Inn," she said. Another image appeared showing him across the street, walking past the Holiday Inn Express, rounding the corner onto 10th Avenue, back tracking a block away from where he had left the van.

Charli knew the street; it was devoid of businesses. *There's no one for you to deliver mail to down there.* "He'll have to come out on Commerce Street," she said. "Should be two minutes later."

There was a long pause. "Come on Commerce Street," she said in a deep tone.

The young agent, Riley, called out. "I've got nothing. He didn't come out."

"The parking garage," she said. It made sense. It was attached to the Holiday Inn, and if the motorcade was diverted, it would provide a good viewing position. "Alright people, we have a hostile at the Holiday Inn. He might backtrack into the hotel itself from the parking structure, or he's there." She paused, carefully choosing her plan of action. "Contact

Nashville SWAT and apprise them of the situation. Get them photos of our suspect ASAP. No one leaves that hotel until we give the go-ahead—that is to be made clear. Have them secure all access points; place people to cover the parking garage entrances, but I want them to provide cover only. Inform our DHS team to deploy to the exterior of the parking structure, lower deck."

He will know something is amiss if the motorcade doesn't show up. "Inform the motorcade of the situation. I want them to come in slow; use the approach pattern Delta. Have them stop for a few minutes for his diversion—let him think that things are still going according to his plan." The DHS team was in the Southern White House and could move fast, but the Nashville PD was going to take a little longer. *As long as he thinks he has a chance, we have an opportunity to catch him.*

"Comms—I want to shut down the cell towers covering downtown," *I hope Caylee is right about him using a cell phone to trigger the bomb.* She had strong-armed AT&T and Verizon to install a kill-switch control, similar to the ones they used to have in Washington DC before the Fall. They complained, but Jack had backed her call. "Yes, Chief," the agent in charge of communications called out. "They are off-line."

"Tell our rooftop teams that I need eyes on that parking structure.

"People," she said, louder than she had called out before. Heads turned, and she felt the eyes of everyone in the room on her. "Get me a countermeasures and rapid response teams positioned on the Commerce and 10th Avenue exits, full assault gear. The person we are going up against may very well be an operative. That makes him a trained killer." "O'Brien, you have the Perch," Charli said. "I'm going in with the teams and will assume command on the ground."

Nashville, Tennessee

Julius took the last flight of stairs to the top level of the parking garage and could feel the strain in his shins. It was the shoes…it had to be. He had crafted his uniform perfectly, including the shoes. Being flat-footed, the shoes had more of an arch than he was used to. *How could postmen wear these things?*

The parking deck didn't have rooftop parking and only two cars were parked on the upper floor. One of them, a yellow Chrysler Strider, looked as if it had been left there for a long time based on the dust covering it. He briskly walked over to the Commerce Street side of the three-story structure. It was a lightly clouded day, quiet. That would all change shortly.

Julius had run enough tests of the motorcade route to know one thing—no matter how they diverted, when confronted with an obstacle, they always passed 9th Avenue. While they would pass nearly fifty feet from the truck, with 2,000 pounds of explosives, it was going to be more than enough to destroy the limousine.

As he came to the deck opening, he leaned out on the thick wire barriers, looking to his right to see the motorcade. It was later than he had expected; no doubt they had driven several blocks around the disabled car with the flat tire…his paid diversion. He caught a glimpse of the progression three blocks away. Julius reached into his carrier bag and pulled out his phone.

The presidential progression of five vehicles turned and was about to pass the truck bomb. Weeks of work and planning were finally paying off, so much that Julius cracked a smile. He called the number and waited for an explosion.

None came.

He dialed it again—again nothing.

Something is wrong! They must be jamming the cell towers. Damn! Leaning back from the edge, he reached into his postal bag and pulled out a sleek Kel-Tec SUB-2000 Carbine, and extended the stock. His mind went over his contingency. Get to the truck; activate the timed switch—mostly to destroy evidence; and then he could reach the getaway vehicle parked six blocks away. The blast would damage a lot of downtown Nashville and while it wouldn't kill the President, it would send ripples of fear in the fledgling American administration. If all went as planned, he'd be on his way out of the city by the time the truck exploded.

Turning quickly, he started to jog toward the staircase. Suddenly, he saw a figure wearing body armor emerge from the stairs. He brought his carbine up and fired two shots, one of which hit the officer square in the chest.

Julius dove for cover behind the yellow Chrysler as he heard the voices and footsteps of police.

Damn it!

Nashville, Tennessee

Charli heard the gunfire above her and shot up the stairs, two at a time. The only thing slowing her was the Secret Service Rapid Response team that was in front of her. As soon as she reached the top floor landing, she went low, motioned to by the team leader, Agent Romler, who had gotten there first. She had her MP5 out as she joined Romler. Glancing down, she could see the hit he had taken. “You alright, Troy?”

He nodded quickly, wincing. “Behind that Chrysler,” he said, nodding his head toward where the agents were clearly aiming. “He’s huddled behind the rear tire.” At least five agents were crammed in the tight space, all with weapons drawn and aimed at the vehicle. Charli rose slowly enough to get a quick glimpse of the car sitting alone near the center of the parking structure.

Grabbing her shoulder mike, she triggered it on. “This is Slingshot. Be advised Perch; we have a suspect on level three of the parking structure.”

“Roger that, Slingshot,” O’Brien replied. “Decoy has made their run.”*…and the bomb didn’t go off. Good!* Charli let the mike control go. Now came the hard part. This was likely an operative that she faced, someone who was the equivalent of Caylee. That made the would-be assassin very dangerous. “Do we have a shot?” she asked. Romler shook his head.

We are three stories up. Grabbing her mike control stud, she called again. “Be advised; we need cover for the first floor of the parking structure exterior.” A flurry of voices confirmed that. A three-story jump was high, but survivable. *I want this guy.* Having him slip through her fingers would be a disaster.

“What about going low—shooting under the car?” she asked in a soft voice.

One of the agents slowly went prone, lying flat in the open doorway. “I have a foot visible,” he whispered.

“Take the shot,” she said, rising to watch.

Two shots cracked from his gun. Echoes in the parking structure made it sound like more than two. There was a sound—an argh!—from the vehicle. Then a spray of semi-automatic fire came from under the vehicle; the flashes from the gun were visible. The prone agent rolled over twice and moved behind a concrete structural support as bullets ricocheted off of the concrete and hit the lower concrete structure that Charli hid behind.

"Got him," the agent called from his new position of cover.

Being hit would make her perp more desperate; she knew that. "Bull horn," she ordered, and a half minute later, one was handed to her. She rose enough to broadcast her message. "This is the Secret Service. There is no way out. Surrender and you will be treated fairly."

Nashville Tennessee

Julius had never been shot before this, but the pain was intense. Looking down, he saw a bit of white bone poking through his sock, bone from his shattered ankle. Blood from the wound squirted over the ground as he painfully repositioned himself so he was lying flat, behind the rear tire, perpendicular to the Secret Service. The blood flow didn't show an artery being hit, but Julius knew he would be getting weaker by the minute.

He heard the booming female voice calling for his surrender though he wished he hadn't. Training took over as he mentally processed his options. His bomb had failed to go off, and he had no way of getting to it, not on a shattered foot. Using the tire for cover was not a good position, not for long. *If they open up, this piece of shit car will disintegrate around me.*

Julius didn't want to die; nor did he want to be a prisoner. He considered sticking the Kel-Tec to his head and pulling the trigger, but that seemed strangely like a cowardly action. If he chose to shoot it out with them, he would be gunned down the moment he poked his head up. Looking past his legs and the growing puddle of blood, he saw the open bay window with the wires he had been leaning on a few minutes earlier. *Even if I could make it there, the jump with one good leg would make me a prisoner.* Raw frustration tore at him. *Come on Julius, you always find a way out.* Looking around he found nothing but frustration. *Damn!*

I overplayed my hand; they knew I was coming; they jammed my signal. There was no recovery, no chance of getting away. He had underestimated the Secret Service. A searing hot stab of pain rippled up his leg from his ankle into his hips. Despite the cool autumn air, he was drenched in sweat.

If I die, it sure as hell isn't going to be in a postal uniform. He had options—shoot himself, shoot it out with the Secret Service and die, or surrender. Shooting it out had some appeal, but there was an equal chance he might survive. He knew that the NSF Secretary would disavow him, or worse, have another operative come and kill him if he surrendered. As much as he was loyal to Newmerica, he now had to cope with the thought of dying for his country…a country that didn't even acknowledge it had operatives like him. *Hell, they would kill me just to distance themselves from this.* That realization made his decision for him.

Julius tossed his gun off to the rear of the vehicle, in plain sight. "Hold your fire!" he called. "I give up!"

Nashville Tennessee

Charli returned to the command and control center to a team that was on the verge of celebration. When she walked in, she noticed that her hand was still trembling as she rested it on the armrest of the Perch. The eyes of her team fell on her and several applauded. *They have every right to be proud, but the threat is far from over.*

"Good work everyone, but for all we know, this person might not be operating alone. Has bomb disposal arrived at the target vehicle?"

"Yes, Chief," O'Brien said. "It's going to be a few hours though. We are evacuating surrounding bodies."

"Inform Rabbit of the situation. Tell him that until we have disabled the device and done a full sweep of the area that Silver Eagle is going to have to operate elsewhere."

"Roger that," he replied. She felt a slight wobble as she moved into the elevated seat. Glancing down, she saw that both of her hands were quivering. O'Brien approached with a cup of coffee which she reached for. "Adrenaline, ma'am?"

She nodded. It wasn't adrenaline; that passed after they had seized the assassin. No, this was something else. Memories of the last Presidential assassination came rushing to her as she left the parking structure. As if it ached, she rubbed the scar on her body where the bullet had torn through her and into him.

She sat the coffee down and closed her eyes for a moment, tuning out the din of voices around her in the command and control center. Charli felt an emotion surge, one of relief…and redemption. *I failed to save the life of the last President. Today I reversed that.* A part of her wanted to cry—while another part wanted to cheer.

Charli found herself wanting to be with Andy…if only to be able to share what she was experiencing. *That can come later…for now, we have an investigation to complete.* As she opened her eyes, she felt an invisible burden lift from her, a burden she had been unaware of.

Charli Kasinski smiled at a job well done.

Broadway, Virginia

The small caravan of vehicles exited I-81 in Broadway, Virginia—little more than a 7-Eleven and rolling farm fields. Maddie watched the farm fields roll by as they turned onto a side road. Off to her left was the majesty of the Blue Ridge Mountains; on the right were the now barren fields. After they had gone another five or so miles, the trio of vehicles pulled off the road near a small creek. "We're getting out to stretch our legs," Brad said.

She zipped her hoodie up a few inches more as she stepped out. The students were aimlessly milling about. Some wandered near the edge of the creek bed, near where it flowed through a culvert under the road. Clarice seemed nervous. "Where can I go to the bathroom?" she asked. Tina pointed to a small clump of brush some 30 yards away, hovering over the creek. "You can go behind those," she said. Clarice looked like she wanted to protest, but didn't.

Brad went back to the van while the students began to huddle. "We got out OK," Francine said, beaming a big smile. Maddie felt relaxed as well. She had spent years looking over her shoulder. Even when she went out with her parents, she had to watch what she was saying. There was always an undercurrent of tension in her life, especially when on the campus. Now it seemed that was all behind her. It was a strange feeling, one she could only describe as relief. She smiled, not forced, but naturally.

For a minute or so the student refugees chuckled and chatted, not about what they had been through, but about nothing in general. Brad and Tina moved outside of their little circle, but she barely paid attention to them.

After another minute she turned, and saw Tina holding a shotgun. *When did she get a gun?* Her head snapped over to Brad and she saw him with a rifle. Beyond the group was the man who wore the lacrosse hoodie; he too held a gun—though his was a pistol.

"What is this?" Maddie asked. The students heard her and turned, realizing suddenly that they were surrounded.

"This is us, taking care of a problem on campus," Tina said.

"More like a cancer," Brad added.

Maddie understood instantly that Brad and Tina had set her up—set all of them up. She moved next to Francine whose eyes were huge and her trembling mouth hung open. Maddie positioned the girl between her and Tina, enough to block Tina's line of sight.

"We do this every year," Brad said, levelling the rifle at the students.

"You lied to us!" Lonnie cursed.

"Of course we did, and you fell for it," Tina said with a single chuckle at the end of her words, as if she were going to enjoy what happened next. "We are social justice warriors—the Grays," she said proudly.

"You can't just kill us here," Lee said.

"You aren't the first ones," Brad said. "But I guarantee we can and will. We'll throw your bodies where we threw the other ones, along the creek. Too bad they banned hunting. Back in the day, someone might find your bodies while out hunting deer. Out here, well, no one has found any of the other ones we've left."

Clarice began to sob. Maddie reached down and felt her pistol in the waistband of her pants. Her hand slowly wrapped around it. Her heart was pounding in her ears and chest as she pulled it free and flicked off the safety.

Tina was the closest of them, and with the shotgun, she was the biggest threat. Her eyes tracked Brad off to her right. *If I move fast and aim well, I can take the two of them.* That still left the one with the pistol. *He's only got a few shots. If they rush him, they might be able to take him.*

There was no choice other than to stand there like sheep being slaughtered. Maddie wasn't deeply religious, but in that moment, she closed her eyes for a second and asked God to help her.

Her actions were a blur in her mind. She pulled the gun out, moving around Francine, and leveling it at Tina. For a millisecond, Tina didn't see her; she was looking off to her right slightly. Then she saw Maddie and began to swing her shotgun around. Maddie didn't panic fire; she remembered what her father had taught her. Her Smith & Wesson kicked twice as she fired into Tina's center mass.

One shot hit her on the left arm, causing the shotgun to swing hard in the same direction, firing more into the air than anything else. The second bullet hit right after the shotgun blast, catching Tina in the left cheek. Her head seemed to deflate like a balloon for a moment as she swung around, twisting and falling all at once.

Maddie turned towards Brad and started to drop to one knee as she aimed. Another shot went off behind her, but she ignored it. Screams tried to penetrate her ears, but only the throb of her heartbeat reached her. As she went down, Brad spun on her, raising the rifle and firing at almost the same instant she did.

The tug of her pistol, the crack-boom of the shot being fired, and a violent jerking happened all in the same moment. She flew backwards, a hot searing pain stabbing her lower chest. More screams and shouts called out as she toppled over backwards, looking into the brilliant blue sky overhead.

Maddie could feel the pistol in her hand and knew she had to sit up, but she couldn't, no matter how hard she tried. Her legs and torso felt as if they were on fire. She surged past the pain for a moment, using her free hand to pull herself on her side. Around her she saw legs and feet running, fleeing. Someone lay on the ground about ten feet away.

Suddenly her vision began to tunnel, going black around the edges. Dizziness swept her and she struggled to get breath—hyperventilating. The more she tried to move, the more the darkness came.

A tornado of thoughts and memories whipped her brain. *Mom... Dad...David...*everything that she held dear. Her mouth opened as she tried to call them, but only a scream rose from her lips, a mix of agony and fear.

In one blink of an eye, everything went black and Maddie Steele collapsed into the darkness.

CHAPTER 22

"If it is not for the betterment of all; it is not for the betterment of one."

Arnold Air Force Base, Tennessee

Caylee moved the police caution tape aside as she followed the Air Force Office of Special Investigations (AFOSI) lieutenant into the place she had called home. She noted that the door had been kicked open; the boot print was clear on the lower panel of the door, and the door frame was splintered. The safety chain, along with the slide, hung at the side.

Blood stained the carpet in the tiny foyer, and she carefully stepped over the largest spot, now long dry and fading to a maroon color. The blue shoe covers almost made her slip, but she maintained her balance. Standing along one wall near the front window, she drank in every detail of the room. In her mind, the scene played out. The ejected cartridges on the floor meant that Raul had fired and hit one of his assailants. Normally that would have made her smile a little, but Raul was gone, and that infuriated her.

The lieutenant moved near her side. "The back door was also broken open. That means a minimum of two, if not three assailants," he said.

"A fucking Domino's Pizza delivery driver," she growled.

"She used false ID—no surprise there," he said as she continued to observe the room. The new FedGov IDs that were required of all citizens had been easy for profiteers to fake. "We are pulling camera footage of her car parked in front of the place—hoping for better images. The security gate got a shot of her and the perp we found dead here," he added.

"And he is?"

"We ID'd him as Dale Gallagher, NSF. Before they were rolled into the NSF, he was a Detective with the Lexington Kentucky PD. Most recently he was assigned to the Cincinnati Branch of the NSF doing special investigations. We have no idea why he was down here."

"He came for Raul," she said flatly.

"We got the DNA tests today—nothing from Mr. Lopez," the lieutenant said. "I think if they were going to kill him, they would have."

"They didn't want him dead; they just wanted him." Her mind went into full investigative mode. *If they found him here, someone had to have tipped off the NSF.* "I need you to run the cell records for the last few weeks of every airman on this base," she said as if it were an easy task. "I want to know if anyone called the tip line. I want to know if they used their girlfriend or boyfriend's phone to contact the NSF. Someone on this base tipped off the NSF that he was here."

"That's a big ask," the lieutenant said.

"I'm not asking," she said with a glare.

"We put up roadblocks on the state line," he said. "The problem is they got a head start. We didn't find the body for almost two hours after the reports of shots. We didn't know where the shots had come from and did a door-to-door sweep; that's when he was found. They could have slipped out of state before we got them in place. Word has gone out to the KSP too. So far no luck."

"Logic says they will be heading north or east," she said firmly. The officer was right; it was probably already too late. "They may head west—try to get to the left coast." The lieutenant nodded.

"I will want a copy of your file," she said. "I want the video footage from the security checkpoint too. Everything you have."

The AFOSI officer looked a little flummoxed but nodded. "The White House made it clear that we were to fully cooperate with you and any requests you have. With tomorrow being Election Day, we have a lot of people on duty, just in case, well, we're needed. I will have my staff copy it all."

Caylee nodded in response, not wanting to talk.

This place had been the closest thing to a home for her, and now it was splattered with blood and a feeling of failure. *I should have been here.* She remembered sitting on the now disheveled sofa, eating popcorn with him. All she had were those memories. *I left, and I let him down.*

It wasn't that Caylee never failed, but this one hurt, deeply… personally.

Stepping out of the crime scene, she went under the police tape and back into the front yard. She knew the people that had taken him…they were ruthless. *They will put him on display like a trophy, rub our noses in it. Then he's a dead man.* Her jaw slid forward and locked into place as she mentally pictured her friend and what he was facing.

That isn't going to happen, she silently resolved in that moment. *I won't let it.* "I'll be at the White House. Send the material over to me there," she said to the lieutenant without even looking back at him. *I need to get my bearings—then I need to go and bring him back.*

Soldier (Sacrifice) Field, Chicago, Illinois

The day before Election Day, Colonel Trip Reager's 36th Infantry Division had raced out of Michigan City, driving along the southern coast of Lake Michigan. The wind coming off the lake was bitter cold, but he was more than warm where he was tucked in the tight space on the right side of the turret of the second tank in the formation,.

The Texans had come in initially on three highways, staying off of I-94, which would have been the obvious path to head to Chicago. There had been roadblocks—crude highway construction concrete barriers, piled four deep and high—that had been thrown up in several spots just inside of Illinois. Trip's G2 intelligence officer had warned him they might set up ambushes and try to divert the tanks into traps. He responded using the full fury of his unit. The tank crews followed his orders to the letter, using HE rounds to blast the barriers into dust, and then driving right through them. Windows shattered for a block and people panicked, which was fine with him. *Word will spread that we mean business.*

Occasional small arms fire came at the tanks, along with two Molotov Cocktails, which did little but burn the paint on the vehicles as they raced by the throwers. Trip wasn't there to stop and fight a battle in East Chicago or Whiting. He was there to secure ground for the federal elections. As such, he ordered his tanks to maintain a steady rate of speed, around 35 mph. For a car, that seemed slow, but for 67.6 tons of turbine-powered tank, it was intimidating. The formations converged near Lakeshore Drive and in a matter of a few hours, they reached Soldier Field, one of his three objectives. While Newmericas referred to the area as Sacrifice Field, Trip had told his officers that as far as he was concerned, it was Soldier Field.

The Missouri National Guard units, coming in trucks behind his forces, were deployed quickly to Grant Park, securing the access points, and then they moved out to Wrigley Field. There, one squadron of armor and additional ground troops were deployed to augment them. At the last minute, he had been given a regiment of the Kentucky National Guard engineers, which he had integrated into the defense of the Grant Park voting location. Being engineers, they came with vehicles and gear that he put to use digging trenches and putting up defense points around the long park on the Lake Michigan shoreline. The entire operation took less than eight hours, so fast that the city had done very little to interfere, short of massive traffic jams near Wrigley Field, no doubt out of the sight of tanks roaring into the city.

The Sons of Liberty had been in position for several days already—hiding themselves outside of the immediate defense zones in abandoned buildings or on rooftops. The warnings they provided were useful. The SEs had equipped themselves with Technicals armed with machine guns. They had also passed on other useful information—that the Illinois National Guard had a reinforced battalion that was deployed to the north of Chicago. Their presence was serious and Colonel Reager adjusted some of his plans accordingly. He assigned an armored squadron as a floating unit that could be rushed in where needed. That command fell to Captain Trigger DeYoung.

While he hoped he would not have to square off against the Illinois troops, it seemed inevitable. Busloads of Social Enforcers had been brought into the city at the behest of the mayor and Governor, "To ensure the integrity of the voting process." It was the kind of lie that only politicians could craft. Where the President had federalized the election, declaring the only official voting locations, the governors loyal to Newmerica had declared their own Voting Sanctuary Zones—which, in the case of Chicago, was Sacrifice Field, where his troops had already started to dig in. Confrontation had been manufactured and was inevitable in Trip's mind.

Trip moved around the map of Chicago, which was laid out on the folding table in the center of the tent. Major Thomas Coleman of the Missouri National Guard stood at the far end of the map, arms crossed, staring at it as if the map were the enemy he was about to face. Captain Keller was busy handing out orders behind him, and Major Turner Settle was busy directing his people. "People," Trip said, getting their attention. "The federal election people have arrived and are getting set up. This is likely our last chance to meet face to face before things get hot." They all stopped what they were doing and moved around the table. Lieutenant Judy Mercury joined them, cradling a cup of steaming coffee in her hands.

"What is the latest, sir?" the impassive Major Coleman asked.

Trip leaned out over the map. "The Illinois National Guard have established their base in Irving Park," he said, pointing to the map. "That means they are situated closer to Wrigley Field at the moment. They are an infantry unit with some anti-tank capabilities and a few armored vehicles. To the north we have anywhere from six to ten thousand SEs forming up as well," He pointed to Rosehill Cemetery where the Sons of the Liberty had identified their rally point. "They have positioned their people to, and I quote here, 'counter protest' the SEs." With the voting destined to start in only six hours, that clash was bound to become violent. *The SOL knew what they were signing up for...they also know that if they can tie up the SEs fighting them, the voting will continue.*

"Soldier Field is the key to this," Trip said. "Both governments have declared this as their own sanctioned voting location. This is where they have to come eventually."

"They are bound to try to keep voters from doing their duty," Captain DeYoung said.

Trip nodded. "The key is the corridors we are establishing to protect voters coming in." With the TRC seemingly out of commission for the last few days, word had spread on the Internet like wildfire, encouraging supporters of America to get out and vote. The Sons of Liberty promised them protection, and web pages went up everywhere telling people the importance of their votes. Usually such information was suppressed, but for a few glorious days, dissenting opinions were voiced. Big Tech was clearly struggling and trying to take down the information, which gave Trip a bit of satisfaction.

"The ROEs still hold?" Captain Keller asked. Trip knew that the rules of engagement were bound to come up.

Trip nodded. "Nonlethals. If you are fired upon, relay that information to me. I alone will make the call if we are to switch things up. I want that conveyed to everyone in your commands. The last thing we want is a massacre if it can be avoided."

There were nods of agreement, and Major Coleman replied with a, "Yes sir."

"This isn't going to be easy. They are going to push and prod us, try to make us out to be the bad guys. Restraint is hell when people are lobbing bricks at you, but we need to demonstrate it. By the same token, I'm not going to have our people come under enemy fire and die while we throw harsh language and rubber bullets at them." Trip knew why he was there in Chicago. He had made the same tough call before, four years ago. He prayed that it would not come down to that again, but in the pit of his stomach, he sensed it would.

Ten hours later ...

The first salvo in the Battle of Chicago was verbal, not ballistic. It had come two hours earlier when the Newmerica voting steam showed up at Soldier Field, demanding that Trip vacate the area immediately. "This is a Voting Sanctuary," the young woman leading the delegation declared arrogantly. "Your administration of this location is against the law."

"We were sent by the President of the United States of America," he said slowly, letting his Texas drawl out for a verbal vacation. "So missy, you and your folks need to pack your asses up and get out of here."

"There is no America!" she proclaimed. "The Ruling Council—"

Trip cut her off. "I want to be clear with you, so there is no misunderstanding." He paused and closed the gap with her to a matter of inches. "The Ruling Council can go fuck itself."

She erupted, responding to his bluntness and being cut off. "You asshole!" she snarled. "I will see you face social justice for that slur."

Trip had eyed her and smiled. "Lieutenant Mercury," he barked.

"Yes sir."

"Zip-tie these people and place them in protective custody," he said.

Mercury snapped her fingers and instantly two soldiers were on each worker. "You can't do this…it's illegal."

"You threaten me and expect to waltz your ass out of here? I don't think so."

Word of the encounter had spread with the troops, and it seemed to briefly ease the tensions. For a long time he had wondered if the voters would actually show. Five years of suppression, being pummeled to silence—would anyone actually show up? Then they started to come, a trickle at first, but then more. They weren't all going to vote for the President, but the voting would be fair—he could see to that.

The first 'protesters' showed up near Wrigley Field, clashing with some of his infantry at a voting corridor that led to the baseball field. Rocks and glass bottles were being thrown, and his people responded with rubber bullets and tear gas. The SEs had experience, albeit five years, in responding. They had riot shields, no doubt provided by the NSF, which protected them. Many had batons, but some still carried bats or other clubs. Gas masks were present, making the tear gas less than effective for some of the protesters. Major Coleman contacted him almost immediately to relay the situation. "Our northern corridor is collapsing, Colonel."

Trip went to the map and studied it. He knew from experience that once they started to give ground, it would be hard to get back. "I'm sending help," he commented. "Get me Trigger," he said to his communications person who nodded back. "You've got him on Tac-two," she said as Trip switched to a different channel.

"Trigger," he said. "They have some problems north of Wrigley. SEs are starting to push our people back."

"Give me the word, sir," he said. "I'll make them regret that."

"Trigger—plow the road."

North of Wrigley Field, Chicago, Illinois
Eighteen Minutes Later

Captain DeYoung sat crunched into the right side of the turret as his M1 Abrams roared down the streets of Chicago. Cars were in the way, but he made his intent clear by driving over them, sending their occupants scrambling for safety. He had to admit there was a bit of glee, driving over the cars, hearing their grinding crunching under him.

The first view he had of the riot was on North Sheffield Ave. The smoke rose from the mass of rioters; the air was filled with projectiles. "Squadron slow," he said as he contacted Major Coleman. "Major, this is Captain DeYoung. My squadron is to your south, at Sheffield and Dakin."

"Glad to have you, Captain. Do you think you can break these bastards up and get them back?"

Trigger grinned. "Oh, we'll move 'em." He switched back to the rest of the squadron. "We advance abreast, nice and snug. Follow our pace—do not slow down or stop for anything." He then called down into the tank. "Driver, 10 mph as soon as the others form up on us."

"Yes sir," Sergeant Watkins called back from the driver's seat.

The tanks and Bradley fighting vehicles of the squadron flanked his tank with barely a yard between them. They filled the width of the entire street.

"Advance," he commanded. The turbine engine of the Abrams roared at a higher tempo as the tank started to roll. From his observation visor, he saw them heading right where the Missouri troops were under assault. Heads turned as they approached, and the infantry understood they needed to get out of the way. They parted like the Red Sea before Moses, and the armored squadron filled the void.

"Keep going," Captain DeYoung called.

The rioters started throwing bricks and bottles at the tanks, which almost made him laugh. Other things were thrown as well—at least a pair of Molotov Cocktails exploded in front of the tanks, but he did not order a stop. The SEs were unsure what to do as the tanks rumbled even closer. Off to his left, the weight of the squadron must have broken a water main, and a geyser shot into the air and rained down all around them—but the tanks lumbered on.

A few brave SEs rushed forward, thinking that if they stood in front of the tanks, DeYoung would stop. He did not give that order. At 10 miles per hour, he was not violating the nonlethal orders that the Colonel gave them.

If they're stupid enough to stand there, we will drive right over them.

Soldier (Sacrifice) Field, Chicago, Illinois
Thirty-Two Minutes Later

Word came from Captain DeYoung that he had broken the lines of the SEs north of Wrigley Field, but Trip knew that was a start. *They are testing our resolve.* Major Coleman had given him a short burst report about the tanks driving into the protesters, forcing them into a panicked retreat after they realized the folly of their efforts. *They are going to come at us again, next time with more force.*

When his communications officer had relayed the next message a few minutes later, he knew the moment had come. As he put the headset on, he heard the staccato of gun fire in the background as Major Keller's voice came on. "Colonel, we have Technicals on the perimeter of Grant Park, and they have opened fire."

"Casualties?"

"None yet, sir, but it is scaring the shit out of the civilians and making voting here all but impossible with everyone sheltering. We have eyes on approximately 5,000 protesters backing them up, coming in from the north and the west."

"I'm on my way," he said moving to the desert tan Humvee that served as his command vehicle. A corporal stood in the top turret and his driver was ready. "Where to sir?"

"Grant Park," he replied, slamming shut the armored door to the passenger seat. "Make it quick."

The driver checked the Inertial Nav System display and gunned the engine. The Humvee rumbled north toward Grant Park and as they got close, Trip could hear the popping of automatic gunfire. *Big guns—they aren't messing around.*

Grant Park was a large, green swath with fountains and a view of Lake Michigan. There were little rolling hills, and the shallow areas filled with troops. They had established a voting center in a series of large tents surrounded by a low wall of sandbags in front of the massive Buckingham fountain at the end of Congress Parkway. When he caught a glimpse of the fountain, he remembered seeing it in the opening of the old TV show, *Married with Children.* For the Colonel, those memories were from a lifetime ago, when he was a kid. The driver aimed for that, going cross-country through the park. Each little hill they crested, Trip could feel himself float off of his seat. The old war-weary Humvee had a rattle on each landing, and the cushion power of a piece of plywood.

At the peak of each little hill, he caught a view of the defenses that the engineers had thrown up. His troops were huddled in quickly dug trenches; some were lined with sandbags. Tracer fire from at least a half-dozen machine guns stitched the autumn-brown grass. He pointed to the Bradley that was the mobile command post, and the young driver aimed for it.

Trip popped the armored door and sprang out, running to the open rear of the Bradley. Captain Keller was there on the radio when Trip moved in alongside him. "Colonel, good to see you."

Bullets hit the front of the fighting vehicle, tinging and dinging off of the front armor. Trip didn't flinch, but he saw a private jerk with the hits.

"What do you have, Marc?"

"As you can tell, they have lowered their shots onto us," he said, putting down his headset. "Now we are pinned down. Needless to say this is keeping the voters from showing up."

Trip nodded grimly. "Any casualties?"

"Six wounded," he confirmed. "Those Technicals are keeping us hunkered down, but they are spraying pretty indiscriminately." As if to confirm his point, another burst of fire rattled off the turret of the Bradley above them.

Colonel Reager knew that his next actions would be questioned, perhaps for years to come. If he did nothing, people were going to get killed and the voting would never happen. If he gave the order to open fire, it would be San Antonio all over again, most likely worse. *I can't win, but there are lot of levels of losing.*

His first obligation was to protect the voters—then his people. Trip closed his eyes for a moment, thinking back to San Antonio four years earlier. It was a ghost that haunted him, followed him everywhere he went. Every time people saw him, that was what they thought of. He had heard the nicknames too—hating the Butcher of San Antonio, which had been the title that the TRC had slapped on him. *Now I am facing the same decision ...*

CHAPTER 23

"History without proper interpretation is nothing more than myths and lies."

Four Years Earlier...
San Antonio, Texas

The Alamo was under siege for a second time in its history, and Major Trip Reager was in the middle of it. The rioting mob numbered in the thousands and were converging on all sides. From the dark masses of the mob came bricks, rocks, and ice-filled glass bottles that rained down on the National Guardsmen. Colonel Caine had already ordered them to fall back once, forming a ring some two blocks out from the Alamo. The retreat had allowed them to tighten their lines, but it had also emboldened the rioters. Fireworks mixed with the rain of projectiles, playing havoc with night vision gear.

Trip remembered the attack on the White House the night of the Fall. They had done the same thing. They also used mortars…and that thought worried him as well. Not only could they kill a lot of his personnel; they could potentially shell the Alamo itself. He hugged his M4 carbine tight to his body-armored chest as he sprinted over to the command tent. The radio on his helmet had taken a hit from a brick and had gone on the fritz, not to mention shaking him up for a few moments.

Colonel Caine was barking orders into his microphone when Trip entered the tent. "Sir, I have men injured. I've had them pulled into the Long Barracks for cover. Our medics are using it as a field hospital."

Caine was overwhelmed. Trip could see it in his deep brown eyes. Before he could respond, there was a series of pops down the street, gunfire. "What in the hell …" Caine started. "Is that us or them?"

A shotgun blast followed, confirming what Trip was hearing. "Those are not our guns, sir. We are under fire."

The older Colonel shook his head. "We need to fall back," he said anxiously.

Then came the first big explosion, off to Trip's right. Moving out of the tent, he looked down toward the Alamo plaza. Smoke rolled skyward, illuminated by the headlights of vehicles. It was what Trip had feared—mortars or rockets.

Turning back toward the tent, he was about to enter it when an explosion threw him back hard, grinding on the pavement of East Crockett Street. He struggled for a moment to get air; the wind had been knocked out of his lungs. Every joint in his body ached from the impact and his ribs throbbed as he finally was able to suck in air.

He rolled to his side and slowly staggered to his feet. The command post was hardly recognizable. The tent material that remained was nothing more than shredded scraps. Two soldiers lay on the sandbags that surrounded the tent, one missing his left arm entirely. Trip rushed over to check the other one but could not get a pulse. Smoke hung in the air around the remains of the tent, reeking of the smell of detonated high explosives and the smell of charred paper.

Turning to the center of the tent, he found half of Colonel Caine. His eyes were open; his helmet was gone—as were his legs. The Colonel's eyes stared skyward, and his mouth hung agape. Trip stared at him for a second, not bothering to check whether he was alive.

Gunfire spat from down the street, tracers going off to his left, hitting his command Humvee and ricocheting into the night with metallic pinging noises. Crouching low, he moved to the far side of the vehicle and jumped in.

"Drive!" he ordered the corporal in the driver's seat. The young enlisted man didn't ask where; he hit the accelerator and turned toward Alamo plaza as Trip grabbed his headset. "This is Major Reager to all command officers. Colonel Caine is dead; the command post has fallen." Another thudding sound of a mortar round went off in front of him, half a block away. Tracer fire flashed in the night from the far end of the Alamo complex, up past Houston Street.

Captain Keller's voice came in the earpiece he squeezed under his helmet. “Major, they are throwing Molotovs up here and firing at my men. I have four down.”

The Humvee swerved at something in the road; Trip didn’t see what it was, but the driver was still racing, coming up on the plaza in a matter of a few seconds. “Can you hold?”

“I don’t think so,” he said.

Another voice came on, “This is Captain Davis of the Rangers. One of my spotters says they are bringing barrels of some sort on the side streets to the rear of the church on Bonham Street,” he said. “I can’t hold my men back much more, Major.” Trip was impressed for a millisecond that the Rangers were holding their fire.

Barrels were no doubt filled with either explosives or gasoline. They won’t be satisfied until we are all dead and the Alamo is taken to the ground. That tore at Trip deeply. Few places existed that were considered sacred soil, but the Alamo was one for every Texan. *God damn it! I didn’t bring this fight on, but I sure as hell will end it.*

“This is Major Reager,” he said smoothly. “The use of live ammunition is authorized. I say again. All units, all commands, you are authorized to use deadly force.”

Suddenly all around the Humvee, the tempo and intensity of fire increased tenfold. Machine guns sputtered, spraying bullets into the black clad mob. “Head around the Alamo. Get me up on Bonham Street,” he ordered the corporal behind the wheel. The Humvee skidded, almost doing a donut as he cranked it around. The turret gunner in the rear of the vehicle fired off small bursts as they raced down the street. Shots peppered the Humvee, one hitting the armored glass right next to Trip and deflecting off into the night. Another chest-rattling explosion of a mortar round went off somewhere in the distance. For a moment, it was hard not to feel like he was back in Iraq, rather than in his home state.

As the Humvee skidded onto Bonham Street, he wondered if they had driven into an ambush. A shotgun blast rattled the entire passenger side of the vehicle, and the intensity of shots rattling the vehicle increased dramatically. His gunner’s M60 burped in much longer bursts. Tracers from the rooftop positions of the National Guard rained downward, over his vehicle.

The black bloc rioters did not seem deterred by the gunfire, returning with fire of their own—everything from pistols to Roman candles. It was undisciplined, erratic, and hopeless. The driver halted in front of a concrete road barrier and Trip jumped out, raising his M4 and aiming down toward East Houston Street where the largest concentration of rioters seemed to be. His own Humvee gunner fired bursts in the same direction. Sparks danced off of the pavement and parking meters.

To his right, near the Crockett Hotel, he saw several rioters rolling out large, blue plastic barrels. Reeling about, Trip took aim and unleashed bursts of three shots, hitting two of the men rolling the one barrel and puncturing the plastic of the container. The liquid shot out of the holes at first, as the other rioters rolling the second barrel broke and ran. He fired another burst at a second barrel and it instantly exploded in a massive fireball, followed a millisecond later by the first container.

The heat from the rolling and billowing mushroom clouds soared skyward. A nearby truck exploded as well. He could feel the intensity of the flames. He fell back into the vehicle, having blunted their assault, closing the door behind him. He reeked of a burning smell. "Take us back to the plaza," he ordered. Two of the people that had been rolling the second barrel were engulfed in the flames and running madly back the way they came toward the hotel, screaming in agony. The plume of flames devoured an oak tree planted along the street, setting ablaze parts of it high up.

"What in the hell was that?" someone called as he put the earpiece under his helmet. The Humvee lurched around and the driver backtracked to the front of the plaza. "Can the chatter," he ordered. "Sit rep, now!"

"We are driving them back here on Houston," came Captain Keller's voice. Another mortar round went off in the distance, this time throwing bits of pavement onto the hood of the Humvee as it roared into the night and around to the front of the Alamo.

"This is Captain Thomas of Texit. We think we know where that mortar is. Down by Elm and McCollough."

"This is Lieutenant Drake of the SWAT team; we are closing on that position," he said. The rat-tat-tat of gunfire almost drowned out his voice.

"This is Lieutenant Mercury. I am hold up in Travis Park. Need reinforcements," she said. *She's pushed out far—too far.* He was both proud and concerned at the same time.

"This is Deputy Bergman, San Antonio PD. We are almost there—hold on," she replied as Trip's desert tan Humvee came to a stop in front of the Alamo.

Climbing out, he glanced back at Texas's most cherished icon. Another massive fireball plume of orange and yellow rolled skyward from behind the church. The burning tree behind the church was visible as well with several of the upper limbs ablaze, further silhouetting the landmark. A bit of burning wood landed in the court not far from him. The Alamo still stood proud, lit up by its exterior lighting, though the orange and yellow flames behind it almost overpowered what he saw.

The flames from the gasoline barrels he had shot up were still burning in the block behind the Alamo mission church, framing it in the night. A few errant tracers stabbed skyward in the distance. He saw the crater from one of the mortar attacks. It was near the entrance to the Long Barracks…a smoking hole in the cobblestone. Small bits of stone—either from the pavement or the damage to the Long Barracks exterior—littered the ground around the structure. The flagpole in front still stood, stabbing skyward, with the Texas flag barely moving in the chaos of the battle raging all around him.

We held…thank God we held! While the fighting was still going on, he took a moment to commit the image of the old church to memory. "Get over to Travis Park," he ordered the driver of the Humvee. It roared off into the night as he made his way to the Long Barracks to check on casualties.

Four Hour Later …

Sunrise over war-torn San Antonio revealed the carnage from the night's fighting. The rioters were not used to real bullets being used. *Too many video games…they thought they could just rush us.* In some areas the dead were heaped three deep. Spent brass was so plentiful; he had nearly tripped as he walked among the dead.

The battle had raged for another hour, mostly with the National Guard, police, and volunteers running down the rioters. When they reached the buses that had brought them, they were assaulted—the troops were in such a frenzy from the fighting. Trip had been hit by a .22 in his chest, but his body armor prevented penetration—though not the hard kick of the impact. He had emptied his 1911 at the attacker, who had been hiding behind the car, a young woman refusing to flee or surrender. Now, in the morning light, he went back to where she had fallen only to find a puddle of blood. Either she had been wounded and got away, or friends had dragged her off the street.

The dead and injured were still being accounted for. It had taken several hours for the fire department to finally show up. He didn't blame them for not rushing in; the battle was erratic and dangerous for anyone that was an authority figure. It seemed ambulances were everywhere; flashing lights added to the smoke that seemed to hang like a fog around the epicenter of the fighting, the Alamo.

Looking at the bodies of the dead, he saw mostly young people. He thought of his daughter Jessie, and prayed that she had not been in the rioters' ranks. Staring at several of them, he wondered how they could be so angry, so filled with hate that they would risk their lives to destroy an icon of history.

Was it their fault or that of their parents? He had believed one or the other was to blame until Jessie had turned against him and his wife. Was it the schools that had indoctrinated them? *Why would they try to start a war that they couldn't possibly win? Who was to blame?*

As Trip Reager looked down Alamo Plaza at the dead, he realized that the only person that could be blamed for this was him. *I gave the order. I caused a massacre. This will haunt me for the rest of my life.*

Grant (Sanders) Park, Chicago, Illinois

God damn it! It was San Antonio all over again. From the rear of the Bradly fighting vehicle, he could see no choice. "The use of live ammunition is authorized," he broadcast on the tactical channel. "All commands, this is Colonel Reager. You are authorized to use live ammunition." He repeated the last sentence.

The Texas National Guardsman did not have to be told again. Trip stepped out of the back of the command vehicle and heard the roar of battle echo off every building surrounding the park. The entire north and west end of Grant Park erupted with weapons fire. A Technical or some other vehicle exploded off to the north, devoured by the precision fire.

Then he saw the smoke plume of a shoulder-mounted missile unleash.

One west-facing Bradley exploded, throwing its turret off and into the air. This was not like San Antonio in that respect. *They have gotten into the armories and armed these punks with dangerous weapons.*

An Abrams tank responded with its big cannon booming so loudly that the concussion shook dust off every building for a block in every direction. Off to the west one of the buildings took a hit from an HE round, exploding and spraying the streets with debris. Smoke rolled from the hit, followed quickly by flames lapping skyward.

"Get me Soldier Field, now," he ordered the communications officer in the back of the Bradley. As the channel came on, he could hear the popping of gunfire. *Shit, they were hitting us down there too.*

"What is your situation?" he demanded.

"Captain Settle, sir. They made a push with weapons, apparently coordinated with the other locations. They firebombed some of our advance units. I have one Bradley hit with a 105 round and we lost that crew. Initial reports are around ten dead; probably three times that wounded. We are returning fire and they are scattering from the looks of it. They don't seem to like it when we shoot back. I hope to have our voting corridors cleared in half an hour, assuming they don't rally and counterattack." That was good news. It wasn't enough to deal with the attacks; he had to make sure that voters could get through. *With all of this gunfire, it will scare away a lot of them.* "Push them, Captain; don't let them pause and rally; they have interfered with this election enough already."

"Yes sir," he said. The communications officer caught his attention. "I have Wrigley Field, Major Coleman, sir." Trip gave him a nod and there was a snap of static as the new voice came on.

"Major, how are you doing?" he said, the sound of gunfire rattling off in the distance from his own battlefield.

"Colonel," came a ragged voice. "We are doing OK. I've got three dead, a dozen wounded—but we have routed them completely. Captain DeYoung drove a path which broke up their formation. They tried firing on us, but DeYoung and some of the SOL tore into them good. The voting corridors are open here. We have cleared at least four blocks to the north and west of our position. We have problems only slightly to the south. There's a sniper unit, probably NSF that is giving us fits and has a lot of Addison covered."

Trip paused. A single sniper could prevent people from using the streets to get to Wrigley to vote. If we were in Iraq or Afghanistan, I'd drop artillery on that building. This is an American city though. He heard the banging of a Bradley firing down a street north of his position. *This is war, regardless of where it is.* The decision came to him easily.

They are counting on us not using our full force. "Major, take down that building if you have to. We can't have some sniper team taking out us or the civilians."

There was a pause, and then Colemen responded. "Yes sir."

Captain Keller came into the rear of the Bradley covered with a film of sweat and gray dust. "Major," he said with a fast salute. "We have a problem."

"What is it?"

"We are getting word from the north end of the park. Those SEs have fled, but what is taking their place is the Illinois National Guard."

The words could have been a gut punch to a lesser commander, but Trip had anticipated them making a move. "Show me," he said and Keller pointed to the map. "How'd they get past Wrigley?"

"They went along the lake shore—as far as we can tell—skirted our corridors," he said.

That means that their commander has at least a half a brain. Keller continued, "They are coming down North LaSalle Drive. Humvees, Bradley fighting vehicles, and at least two tanks—two companies of infantry."

Looking at the map, his mind raced with options. Grant Park was a defended position. *We are in a well-entrenched position, open fields of fire.* He glanced over at Wrigley Field to the far north and west of the park on the map. *If he can take us out here, he can isolate Wrigley and Soldier Field.*

It was tempting to let the Illinois troops come to him, bleed against his forces. Urban combat environments favored the defender, but if the Illinois troops could get into the park itself, it would negate some of the defenses they had dug there. If we hold them in the city, it limits how much firepower they can bring to bear. The problem with that strategy was that it would all but prevent voting in Grant Park and could turn the ground into a meat grinder. *They want to break up the voting. They are counting on us fighting a holding action. So we need to do something they won't expect.*

"Get me Captain DeYoung," he ordered the communications officer. A moment later he got the nod and adjusted the microphone. "Trigger, this is Colonel Reager."

"Yes sir," came back the fiery officer's voice.

"You in good shape?"

"Yes sir. It turns out no one wants to have a tank drive over them." Trip could picture the smirk on his face as he spoke.

"We have a problem, and I think you may be the solution. The Illinois National Guard is south of you, heading for Grant Park on LaSalle. I'd like your force to come in on their rear and hit them hard; get their attention, and get them to turn around. We will then launch an assault out of Grant Park, and catch them in the middle." His eyes fell to Captain Keller, who slowly began to realize his role and crack a broad grin.

There was no pause, no hesitation from DeYoung. "We will be rolling in a few minutes sir; there's some support forces here I might want to bring along."

"Understood. Coordinate your timing with Captain Heller directly," he said, and Heller gave him a nod of agreement.

"Tear them a new asshole, Trigger."

Lake View, Chicago, Illinois

Captain "Trigger" DeYoung rose out of the turret hatch and saw a yellow flag being carried by a member of the Sons of Liberty. "Hey," he called over and three members of the SOL turned to face him. "Who's your commander?"

"I am," a dark-skinned woman said. "Rita Presley, Southside Irregulars." She walked up alongside the idling tank with her AR-15 clenched tightly to her chest. She held her trigger finger straight, demonstrating that she had learned her weapons discipline in the military.

"I need your help. The Illinois National Guard are moving on Grant Park. I'm about to give them a 105 millimeter enema. I could use a little infantry support."

"You've got it," she said, and then whistled loud enough that it could be heard over the din of the three tanks. The Sons of Liberty emerged from around street corners for a block away. Most were wearing hunting attire, but, given the camouflage on his tank, he was in no position to point out the folly of their colors. Almost thirty of the SOL converged on Rita around his tank. "Mount up," DeYoung said. There was no hesitation as they clamored on the tanks and clung to the exteriors of the Humvees and the two Bradley vehicles. Rita took a seat next to him on the turret. She motioned to one of the men who handed her the big, yellow flag. DeYoung looked up and saw the coiled rattlesnake in black with the words, 'Don't Tread on Me" at the bottom.

"Once the shooting starts, you will need to get off," he said to her.

"Like you had to tell me that," she replied sarcastically. "Roll this bitch—let's get it on."

"Glad to have you on board, ma'am," Trigger replied with a smile. "You heard the lady. Let's rock and roll," he ordered. The massive M1 Abrams rumbled to life and jerked as it started out.

Grant (Sanders) Park, Chicago, Illinois

Colonel Reager moved up to the front lines; the firefight intensified with each step that he jogged. Leaping down into a fresh trench, he raised his M4 and swept the front field of fire, but saw no immediate targets. The Illinois Guardsmen had pressed hard, reaching the edge of Grant Park, emerging from the city with guns blazing. His defense forces replied in kind. Bullets whizzed overhead, a sound that was far too familiar.

Come on Trigger—where in the hell are you? He reached up for his shoulder microphone when suddenly there was a massive explosion in front of his trench. The entire side of the trench and the piled up dirt in front of it came at him like a tidal wave of black soil. His mouth caught some of the dirt and for a few moments, he couldn't see. Trip felt like someone was sitting on his chest, and he wondered if he was buried. Hands grabbed at him, but everything was muffled. Damned ears popped. As a sergeant pulled him up, his hearing seemed to hiss, and then come back. "You alright, Colonel?'

He spat the dirt from his mouth and patted himself down to make sure everything was where it was supposed to be. He fumbled with the earpiece in his helmet, banging the side of the helmet a few times before it crackled back on. “Colonel, this is Captain DeYoung. We’re engaging three blocks north of you.”

Trip shook his head, his neck aching from the blast that had brought most of the trench down on top of him. “Captain Keller,” he said as he toggled his shoulder mic. “It’s time.”

Keller’s voice came back over the purring of a machine gun blazing away in the distance. “Give the word, sir; we’ll charge ‘em.”

Trip felt every muscle in his body tense up. “Alright then—all units advance. Charge!”

Keller’s voice came back, this time being broadcast to every open microphone in the park. “All units—charge!” There was a moment of pause, then another cry, this time not from Keller. “Remember the Alamo!”

Screams of, “Remember the Alamo!” cascaded, not only on the microphone, but from the troops that surrounded him. Trip could never forget that night; by the same token, the words seemed to turn the personnel under him into raging warriors. He saw the sergeant that had helped free him rise on the blasted trench, rushing forward, yelling, “Remember the Alamo!” A Bradley roared by at the end of the trench, a Texas flag hanging off the back, billowing in the wind as it went past, its 25 mm gun rapid firing off into Chicago at some target he didn’t see. The Kentucky National Guardsmen rushed out, yelling the same chant in the air, caught up in the frenzy. After years of being suppressed, the men and women in the armed forces savored the chance to strike back.

Trip Reager clamored over the trench, clutched his M4, and ran off into the heat of the battle yelling, “Remember the Alamo!” like those men and women around him.

Two and a Half Hours Later ...

The line of prisoners who had surrendered to the Texans was short. Some of the captives were helping wounded infantry limp in, while others manned stretchers that carried injured SEs, their black bloc attire slick with blood. Trip watched them march into Grant Park; some were injured, but most were merely sullen at having been defeated. DeYoung and the Sons of Liberty had slammed into the rear of the Illinois Guard’s columns, blowing up two of their M1s and a number of smaller fighting vehicles. They had turned to face the new threat when the Texans in Grant Park had surged out.

The commanding officer of the Illinois force, realizing he was flanked, retrograded to Lake Shore Drive and used that highway to fall back to the north. Only one third of his battalion had managed to get out; the rest tried to slug it out, and then eventually surrendered.

As Trip looked back over the city, he saw plumes of smoke, gray and black, rolling skyward from several points in the city. Sirens wailed everywhere in the distance. There was no more gunfire, not near enough for him to hear anyway. As he slowly walked back toward the command Bradley, he cleared his weapon for the first time all day.

He slumped against the fighting vehicle for a moment, noting the pain in his ribs and his lower back. *I am getting too old to be doing this shit.* A passing private handed him a bottle of water. "Here sir," he said, and Trip took the bottle and gulped half of it down. His beard stubble was filled with sweat, dirt, and other filth. None of that mattered to Trip Reager.

Voting was still happening at all three locations and would finish up shortly. Then they could fall back to Soldier Field where helicopters would come in and take out the ballots and the tallies. His battered Texans and their allies from Missouri could start the trek out of Chicago.

The dead were everywhere, all over the city. Trip had ordered that his people's remains were to be extracted and he sent out teams to do that. The dead SEs...he left them for the locals to deal with. He had faced them in San Antonio and now Chicago and his opinion of them had not improved. The bitterness of them firing on American troops was not something that he was likely to shake anytime in the near future. *They don't deserve the same honor we give our dead.*

Trip finished the last of the water, crumbling the plastic bottle in his hands. Looking over he saw a pedestal with mangled bronze atop it. The words, 'Abraham Lincoln,' were etched in the circular stone pedestal. The words were hard to read with the graffiti and deep chisel marks in them, but he saw them all the same. No doubt the statue had been torn down during the Fall.

He had not noticed it until the fighting was over—his attention had been so focused. Now he saw it and stared at the mutilated remains and felt a pang of disgust. *They will never deserve the honor we give to our people.*

CHAPTER 24

"The only fair elections are the ones that we say are fair."

The Southern White House
Nashville Tennessee

Caylee entered the conference room that Jack Desmond had invited her to and saw a flurry of friendly and familiar faces. Travis Cullen had several empty beer bottles in front of him; he smiled when he saw her and tipped his bottle toward her. Charli Kasinski was there, and she came up and greeted Caylee. Andy Forrest was assembling a sandwich from the meat and cheese trays that filled most of the conference room table. He smiled when he saw her, but she could not return the courtesy.

Her thoughts were not on the election night results; nor were they with the people in the room. All she could do was focus on one thing, Raul Lopez. It was a difficult issue for her to resolve. She could find him; she was sure that her skills and contacts could help with that task—but getting him free from whatever prison he was in was not going to be easy. And once she did, getting him to safety seemed insurmountable. *They won't let him get away again.* As far as she knew, his family was still being held as well. *I have to come up with a solution to get them to safety.* Caylee was good, but she came to the grim realization that she was not good enough for this—and that thought consumed her.

To pull this off, I will need help. That was something she did not ask for easily.

"Can I get you something to drink," Charli asked.

She shook her head as Andy handed her a cold beer.

"Alright, what's the matter?"

"It's nothing," she lied.

"The hell, it's nothing," Charli countered.

"It's Raul Lopez," she finally conceded.

"The kid that was the most wanted? The one that the NSF was bragging that they apprehended?" Andy asked as he returned to his place at the far end of the table.

She nodded quickly. "I got him from Pennsylvania. I was looking out for him. When we went on our last op." She glanced over at Travis, who took a step to close in on the conversation, "They came for him." Caylee paused for a moment. "I fucked up. I shouldn't have left him without someone there with him." *I shouldn't have let myself get so close to the kid. We were living together and pretending we were family. I never should have opened myself up to him.* Kicking herself had become a full time occupation along with obsessing about rescuing Raul.

"So, you go and get him," Travis said. "You've got the skills."

She shook her head. "It's not going to be that easy," she replied. "They'll be waiting for that kind of move—they'll be prepared." *On top of that, I don't even know where he is. The fact that they want a show trial is the only thing keeping him alive.*

A major part of what Caylee liked about being an operative was that she worked alone. Having friends was a burden in her profession. She had let Raul into her life, and they had taken her from him. Admitting that she needed help was hard—almost impossible.

Almost.

"I can't do it alone," she said slowly, the words bitter in her mouth.

For a long moment, no one in the room spoke.

Charli put her hand on Caylee's shoulder. "You won't have to," she said. "I'll go with you."

Travis stepped over. "You helped me take down the entire East Coast's Internet," he said. "Count me in."

Andy stood there with a sandwich in his hand. "Wait! Did you say that you two were the ones that took down the net?"

Travis smiled but didn't answer, which was an answer all by itself. Andy looked at them. "I have zero skills that can help, but count me in."

"Andy," Charli said. "You need to stay here."

"To hell with that," he replied. "You're not leaving me here." Charli didn't bother to suppress her slight grin, but Caylee caught it.

"I appreciate it Mister—Andy," Caylee said. She remembered first meeting him at Mt. Rushmore and was amazed that he wanted to be a part of what she was undertaking. "I can't ask you to do this though. Newmerica isn't going to give him up without a fight."

"We don't care," Charli said.

Caylee looked around. She wanted to argue with them, convince them not to help her. As much as she wanted to, she suddenly felt unburdened by asking for help and getting it. *I'd be a fool to turn them down.*

The Southern White House
Nashville Tennessee

Jack entered the conference room down the hall from the President's office carrying a bottle of Woodford Reserve bourbon. The election results were coming in, and he had been tied up with the President and his cabinet. This room, however, was the room he wanted to be in. "I brought this down, hoping to share it with some friends." He had told the President he needed to spend time with the people that had made the election possible—*and that is the people in this room.*

In the room seated around the table that was covered with meat and cheese trays were the people that had made the election possible. Andy stood at the far end of the table, holding a red Solo cup filled with something he held with both hands. Seated in front of him was Charli Kasinski with a nearly empty bottle of Nashville Amber Lager beer. Across from her, standing at the window with crossed arms, was Caylee Leatrom, who actually seemed to have a smile on her face. Sitting with his cowboy boots on the far edge of the table was Travis Cullen—drinking a Bud Light. When he entered the room and sat the bottle down, he felt all eyes on him.

"How's it going down the hall?" Andy asked.

"As well as expected," Jack said. "You don't have the TV on?" He looked behind Travis at the dark, wall-sized television.

"None of us want to see the results if we lose," Charli said.

"Well, you might want to turn it on," Jack said with a hint of hope in his voice. Charli picked up the remote and turned on CNN. The banner read, 'Too Close to Call' and the clearly frustrated announcer was angrily carrying on a conversation that no one in the conference room could hear thanks to the volume being turned down. Another, thinner banner appeared, 'Chicago turned into a warzone.'

"If CNN says it is too close to call, we must be winning," Travis said grinning broadly as he turned to look at the screen.

"We are," Jack said. "Our ground game was good with the SOL out there ensuring the safety of voters. As it turns out, a lot of people were sick and tired of the BS coming out of the Ruling Council. Their supporters took everything for granted; a lot didn't bother to show up and vote. As it turns out, when you condition people to sit on their asses at home and simply expect the government to do everything for you, people lack the motivation to get up and vote. They expected everything to be handed to them because that's what the FedGov has done for five years. As it turns out, laziness and complacency were our unwilling allies, " Jack said, pouring himself at least four fingers of Woodford Reserve in a blue Solo Cup.

"What happened in Chicago?" Andy asked.

"It got messy," Jack conceded. "The Texas boys and girls kicked some ass, but it came with a body count." He took a sip of the drink and winced as it burned deep in his chest. "We had similar problems in St. Louis, Philly, and what went down in Atlanta was nothing short of a disaster. Add in that the Ruling Council has already announced they will contest the election results…that the only votes that count come from their Voting Sanctuaries." He had expected nothing less from Newmerica. They had turned challenging elections into an art form right up until the Fall. *There's no reason for us to think they will behave differently now.*

"They won't accept the results," Caylee said.

"No they won't," Jack admitted, taking another smaller sip. Several states had already declared their support to Newmerica, regardless of the election results. "It's not important that they admit that we won; what is important is that the *people* believe we won."

"They can't step down, not after all they've done," Travis said firmly.

No, they won't. "We have prepared contingencies for that." *The Razorback Initiative is already being implemented.*

"This doesn't feel like a win. It's not an end. It's a beginning. This will lead to civil war," Andy said.

Jack nodded. "That is what we think as well. It isn't over yet."

"It will be bloody," Charli said.

"It has already started," Jack said. "Technically it began five years ago. It will only intensify after tonight." He turned to Caylee. "I think we are going to need some of your special talents."

She surprised him by shaking her head. "No can do, Mr. Desmond," she said. "I have a mission of my own."

Lopez...she's still kicking herself about his kidnapping. "You can't do that alone, Caylee. We will need to get you a team."

"She already has one," Charli said. Suddenly the people in the room began to move around the table, flanking Caylee.

"Charli, you're the head of the Secret Service. You can't take off. Besides, we have a trial of your assassin coming up."

"Actually I can," she said firmly. "I've been through two Presidential assassinations. I took a bullet on one, and my people saved our charge on the second one. You used to be in the Service Jack; you know that if you save the President's life, you get your pick of assignments. Well, I'm taking this one. Consider me on TDY."

He looked to Travis Cullen, who finished his beer in one long swig. "It sounds challenging," he said. "I love challenging. Besides, she's the brains behind a lot of the stuff we pulled two weeks ago. I figure I owe her. *You* owe her too, Jack. She tarnished the Secretary of the NSF and masterminded taking down the East Coast's Internet. She's owed a one off operation, at the very least."

Jack turned to Andy, who paused long enough to finish the sandwich he was chewing. "I lost everyone in my life that was important to me. My career is toast, and all my worldly possessions consist of a few changes of clothing and some books I've been reading. *Charli* is all I have. I go wherever she goes," he said, nodding to Charli, who flashed him a smile.

Desmond stood there facing all of them. *I owe them this, and probably a hell of a lot more.* "If I can't convince you to not go, the least I can do is sanction it and make sure you get all of the gear and cover you need."

Everyone lifted their glasses to toast him, and he held up his bourbon, slamming the rest down. There were still many hours before the final results would be tallied.

EPILOGUE

"Freedom is overrated. What matters is security."

Newmerica Penitentiary, Administrative Maximum Facility
Florence, Colorado

The Supermax prison in Colorado was stunningly sterile for Deja's tastes. The people kept there didn't deserve to be treated well in her mind. Looking at her prisoner, legs shackled, hands cuffed and chained to the table—he didn't look like he was suffering, other than his lack of freedom.

Getting Raul to Colorado had been tricky and dangerous. They had sedated him when they drove across the state line into Missouri, through the state police checkpoint. In Nebraska their car's heater had died, so they had to hold up for a day to get it repaired. Because of the recharging time on the electric vehicle, the journey took much longer, and each stop brought a risk of someone spotting them. He was blindfolded most of the time and kept in the trunk of the car. In the motels where they stayed, he was gagged. When he struggled, he was hit or kicked—not just as a reminder to remain subdued, but a bit out of revenge.

There were reminders everywhere that she was in hostile territory. The spray painted letters, 'GBA' were on rail cars they passed, bridge overpasses, etc. *God Bless America? Fuck America!* She saw the old American flag far too often as well. *I thought we burned all of them.* The fact that people felt comfortable putting out those symbols of racism and hate infuriated her even more.

Once they got into Colorado, she felt slightly able to relax. When her team arrived at the isolated prison, a light snow was falling and the air stung her nostrils as if she were back home in Minnesota. *It's a hell of a place to build a prison like this—in the middle of nowhere.*

Now Raul sat slumped over in front of her. There would be no escape this time; the Supermax prison was the best that the country had. She pulled the metal chair up opposite of him, sitting on it backwards, and glared at her prey.

They had shaved his head entirely, exposing several fading yellow-purplish bruises. They had him shower, and she could smell the cheap soap on his skin. As he lifted his head and looked at her, she saw her enemy masquerading as a young man. *I'm not falling for that innocent look you project...I've see the shit you've done.*

"They tell you where you are yet?" she asked.

He shook his head, not breaking his gaze with her.

"You are in hell itself. The most secure prison on the planet. We have terrorists here; hell, even the Unabomber is rotting in one of these cells. We are putting you with the scum of the earth. They are going to hold your ass here until the trial. After that, they will hang you, or shoot you full of drugs until you die. That's your whole fucking existence now."

Raul said nothing in response, just looked into her eyes, refusing to convey emotion. "What about my mom?"

There it is—his weakness. "They're likely going to hold her and your sister until your trial. They will tell her if she confesses about your alt-right affiliations that you might get a lighter sentence. Of course, she can never return to Texas—not after the election today. I'm sure she will find some way to survive on the streets."

Deja's words hit home; she could see it in his face, how his cheeks sagged. "I am the center of your whole world, Raul. You cooperate with me; tell me what I want to know; things might go easier on you...you never know. You got that?"

Lopez nodded slowly with resignation.

"To start with, what I want to know is simple. Who was that women 'ou were with in Ohio—the one that was living with you on that base? vould really like to know her name. If you cooperate, it might go a 'e easier on you—you never know." She knew that there was nothing ould say or do to help his case, but she was counting on him not ing that.

Raul Lopez did something unexpected—he smiled. A moment later he even chuckled. "Did I say something funny, you little asshole?" she barked.

"I'll tell you who she is," Raul said, still grinning. Deja leaned in, and his eyes opened wide. "She's the person that is going to kill you before this is over." He then laughed even louder.

The District

The two Newmerica candidates sat and watched the results from their new office in the House wing of the Capitol. When the Pretender came out and declared victory at 2:30 a.m., it had been devastating and infuriating at the same time. Daniel threw his glass across the room, shattering it on the wall and spraying tiny bits of ice and glass as shrapnel. The President's comments were aimed at them like missiles. "The Newmerica people know they have lost this election, but they are likely to lie about it. The people have spoken. Should they decide not to concede and assist in a peaceful transition of power, they and any government that supports them and their doomed cause will be considered to be in rebellion."

Daniel cursed at the large, flat screen image. "We aren't in rebellion. They are! I would see states burned rather than turn them over to that silver-haired asshat!"

The election results were equally disturbing to the VP candidate for Newmerica, but she held her public display of rage in check. Her NSF assets had warned her in reports that upsets might be possible, but this…*this is outrageous! These people have no sense of obligation. We have almost crushed racism; we have corrected the faulty past that had tainted us, and we removed the symbols of hate. After all we have done for them, they repay us with this? Not showing up to vote?*

The assassination attempt on the Pretender normally would have been blocked and treated as false news by the TRC, but the TRC was hamstrung still with the Internet being down. It did something she had not expected; it had garnered sympathy to the old man running against them. *If we had done it right, he'd be dead, and this farce of an election wouldn't have happened.*

She sat next to Daniel whose crimson face betrayed his rage. "We didn't do enough," he said in a low tone.

"What do you mean?" their campaign manager asked. "You mean our ground game? I agree. Someone should be held responsible," she said and glared at their campaign manager, Debbie, whose face went white with fear. "And we should have sent more force in to squash what the Pretender did." The images of Chicago were still burned in her mind.

"No," he said. "We thought that if we put them in Social Quarantine or arrested enough of them, they would learn their place in the new order of things. We thought they'd be thankful. Now I see the error of my thinking. We should have killed them all." It was not idle talk; he was speaking like the Daniel Porter who led the revolutionaries to victory five years ago. She embraced the darkness of his thoughts. *A little too late…but you understand now where I am coming from.*

"We cannot concede," she declared.

"Of course not," Daniel replied. "We will claim victory…that the votes were tampered with, especially in those cities where they sent in the National Guard. We will refuse to go along with the results. Newmerica will not be erased in the voting booth, not today, not ever."

"The electoral votes are only marginally in their favor," the campaign manager said.

"Fuck the electoral college!" Daniel said pounding his fist on the desk. "These people tried to kill us. They messed with the election. I don't give a shit about the electoral votes. This is a matter of national pride! We will have ourselves sworn in—a full ceremony. We will proceed as if we won. We will have all the pomp and circumstance. It will validate our claim that the election was a fraud."

She liked the sound of that. I will be the VP, one heartbeat away from holding all of the power.

"We know the states that betrayed us," the Secretary of the NSF and candidate said. "We can play the same game they did. We can send troops in to take them back, one at a time if we have to." The military overall was sitting on the sidelines, but individuals and in some cases even entire units were defecting to both sides. *We have more strength than we have brought to bear…yet.*

Daniel nodded. "The traitors you have brought in, the ones behind the bombing…I want show trials. I want them to confess publically that they were aiding that damned Pretender. I want them executed…so that everyone can see exactly what we are up against. No one is going to rise up against us once they see what happens to those that try."

Those words made her crack a grin. She had used the bombing to round up not only the conspirators, but a large number of others that had been her opponents. *They'll all go down, one at a time. Each death will remind the people who they need to support.*

"The TRC is working on the messages now," she said. "With the Internet still down, we can't prevent people from spreading the results of the election. The news outlets want statements from us and are going to downplay and edit the Pretender's messages," she reminded him. They had tried for two weeks to get the hubs operational. Each time they thought they got ahead, the system would get overloaded to the point where it ground to a halt.

"His message on CNN that we just watched wasn't edited!" Daniel spat back. "You may need to remind the media who provided them their bread and butter."

"Don't worry," she said. "I will handle it." *Let a few reporters spend time in the camps…that will bring them in line.*

"Sabotage. That's what this was, plain and simple," Daniel said. "We were hamstrung by these terrorists. It is like I always said. They will do anything to seize power."

"It's a rebellion," she declared bluntly. "We are the legitimate government, and those states that defied us, they are in rebellion, regardless of what the Pretender says. We need to label them for what they are—Traitor States."

"Yes," he growled. "Traitors—each and every one of them."

"They have mounted an insurrection against us," she continued. "That makes each person a traitor. Once they see the fate of traitors, many will reconsider. In the meantime, we will cut off their power, their government services, their reparations, everything. Let the Pretender and his people try to take care of them. Sooner or later, they'll come back. They need us…need the government. Without us, they're nothing."

She rose slowly to her feet. "I need to get back to the NSF, and the TRC. I will be back over in time for us to issue a joint statement about this fraud of an election and announce our swearing in."

"Thank you, Alex," Daniel said.

"Don't worry. I'll handle everything ..."

The District
Thirty-Two Minutes Later ...

The NSF Director, now Vice President Elect, arrived at Room J to find the room filled with people. She had ordered food brought in for them, but they were far from a celebratory mood when she entered. Some stood, out of either reverence or fear.

"I had hoped that this would be more of a party," she said, moving to the front of the conference room. "I do want to thank you all for coming. We do have everyone here, don't we?"

There were nods and Operative Ramses Ossege spoke up. "Yes ma'am. We have everyone here that worked on the project." He spoke with pride, which she understood. After all, it was her plan.

"Excellent," she said. "And are you all wearing the security pins you were provided?"

There were a number of nods, and her eyes drifted down to the lapel pins. The people she didn't immediately recognize wore them on shirt pockets, or on their collars. No doubt they were the video editors or the cyber team that helped with the digital manipulation.

"I want you all to know that you did an outstanding job on this project. The bombing attempt was well staged; it gave our campaign a much-needed boost in terms of public opinion.

"Unfortunately, you saw the initial results of the election tonight," she said, sweeping the room with her dark eyes. "Newmerica will always be strong. We are not going to give in just because our enemies have played games with the election results. We will resist, and resist in ways they can't imagine." She stopped, and most of the room applauded.

"I wanted you to know that your efforts weren't in vain. Because of you, we have arrested 150 would-be traitors and terrorists. You have all done a great service to your nation. You will all be in my debt for the rest of your lives."

Many in the room smiled. One young woman had a tear running down her cheek. It was touching. The Secretary reached down to her purse and pulled out a small box, similar to a jewelry case. She opened it and there was a single green button.

She pushed it.

The pins, which everyone wore, flashed bright white as the tiny, shaped explosive charges in them went off. Her ears popped with the staccato of small explosions that rocked the room. Most pins, the lapel-worn ones, blew holes in the hearts of the wearers. Those that wore them on their collars were messy since the force of the explosions devoured significant chunks of their necks, spraying gore onto ceiling tiles and on walls. One or two lay in the heap of dead bodies, moaning slightly as the last bits of their life flowed out onto the marble tiled floor. The air smelled coppery, with a heavy hint of smoke from the tiny, explosive devices.

Her ears throbbed and her heart pounded from the explosions and the excitement. Silently, she put the box back in her purse and stepped over the dead. It was a shame to lose such talent, but they were loose ends—and that was something she could not tolerate. The cleanup team would be there shortly, and when they were done, there would be no trace of her conspirators; nor could any of them reveal her role in matters.

This is war...and there are times when every good general must sacrifice their troops in order to achieve a victory.

A SNEAK PEEK AT THE NEXT BLUE DAWN NOVEL—*CONFEDERACY OF FEAR...*

PROLOGUE

"Most people who use the word 'freedom' mean the opposite."

Four Years Earlier ...
The Pacific Ocean East of Taiwan

Su-Hui Zhou remembered glancing over his shoulder back to his homeland of Taiwan and seeing the swirls of smoke rising from far too many places on the tiny island. The sight of it getting smaller in the distance made him weep, if only for a few minutes. His nation, his cultural identity, his job, his friends—everything has gone. He had saved most of his family, but they were far from safety and his enemies were known to be ruthless.

Su-Hui had been a mid-level executive at Formosa Plastics Corporation when the initial attack began last week. Taiwan's fate had always been precarious on the world stage. It was the last bastion of true capitalism and China resented their freedom and prosperity. The People's Republic, a name that on its own was a contradiction of words, had always claimed they were a 'breakaway republic.' That phrase was both a reminder and a threat to the Taiwanese people. 'We still see you as part of us…and one day you will be again.' For generations, they had lived with the knowledge that across the Straits, a looming monster, 'the red dragon,' as his mother had called the threat, eyed them hungrily, waiting for the right moment to absorb them back into their communist fold.

There were things that had held China in check—namely the United States of America and its pledge to protect Taiwan. With the so-called Liberation, America had morphed overnight into something else—

Newmerica. Just thinking about the rebranded nation made him angry. When China began being aggressive, with dangerous penetrations of his country's air space, and their deployment of aircraft carriers to the region, Newmerica was called upon to do what it had done before—rattle its saber. This time, it was different. The new quasi-socialists of Newmerica did something they had never done before when his people asked for protection.

They said *no*.

Their response was far from blunt. Flowery language about 'self-determination,' and 'China's historic claims to Formosa,' had been like pouring gasoline on a bonfire. Everyone knew what it meant—Newmerica's vast military would not risk itself if China pushed to seize the island. A pending sense of doom seemed to smother his people. *We knew what was coming, and now there was nothing to prevent the inevitable.*

It was not a complete surprise. Almost as soon as the Ruling Council had come into power in the three years earlier, they had knee-jerked the US military out of Afghanistan under the pretense of, "We accomplished our mission there." The Afghan government collapsed and the Taliban took over, only to be replaced by more extremists and terrorists, including a resurging ISIS. The Newmerican press didn't cover the debacle, but international media sources did. Over 100,000 Afghan refugees flooded into the United States as their former nation plunged into utter chaos. Afghanistan had devolved into partisan tribal conflicts and a terrorist safe haven. The botched withdrawal was a signal to the allies of the former United States…all bets were off. *Even the North Koreans have begun firing missiles again…they know that Newmerica has no will to fight a war overseas.*

The Chinese read the tea leaves, eyeing Taiwan like a hungry tiger stares at fresh prey. The fighting started three weeks ago—the air battle over the island was spectacular and terrifying to see unfold. China had the numbers on its side, and slowly the Republic of China Air Force made the mainland Chinese suffer, even managing to counterattack and sink one of their aircraft carriers. That fleeting moment of national pride evaporated quickly. In the end though, the numbers of the enemy prevailed.

The communist Chinese navy forced landings in the Straits and with air superiority secured, the defenders were slaughtered. Helicopter forces deployed in New Taipei City on the north end of the island with devastating results. The surge of the communist army was relentless. *They didn't care what they destroyed or how many men it took to secure victory.*

Su-Hui owned a small sailboat that he used for short trips on the weekends out of Taitung. Once the invasion began, he evacuated his family, loading the boat with supplies and everything of value that they owned, and fled. Now, days later, there were times he felt he could almost hear the wails of his homeland as it fell. The cries were carried skyward in the plumes of fires from the fighting.

The journey thus far had not been easy. His mother was in perpetual fear, trembling and somewhat confused by everything that had happened. She talked constantly about going home. Su-Hui's daughter was seasick one day and had not reached the edge of the boat in time to throw up. Vomit and sea spray had been impossible to clean up. They ate cold food out of cans; there was no means for heating it. His face sported the ragged start of a beard…he didn't want to waste water on something like shaving. Sunburn seared the back of his neck and legs, but he ignored it.

His sailboat was not alone—over a hundred boats of every kind were fleeing Taiwan. They stayed close to each other, in case one of them ran into problems. One motor launch lost its engine, but was being towed by a larger sailing ship at this point. Another sunk, with some of the passengers rescued by boats that could get there in time.

They were sailing east, because there were rumors of the Chinese navy sinking similar flotillas of refugees that were heading south. There was no leadership in the people that were fleeing; they huddled together almost on an instinctive level…a tribal sense of safety in numbers.

On day three of their flight, the wind died down and the small flotilla slowed on the seas. A Chinese fighter jet roared low over them at one point, nearly panicking his elderly mother, who was in the cabin of the boat. The constant bombing during the invasion had terrorized her and his youngest child. Clearly the fighter must have seen them, but it did not launch an attack. The flyover was a reminder for all of them—they were not safe.

Four days into their sojourn, they saw a military ship on the western horizon, closing with the tiny fleet of refugees. Su-Hui watched as it grew larger, using binoculars to finally spy the Newmerican flag on the ship, black with an up-thrust white fist. Word was passed over the radio and by simple shouts to other vessels. The ship, the *USS John S. McCain,* swung wide of the group and then came in parallel to the ship.

Orders were barked out, both in English and Mandarin, telling the ships to slow, that they were there to help. That only made Su-Hui angrier. *If you wished to help, you should have joined us to defend our nation.* The large, gray destroyer pulled alongside of several ships, using cranes and baskets to lift the refugees aboard ship. It was a slow process in the churning seas. He was tenth in line with his sailboat, and carefully tacked its way into position, bumping hard on the hull of the destroyer in the process.

Three at a time, his family was lifted off. Each carried a suitcase or two containing what was left of their worldly possessions. The naval officer, who came down in the first basket, finally loaded him and his son into the basket.

"What about my boat?" Su-Hui asked in his best English.

The sailor shook his head. "Sorry," he said. "We are only taking people at this point." As the basket was winched up, he looked at his ship, now starting to drift away. It had taken two years for him to save up for the down payment on the vessel, and now it was simply cast adrift in the vastness of the Pacific. He watched sadly as it bobbed about like a child's toy in a bathtub. *I worked so hard to save for it...and now it is thrown aside like garbage.* He then felt a wave of guilt wash over him. *My people have lost their nation...their hopes...their dreams. What is a sailboat against that?*

While the navy crew was kind, helping them aboard, checking them for medical issues, Su-Hui fumed. *None of this would have been necessary if Newmerica had answered Taiwan's plea for help.* A part of him understood it far too well. Newmerica was socialist without using that word. The entire world knew it. They called it 'progressivism,' or 'neo-collectivism,' or 'enlightened capitalism,' but he knew they supported China over a free Taiwan. *Their twist on economics has turned me from being a successful business person to being a refugee.*

Someone was going to pay for this. He promised himself that much.

These events will not define my existence. I won't allow that to happen. I will rebuild my life, and when I do, I will find the people responsible for the loss of my homeland and make them pay.

gramcontent.com/pod-product-compliance
g Source LLC
sburg PA
2157270326
B00009B/1561
78195593727 6 *